Engines of Instruction, Mischief, and Magic

CONTES
DE MA
MERE
LOYE

Mary V. Jackson

University of Nebraska Press: Lincoln

*Children's
Literature
in England
from Its
Beginnings
to 1839*

Engines of

Instruction,

Mischief,

and Mag!c

The paper in this book meets
the minimum require-
ments of American National
Standard for Infor-
mation Sciences — Permanence
of Paper for
Printed Library Materials,
ANSI Z39.48-1984

Library of Congress
Cataloging in Publication Data
Jackson, Mary V, 1939 –
Engines of instruction, mischief,
and magic: children's
literature in England from its
beginnings to 1839 /
Mary V. Jackson.   p.   cm.
Bibliography: p.
Includes index.
ISBN 0-8032-2572-5 (alk. paper).
ISBN 0-8032-7570-6 (pbk: alk. paper)
1. Children's literature, English –
History and criticism.
2. Children – England – Books
and reading – History.
I. Title.
PR990.J 33 1989   820'.9'9282 —
dc 19   CIP 88-31144

To my husband, Raymond,

&

my daughter, Mary Harriet

Contents

Preface

When I first considered a suggestion that I write a history of English children's books before 1900, I was uncertain that it could be done or, given F. J. Harvey Darton's monumental *Children's Books in England* (1932), that it needed doing. What of significance could be said that he had not already said so eloquently? And if there had once been anything left to add, had not Mary F. Thwaite in fact done so in her splendid history, *From Primer to Pleasure in Reading* (1963; revised ed., 1972), or if not she, then Brian Alderson, in the superbly revised third edition of Darton (1982)? To be sure, heretofore unknown books and publishers have come to light, and of course Darton, Thwaite, Percy Muir, Francella Butler, and the other pioneers in the field have not pretended to have discussed everything, but did the new material or any new approach actually justify a reevaluation of the field? Such were my misgivings.

Although there have been several important learned books since Darton's and Thwaite's, few are scholarly histories of the field: To cite only three examples that have proved especially helpful, Victor Neuburg's *The Penny Histories* (1968) and *Popular Education in Eighteenth-Century England* (1971) provide crucial bibliographical data on the chapbook industry and the corollary issues of its readership and the nature and extent of literacy among the poor. And Samuel F. Pickering's erudite *John Locke and Children's Books in Eighteenth-Century England* (1981) tackles a vast and complicated body of material from a specialized angle, illuminating many previously half-understood and misunderstood matters. But it was not meant to account fully for this huge motley of a field.

As I pursued my research, which had begun with the study of the debts of Blake and other English Romantics to a variety of children's books at the British Library, what convinced me there might be some value in retelling the story of these fascinating works were numerous questions, the full answers to many of which were not to be got by reading studies in the field. The questions were of two general sorts: First, what were the various conditions and events, beliefs and ideas, that lay behind book trade developments, and how thoroughly did they account for the trade's evolution? Could we determine some of the manifold influences over the years that induced writers to express the attitudes they did and to give their books a specific form? And second, when, how precisely, and with what consistency did children's books come under the influence of adult literature (or influence it in turn)? Could one, moreover, discern systematic, coherent connections between ideological or literary developments in children's books and the larger sociopolitical context, connections pervasive enough to require a general rethinking of the history? The first sort of query involves matters that ordinarily concern social historians; and the second sort concerns mainly literary historians. Yet both are inextricably interwoven in the story of books for children, and, I felt, neither—let alone the two in concert—had been adequately addressed. These I set out to understand.

Darton had created for twentieth-century readers an intimate sense of over three centuries of juvenile literature based on his vast firsthand knowledge of innumerable books, his practical experience as a publisher, and his family's long history as publishers and creators of books. To these were added his wide knowledge of literature, his superb taste, the charming spirit of the best of a bygone age in his style, and as Brian Alderson points out, a maturity that was the fruit of a long and distinguished career. From Darton's pages, many modern readers first learned of some book's existence, of now defunct publishing firms, and of long-abandoned publishing or printing practices. To this day, his work remains indispensable as an orienting beacon to thousands of works and hundreds of publishers and authors.

The second scholarly history, Mary F. Thwaite's *From Primer to Pleasure,* is also suitable for the general reader, though originally intended for librarians. It cogently charts early developments in children's books from various forms of adult literature, contains apercus into the society from which they sprang, provides a number of exceedingly fine though discrete literary analyses, and is moreover replete with superb bibliographies. However, since it was not Thwaite's intent to delineate systematically the interconnections between the social, political, and economic contexts in which children lived and out of which the books proceeded, her explanations of particular developments do not focus on or derive from a theory of coherent progression in the field. She explores the causes of a number of phenomena, but her greater strength lies in the clarity of her descriptions of them.

Yet at every point in its early history, children's literature was rooted in the conditions and imperatives of the adult world and was regarded first and foremost as a tool to shape the young to the needs of that world. If we would truly understand what it is "about," we must master both its overt and hidden texts, its plain statements as well as its tacitly understood messages and veiled directives. To do this, we must apply a thorough knowledge of the field of value and action from which the literature sprang.

In contradistinction to both Darton's and Thwaite's works, the basic premise of this interpretive history is that major developments in children's books reflect diverse influences from the adult world and reflect the nearly universal assumption that children were resources to be molded or engineered to needs and specifications determined by a prevailing social standard. Since the books did not spring up *ex nihilo*, we profit from the application to this field of what is known through our major disciplines and through contemporary documents—diaries, biographies, familial guides, and the like—about life and art in the period.

Given these assumptions, it follows that I propose somewhat different interpretations of both events and trends in the literature from those of earlier historians. For example, my discussion of the role of Puritan books in the field (chapter 2) does not focus on the anomalies of the group that produced them but explains what Puritan writers had in common with their more orthodox fellow citizens, and how and why Puritan values eventually prevailed in the nation's juvenile literature. My analyses (chapter 3) of the effect of chapbooks on the early book trade and the related matter of the role of Felix Summerly and *The Home Treasury* (chapter 10) differ from Darton's. The prevailing class bias of his time prevented him from assessing fairly, I feel, the cultural and marketing implications of chapbook popularity. My appraisal of John Newbery's literary innovations and perhaps unconsciously radical social schemes (chapter 4) differs from any in print that I know, as does my reinterpretation of similar issues in John Marshall's career (chapter 5).

Likewise, though I use some of Thwaite's literary categories, my unraveling of the role of Trimmer, Fenn, and religiously orthodox children's book reformers, as compared to so-called Rousseauist reformers (chapters 7 and 8), yields another explanation, one derived from my elucidation of shared motives fueled by larger sociopolitical events (class strife exacerbated by the French Revolution and Jacobin menace) that overrode religious differences likely otherwise to have divided fervent Anglicans from an ostensibly anti-church party. Instead, events drove these allies to use similar strategies and to reject attitudes and books judged inimical to the establishment. Furthermore, although I naturally urge reevaluation of some forces that shaped juvenile books over two centuries, I also endorse earlier historians' perceptions when they seem valid. Yet even when iterating what has been long agreed to or known, I attempt to qualify raw or discrete data by establishing their true perspective in relation to other facts.

Predictably, the investigation of the sociopolitical elements that shaped children's books yielded a more fully systematic and coherent evolutionary account than could the inquiry into adult esthetic and literary influences. Prior to 1860 or so, there were few books for children of true literary distinction. Though more fragmented, literary influences are nonetheless significant and have received particular attention here. Typically, my aim has been to discover what was adopted from adult polite literature and why, how it was tailored to its new role, how precisely it fit the borrower's propaganda needs, and what artistic leavening it infused, if any.

Thus, my book explains, for example, reasons for the wide use of the tour motif in early books and its comparative lack of success (chapter 4); the rise of the children's trade novel, from miscellanies and from the first juvenile magazine, and its later disfavor (chapters 3 and 4); the borrowing of the picaresque form of works like *The History of Pompey the Little* and *Chrysal; or, The Adventures of a Silver Guinea* and the reasons its satiric elements were anathematized, especially in girls' books (chapter 6); the distorting and grafting of Rousseau's ideals to older fictional archetypes and to blacks (chapter 7); the manufacture of propagandistic fiction (chapter 8); how neoclassical influences generated mock-epic poetry for children (papillonnades), which in turn engendered the trade's first body of successful pedagogic entertainments (chapter 9); the effects of pre-Romantic literature and Romantic poetry, art, and theory on children's prose, poetry, and illustrations, on publishers' practices, and on the rise of juvenile drama (chapters 9 and 10); and how the Romantic ideal of the imagination helped to vindicate fantasy in children's books (chapter 10).

Children's literature, a so-called minor area, is unlike any minor field I know, for the term usually connotes a paucity of authors and works, relative insignificance, and meager esthetic quality as compared to the best of an era. Even to only 1839, children's literature is an enormous field; its significance in terms of influence on major writers is great; and its potential for illuminating the social or human context of major literary periods has barely been recognized until recently.* It is a scholar's paradise of as yet unexcavated bibliographies and unwritten histories of publisher's houses and also of authors' works in their myriad editions, printings, and issues, from which, as my study shows, one can deduce useful insights into matters of taste and intellectual trends. It contains, moreover, a number of works of imaginative and literary success even before 1840 and of poetic genius thereafter. In truth, it is not a minor field at all. Rather, it has been labeled insignificant and given minor attention because of two still potent social and academic biases—a tendency to discount or devalue culture when related to the world of the child and a rooted disdain for whatever seems simple and uncomplicated.

My study seeks to give a clear picture of the inner consistencies in children's books, and between them and their religious, philosophical, sociopolitical, and trade conditions and esthetic and literary contexts. It seeks to explain those portions of the history of the field that legitimately cohere and to show where and, in some cases, why such systematic connections broke down. Though the focus on the larger social context shifts as events dictate, my purpose has been to follow the thread of influence through the labyrinth of major and minor trends in beliefs, social propaganda, and literary developments and to describe and interpret these in as true a perspective as is possible.

As regards the book itself, I wish to clarify certain decisions: First, my study covers juvenile books from their beginnings to about 1839, an era that drew to a close just as fantasy became respectable and the literature gained undisputed acceptance at the highest social levels. I think the next distinct phase in the evolution of children's books runs from

---

* Marilyn Gaull's *English Romanticism: The Human Context* (New York and London: W. W. Norton, 1988) was released shortly after *Engines* went to press. I have perused but not utilized this important volume, which contains a chapter on children's literature.

about 1840 to 1910, that is, through the Victorian and Edwardian ages, during which a number of masterpieces were produced. I hope to explore this literature in a future volume. Second, I wish to comment on my choice of terms, particularly as applied to social classes. At times I make use of phrases like "the lowly" and "the lower orders," two that were often applied in the age to the working classes and the poor by "their betters." Here, as in other instances where I borrow expressions current in an era being discussed, I do so the better to convey a sense of its character as well as its views and not because I endorse its values or want to patronize any of the human beings about whom I write.

Since I began this research in 1978, I have spent many an hour in libraries and collections and am very grateful for the unstinting help I have received. I wish to thank the librarians and staff of the British Library, the Harvard Libraries, the New York Public Library, the Pierpont Morgan Library, and, for many useful facsimiles, Boys and Girls House of the Toronto Public Library. Vira C. Hinds kindly guided me to invaluable library resources. And rare book dealer Justin G. Schiller gave me much sage advice and help in building my collection of eighteenth- and nineteenth-century British, American, and French children's books over the last six years and granted me precious glimpses of rare works and editions to which I might not otherwise have had access.

Like all such ventures, this book could not exist but for the lavish sharing of scholarly expertise and generous encouragement from a number of colleagues. I am deeply indebted to Betty Rizzo, Leon Guilhamet, and Barbara Dunlap for reading several versions of the manuscript. To many others who read and contributed to the final version I owe a debt of gratitude: Samuel F. Pickering, Stephen C. Behrendt, Lois R. Kuznets, Leo Hamalian, Robert Ghiradella, Earl Rovit, Paul Sherwin, Sarah W. R. Smith, Beverly Schneller, and William Crain. I wish to thank Paul Lorrimer and Ketti Melonas for technical assistance in processing the manuscript. Finally, I am deeply grateful to Raymond Jackson for countless readings of the book and for photographing works from my collection; and I am excessively obliged as well to Mary Harriet P. Jackson for keeping me firmly in touch with the real child's world through it all. The flaws in this book are indeed my own, but such strengths as it may possess were made possible by the incredible kindness and unflagging assistance of these, my associates and colleagues, friends and family.

1. The Birth of the Children's Book Trade: Economic and Social Stimuli

In 1744 John Newbery (1713–67) opened his firm in London at the Bible and Crown and published his first children's book, *A Little Pretty Pocket-Book*, establishing in a stroke, as tradition has it, the juvenile book trade and children's literature in England. Although some leisure books for children were available early in the century, the idea of a business devoted wholly or even largely to them was unheard of. Indeed, Newbery continued to publish school texts and adult books and to sell patent medicines, a steady source of income. In 1745, Newbery moved his growing family and still precarious business to the Bible and Sun, outside St. Paul's Churchyard, and concentrated on making his venture a success.[1] By 1760 the new branch of book publishing was known as a potentially lucrative and growing field for those with suitable entrepreneurial talents. Competitors and sometime copublishers— like Richard Baldwin and Samuel Crowder in London and their associate, Benjamin Collins, in Salisbury—vied with Newbery for the barely tapped market.

It became commonplace to see advertisements, or "puffs," for children's songbooks and miscellanies in England's many periodicals, like the *World*, the *Daily Advertiser*, the *Penny London Morning Advertiser*, *Penny London Post*, the *London Chronicle*, and the *London Evening Post*. Parents as well as children eagerly awaited these treats: Adults esteemed the literature, the newest aid to forming the character of the young while entertaining them; and children found its novelty and variety enormously appealing. In short, the new wares combined necessity and desirability, a fact publishers and booksellers emphasized in journal ads, touted in the lists at the back of each volume, and hoped would be further reinforced when patrons visited their bookstores. These marketing devices created business, for they kindled the desire to purchase books

1. "Le Maitre Chat" ("Puss in Boots"). Charles Perrault, *Contes du Temps Passé*, 1700.

2. "Tom repells the turkey's attack." *The New Tom Thumb*, 1838.

and in time fixed the book-buying habit for a significant portion of most classes. Using clever techniques for advertising to whet readers' appetites, and taking advantage of the newly emerging optimism infecting many, Newbery and his compeers eventually transformed customers into consumers and thus assured the increasing volume needed to build a shaky experiment into a valuable and highly influential trade offshoot.

Over the next few decades the juvenile book trade developed from a minor sideline in many firms into a minor industry. Advertising competitively, great numbers of publishers vied for a share in the brisk sales, and profits were handsome for many. The more prosperous companies had "juvenile libraries," their own bookstores, located in or near their printshops, and these were touted as vigorously as the works themselves in hopes of enticing customers to view the firm's special line of books.

Although publishers stocked their libraries with their own editions of material from the public domain, such as fairy tales, romances, and nursery rhymes, their fame and thus their profits depended greatly on their special line of books. These were built up as firms reprinted every saleable original work they had ever published while adding fresh material at regular intervals. Generally, new offerings floated for holidays were aimed to entice new consumers to splurge. Thus, Christmas, New Year's, Twelfth Day, Valentine's, and May Day became customary dates for issuing "brand new" works, many of which in fact contained familiar tales, riddles, and fillers within the framework of a catchy new gimmick, to stimulate the buying habit.

In the early decades of their history, juvenile books were thoroughly controlled by trade or business interests and not, as one might think, by religious or educational ones. It was not uncommon for publishers to collect, edit, or even write their own material. Most also hired professional authors of real talent, like Oliver Goldsmith, commissioned by Newbery to write a history and probably *Goody Two-Shoes*, or like Christopher Smart, probable author of *The Lilliputian*.[2] Yet no matter who did the actual writing, the books were often conceived, printed, and sold under one person's guidance. Most books had no pretension to literary excellence. Being wares in every sense, they usually hewed to prevailing tastes and values; publishers sought to supply their patrons or patrons' parents with what they wanted, not to reshape their views, as would reformist authors after 1780.

In essence parents wanted their offspring to be taught, albeit entertainingly, the skills, habits, virtues, and graces the children likely needed to gain success in a world newly perceived to contain opportunities for advancement. A large, diverse body of literature—ABCs, natural histories, Bibles, "moral-financial account" books (which yoked ethical solvency to sound money management), seasonal miscellanies, novels, and polite-conduct guides—was permeated by a new gestalt characterized but not fully defined by four elements: optimism, humor or play, morality, and business. For the first time in books for the young, the venerable Renaissance formula (borrowed from the Greeks) for literature, "to delight and instruct," was thought appropriate. Within limits, fun was not only good in itself but good *for* children, since it sped learning, ensured cheerful resolution, and generally enhanced their prospects.

Childhood was still a serious affair, though less somber than earlier.

3. A pictorial cover from
a French natural history.
*Histoire Naturelle des
Animaux*, [c. 1850–60].

4. *A Silver Hornbook,* the decorated side, [late seventeenth century].

Increasingly, children's responsibility—to make themselves into proper adults—took on a secular cast, to which purely religious goals became secondary. In the lives reflected in the new books, the winning of worldly success, though reserved solely for the pious and morally up-right (who were also, as it happened, avid book readers), took prece-dence over earlier visions of spiritual or otherworldly rewards; and a desire for self-betterment and advancement challenged the former res-ignation to one's appointed niche in society—dramatic developments spurred in part by the century's new science and technology.

The eighteenth century was as much an era of invention as it was the Age of Enlightenment. Indeed, the two went hand in hand. Human visions in science, industry, agriculture, and exploration were translated into realities at a pace both amazing and unsettling to many. Overnight, it seemed, a stream of discoveries and inventions transformed centuries-old manufacturing procedures. New enterprises sprang up, and new-fangled ways of doing things were adopted in country and town. Businesses became more complicated to manage, and the increased pa-perwork placed a premium on workers who could read and write.[3]

The glories of seventeenth- and eighteenth-century science—Boyle's chemistry; Newton's astronomy, physics, and optics; Buffon's and Lin-naeus's studies in natural science; Franklin's studies of electricity, for ex-ample—were the basis of innovations not limited to manufacture and trade. The Age of Reason adapted the rigors of classical, scientific em-piricism for investigations of the nature of human beings and society, and of the potential utility of the natural world. Eighteenth-century hopes for humankind's perfectibility, or at least for its profound im-provement, and social progress rested on the application of scientific models of inquiry to psychological and social phenomena. Moreover, these intoxicating speculations and researches had long since received the crucial moral imprimatur of the Established Church partly through the intercession, as it were, of John Locke's philosophy.

Within a decade of its appearance, Locke's *Essay Concerning Human Understanding* (1690) had altered the way people looked upon human endeavor in secular matters. His treatise undertook to prove that mor-tals are born with no innate ideas; each enters the world with a mind like a blank slate (tabula rasa). Experience writes on this slate through the medium of the senses, gradually building concepts, principles, and human judgment. But if women and men have no natural, preexistent ideas, then it is doubtful that they are inherently moral *or* immoral. Thus, Locke's logic called into question the doctrine of Original Sin, for centuries the cornerstone of Christian orthodoxy. Undoubtedly, he did not intend his philosophy to undermine religion, for he attempted in Book II to place proofs of the existence of God beyond all doubt.[4] These notwithstanding, by successfully compromising the idea of inborn principles, Locke subverted the all-important tenet of innate human evil. Of course, if humans are not sinful from their origin, then neither are the products of their reason automatically suspect, even when rooted in secular concerns.

Predictably, the religiously zealous and vigilant conservatives of the Established Church and Dissenters alike at once scented out and attacked this dangerous heresy. For on the faith in Original Sin rested other cherished beliefs, such as the presumption of a natural world that had been decaying since the fall of Adam, and the corollary suppositions that all worldly interests and any idea of earthly progress were suspect, if not downright evil.

Despite vigorous opposition, however, Locke's arguments were adopted by English and European scientists, thinkers, and churchmen, with amazing alacrity—as though Europe had been on the lookout,

5. XIX, King David playing on his harp. XX, Absolom hanging in the oak. Sarah Trimmer, *A New Series of Prints . . . from the Old Testament* [Illustrated, engraved by/ after William Blake?], 1808.

though unconsciously, for a sufficiently persuasive spokesman to midwife its own intellectual progeny. Little more than ten years after the
publication of *Human Understanding*, William Sherlock, dean of St.
Paul's, incorporated John Locke's arguments into his discourse on salvation: "Whatever ideas we have latent in our Minds . . . *we gain no
actual Knowledge of them, but as they are awakened* for us *by external Impressions*," he declared. "Actual Knowledge [is] . . . acquired, and possibly much in the same way that Mr. Lock [*sic*] represents it."[5] Thus did
the spotlight shift from human beings' congenital wickedness to those
crucial processes whereby they acquired their impressions.

If humanity was not precisely acquitted of Original Sin, and of
course it was not, then it was at least viewed with a new forbearance,
and the issue of its inborn defectiveness was moved from center stage in
the drama of human affairs to a still prominent but decidedly secondary
position. These developments were reinforced by the latitudinarian
spirit (the will to tolerate individual differences of conscience as gener-
ously as possible) bequeathed to eighteenth-century England by seventeenth-century divines like John Tillotson, archbishop of Canterbury.

By 1740 the medieval view that earthly progress was a snare of the
devil was a thoroughly discredited notion to which only extremists subscribed. Secular learning was unfettered: Clearly, human beings had
both the capacity and the obligation, the duty, to fathom all they could
of God's creation by the rational use of their God-given senses. Thus
was nature renovated and progress made part of the Divine Plan. Moreover, through progress lay humanity's path to intellectual, social, and
even spiritual improvement. The timely return, as predicted, of Edmund Halley's comet in 1758–59 may have seemed providential to many,
a clear, heavenly confirmation of their enlightened views and aspirations.

As in lofty matters, so it was in everyday life during the period. At
every level, numerous improvements wrought by the impressive scientific and industrial developments fed individual hopes and ambitions.
More and better food was available even to the lower classes; milk, previously very scarce in winter, began to be more plentiful. The infant and
child mortality rate began its slow decline, and indeed the health of the
entire population improved slightly. But even a small drop in the death
rate meant a much-needed rise in the number of workers and of children, whose purchases in turn augmented the nation's commerce. Epi-

44 PIZARRO.

a hope of gaining his liberty. The room in which he was confined was twenty-two feet long, by sixteen wide. The Inca offered to fill it with golden vessels, as high as he could reach, for his ransom. This offer was accepted. And Atahualpa dispatched orders all over his empire, to bring in the needed treasures.

But when all was punctually paid, in vain did the Inca solicit for his liberty. Nothing like justice, or kindness, had place in the heart of Pizarro, or his companions.

24. *Discovering that Pizarro could not read.*

There were none of the European Arts which so much delighted the Inca, as reading and writing. He wanted to know whether this was natural to them all, or acquired by education. He requested therefore one of the soldiers who stood guard over him, to write the name of their God, on his thumb-nail. He then presented his thumb to every one who came near him; to his great surprise he found them all pronounce it ex-

6. 22, "Discovering the [Cinchoa] Bark [Quinine for fevers]." 23, "Pizarro seizes the Inca." 24, "The Inca discover Pizarro could not read." The Rev. Isaac Taylor, *Scenes in America,* 1821.

demic plagues occasionally afflicted the population, but with the realization that filth (especially in impoverished urban districts) fostered the plagues, and with innovations like the water closet, forerunner of systematic sanitation, came hope for control. Faster travel on land for people and the mails, and on the expanding river and canal system for raw materials, produce, and manufactured goods, meant more and cheaper staples. The conditions that nurtured these domestic improvements were further stimulated by expanded foreign markets in the colonies. The explorations of Captain Cook and others seemed to lay open the very world to ambitious and enterprising Britons.[6]

To be sure, poverty was still widespread and life was often brutal. But in England the poor seemed to fare better than in many European nations, especially during this period of expansion, before the full onslaught of that concatenation of social and economic events known as the Industrial Revolution. Certainly laborers and the artisans and small shop owners of the lower-middle class not only lived better but also began to glimpse tantalizing prospects for their sons. Even a modest rise in income could mean money for books and chapbooks.

A boy who "learned his Book," as Newbery never tired of emphasizing in his one-, two-, and sixpenny volumes, was sure to achieve enviable material security. In this, Newbery was following both the ideals and the substantial practical efforts of at least two generations of Britons of all classes and faiths who had mounted and privately financed the most massive system of general education Europe had known; their purpose had been profoundly religious and only secondarily nationalistic and economic. Along with the 128 elite grammar (Latin) schools instituted in England between 1700 and 1799, these men and women established thousands of charity schools, endowed by the rich or, remarkably, supported by subscriptions from the middle classes. The Society for Promoting Christian Knowledge, founded in 1699, reported 1,327 schools with 23,421 students enrolled in England in 1723, the organization of 170 charity schools in Ireland between 1700 and 1733, the instruction in Wales of over 158,000 children (and uncounted numbers of adult poor) between 1737 and 1761, and in Scotland the *addition* of 500 charity schools between 1707 and 1730, this in a section that boasted at least one charity school in nearly every parish.[7]

Since the SPCK did not report on non-Anglican institutions, these figures do not indicate the substantial efforts of Dissenters, whose academies were famous, or of Nonconformists, Methodists, Quakers, Jews, and Huguenots, all of whom undertook to some extent similarly financed and operated schools for their laboring poor and paupers, as well as for children of the middling classes. In 1766 Jonas Hanway reported that England "abounded in charity schools." In 1776 Adam Smith made a similar estimate, also pointing out that Scotland far outdistanced England in the number of children taught and in the number of schools. And from 1787 to 1797, when the Sunday School movement had begun to reinforce the weekday charity schools' efforts, in the Sunday Schools alone over a quarter of a million poor children received rudimentary instruction in reading if not in writing.[8]

Despite his unarguable intention of profiting by encouraging children to buy as well as "learn their" books, Newbery was allied—by his demonstrably genuine, if secular, concern—to those English men and women who had created and supported the national charity school system and who had urged the spiritual and mental improvement of British

7. Exod. 20:17. *A New Hieroglyphical Bible*, 1842.

youth, especially the poorest. Moreover, in his emphasis on the worldly personal gain in such learning, he was in complete harmony with his own era, but in his insistence on the importance of educated middle and lower classes to the nation's future in emerging world trade, he anticipated nationalistic and economic developments of the next century.

With businesses requiring ever larger numbers of competent clerks, many parents of the lower middling classes nursed hopes for their sons' advancement and willingly parted with the pence for a dame or domine school (held in a schoolmistress's or -master's home) and for books likely to help them realize their dreams.[9] This imposed a double financial drain on some lower-middle-class families, first to pay for the rudiments of a primary education, and second to forfeit all or part of the child's wages from odd jobs and seasonal labor. A real inducement to such parental complaisance was the growing hope among Newbery's lower-middle-class customers that learning and hard work might bring not only wealth but also the means to rise socially, for a boy and his family—no small matter.[10] Naturally, the affluent and respectable classes needed no such rationale for expenditures on publishers' enticing new wares, for they assumed that little Master and Miss would be educated as befitted their station and were entitled to the pleasures of books. Advertising appealed to the needs of both, with books for different purses.

There are indications that among children of virtually all classes and even among poor adults, early children's books played a significant role in disseminating information about the principles and practical advances of the Enlightenment.[11] Often the information was watered down, sometimes a little garbled, and on occasion, so distorted as to fail altogether to be transmitted. But enough got through to young and old to fuel the demand for learning and books. In a very real sense, the Enlightenment percolated through English society from opposite directions: from the top down through the writings of philosophers, scientists, and their popularizers; and from the bottom up through a variety of humble, popular books, including that upstart, children's literature.

The lessons of Enlightenment thought and science were taught in a variety of ways in the literature, sometimes very directly as in *The Newtonian System of Philosophy Adapted to the Capacities of Young* GENTLEMEN *and* LADIES, *and familiarized and made entertaining by Objects with which they are intimately acquainted: Being The Substance of* SIX LECTURES *read to the* LILLIPUTIAN SOCIETY, *By* TOM TELESCOPE, *A.M. And collected and methodized for the benefit of the Youth of these Kingdoms, By their old Friend,* MR. NEWBERY, *in St. Paul's Church Yard* (1761). *The Philosophy of Tops and Balls,* as *The Newtonian System* was also known, was perhaps Newbery's finest product. It conveys lucid instruction in Locke's psychology and Newton's physics and optics, frequently punctuated by humorous verbal jousts between the young lecturer, Tom, and the more inattentive or obstreperous members of his audience.

Sometimes homilies about perseverance in hard times, careful attention to the duties of preparing oneself for adult responsibility, and the

material and spiritual rewards such measures brought were instilled through the funny, adventurous doings of contemporary male and female Dick Whittingtons and Fortunatuses (owner of an ever-full purse and wishing cap). Two of the most popular heroes of this type were Giles Gingerbread, a poor and ragged urchin who pines to drive his own "coach and six" (i.e., horses) and who makes a sound start by mastering his letters; and Margery Two-Shoes, who enterprisingly rescues herself from both starvation and illiteracy and rises to become the greatest lady in the district. Of course, *The Renowned History of Giles Gingerbread* (1764) and *The History of Little Goody Two-Shoes* (1765) were trade wares created expressly to "delight and instruct" in the new spirit. But efforts to make lessons lighter and more amusing came also in quite unlikely forms. *The Childrens Bible* (Ann Law, 1759, 1763, 1769) declares it will offer "Passages of the Old and New Testament . . . in a method never before attempted utilizing . . . a *lively* and *striking* Abstract . . . so as to take firm Hold of their young Minds and Memories" (title page, italics mine).

It is important to realize that a mere twenty or so years before *The Childrens Bible* appeared, the most popular religious work for boys and girls—apart from Issac Watts's *Divine Songs for Children*—depicted the spiritual rapture of young Christians enduring slow and painful deaths and solemnly urged tots (and their parents) to consider that they were "not too little to go to Hell." The book was by James Janeway, *A Token for Children . . . An Exact Account of the Conversion, Holy and Exemplary Lives, and Joyful Deaths, of several young Children* (1672). So successful was this that a sequel immediately followed: *A Token for Children. The Second Part. Being a farther Account . . . of several other young Children not published in The First Part* (1672). These books went through innumerable editions in standard, costly book form and as inexpensive chapbooks, thus reaching all levels of society over the next 125 years. Significantly, the main complaint or criticism leveled at the *Tokens* was the fear that Janeway's patterns of perfect faith and unregenerate depravity were not the true biographies of actual children but were partial or complete fictions and therefore were unreliable and dangerous.[12]

To late-twentieth-century tastes, however, even the comparatively lighthearted "histories" of admittedly fictional children in books published between 1740 and 1770, like *Giles Gingerbread* and *Goody Two-Shoes,* might seem very heavy going and impossible to sell, burdened as

10. Chapbook cover. *The Popular Story of Blue Beard,* [*c.* 1846].

11. "The Giant threatening to kill Jack's Mother." "Jack and the Bean-Stalk," *Popular Tales of the Olden Time,* [*c.* 1830].

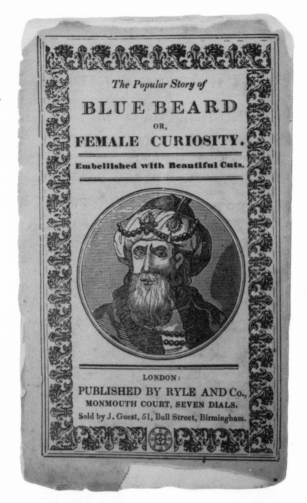

The Popular Story of
BLUE BEARD
OR,
FEMALE CURIOSITY.
Embellished with Beautiful Cuts.

LONDON:
PUBLISHED BY RYLE AND Co.,
MONMOUTH COURT, SEVEN DIALS.
Sold by J. Guest, 51, Bull Street, Birmingham.

they are with moral and practical lessons. Yet clearly they were considered by many, young and old alike, to be buoyant, even playful, despite their purposefulness. Perhaps insight into how the new trade literature struck its contemporaries can be arrived at only by comparing early trade books with those that children read, or had read to them, before 1740. For only in this context can we gauge the modulations in tone, the shifts in attitude, and the emergence of new goals and aspirations.

To make this comparison, three bodies of early children's books require consideration: the mixed bag of works written for adult entertainment but usually enjoyed by the whole community, including the young who eventually monopolized portions of it; purely instructional books for the young that evolved into lighter fare; and a variety of books written for children's leisure, mainly by or for Puritans. Some scholars have disputed the validity of considering some or all of these to be bona fide children's books.[13] But the quibble is academic, since (1) examples of these types—communal, instructional, and Puritan—were successfully adapted by early trade publishers, and (2) a large number of genres and actual works from the three groups remained in print not only throughout the next century but also well into our own. Moreover, no mere choice of labels can obviate the usefulness of a literature whose lines of development over two hundred years provide invaluable insights into the evolution of taste, moral values, reading habits, and the applications of books to real lives, as well as supplying information about the rise of adult and child literacy.

For one fact remained a constant, in 1650 and in 1850 (and to this

The Giant threatening to kill Jack's Mother.

page 11.

day): Whether subtly or blatantly, children's books were largely propagandistic in nature. They were tools for social, moral, religious, and political conditioning. They represented the enormously powerful collusive efforts of parents, producers of books, and indeed most adults—in a word, of society—to program the young, to engineer conformity to the prevailing cultural values. As such, they often parallelled "polite" adult tastes in literature. On occasion, they may seem to diverge from the norm, when they may in fact be anticipating newly emerging aspects of or ideals implicit in the dominant cultural set.

Analyzing changes in the early literature yields then a number of valuable insights into the social history of the nation. It is from this that we can deduce the rationale for most developments in children's books in this period. Such a study also offers the only reliable means, contextualism, to comprehend how books that seem to us to be loaded down with moral advice, businesslike socioeconomic lessons, and thinly disguised schooling could have been joyfully welcomed as light reading and even suspected of frivolity, as in fact they were by certain austere mid-eighteenth-century souls, and could thus have been sold not only for their improving qualities but also for the "delight" they gave.

2. Puritan and Other Religious Prototypes for Juvenile Literature

What was available for children's idle hours before 1744 and how was it adapted to the needs of the new trade? Thomas Boreman, Mary Cooper, and John Newbery, creators of many of the earliest examples of the genre, developed their books from several basic prototypes, few of which were originally written for the young: ABCs and hornbooks, romances and fairy tales, ballads and street-game songs, fables and bestiaries, abridged prose fictions, Puritan children's literature, and certain kinds of chapbook literature.

With the exception of Puritan books from about 1680, schoolroom texts, and training manuals, little was written specifically for middle- or lower-class children. The young grandson of Louis XIV of France had Fénelon to create moral fairy tales, myths, and fantasies to entertain and instruct him, as in the much-esteemed *Les Aventures de Télémaque (The Adventures of Telemachus*, 1699) and *Fables* (1718), but youngsters like "Little Master Tommy and Pretty Miss Polly" had to wait over half a century before any but the religiously motivated undertook to write books for them.[1]

Most of what the young read or heard read in their spare time before 1740 was intended for a communal audience, for adults as well as children. Only gradually, and largely from the impact of the juvenile book trade, did clear age distinctions emerge. Well into the second half of the eighteenth century, semiliterate adults still partook of readings that would soon be monopolized by the young. Then, as at the start of the century, children chiefly read once popular and fashionable adult cast-offs, which by some unerring sonar they selected from the numerous less palatable fish in these cultural backwaters.

Why one thing was eagerly pounced on by the young and another resolutely ignored is not easy to say, though most of us recognize a cer-

12. Alphabet, vowels, and prayers. *A Silver Hornbook,* [late seventeenth century].

13. Gen. 2:22; 3:1: *A New Hieroglyphical Bible,* 1842.

tain special quality in those works so honored by children. It was not only the fanciful or frivolous that was embraced, yet imaginative and whimsical works were more likely to survive than not. Clearly, whatever answered a need or hunger in developing minds was adopted. The fact that so much in the first decades of the history of the trade still appeals nearly two-and-a-half centuries later attests more to that abiding and unerring sonar of the young than to any calculated perspicacity in eighteenth-century booksellers. It also accounts for the fact, surprising at first, that virtually all the earliest prototypes persist today in some form, not just the predictable fairy tales and nursery rhymes but also ostensibly defunct fare such as medieval courtesy books.[2] It is fitting to begin, however, with the most important single source of "modern" trade books, Puritan children's books.

Unlikely though it may seem to moderns, both Puritan children's literature and child-rearing practices had a decisive role in the creation of English juvenile literature and in its subsequent development throughout the nineteenth century. Various "Puritan" groups were the first to write and publish books for youthful leisure reading, aimed not at an

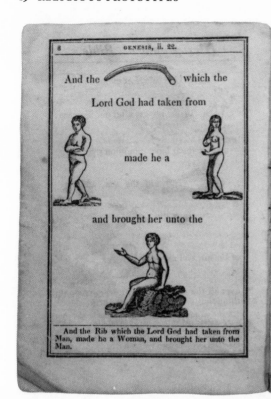
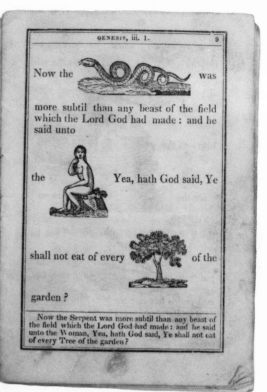

elite but at the ordinary child. Many of these have an otherworldly focus, a (to us) morbid preoccupation with death, damnation, and hellfire, and a grim and relentlessly preachy tone. But what may not be clear is how this literature of an apparently despised and disenfranchised minority managed not only to hold its own—and this in a political and religious environment often hostile to any vestiges of the Cromwellian years of irksome control—but also eventually to spread its influence into nearly every branch of the burgeoning book trade.[3]

From the first, *puritanism* was to many a catchall term, a comic or contemptuous epithet for pious display or for the excessive insistence on the continued purification of the Church of England of all vestiges of Roman Catholicism. In short, it was synonymous with extreme Protestantism, which in England came in many varieties. There seems to have been no one "Puritan sect," at least not until one was forged as a military, political arm of the religious state under Oliver Cromwell (1645–58).[4] With the restoration of the monarchy and civil order after 1660, fear and hatred of possible Roman Catholic intervention in England's affairs and of Puritan disruptions slowly waned. This is not to

St Polycarp burning at a stake.

say that the return to a balanced national mood was easy, smooth, or unmarred by injustice;[5] but gradually, lines dividing groups of like spirit within and without the church softened.

14. "St. Polycarp burning at a stake." *An History of the . . . Martyrs*, 1764.

15. XXIII, The Prophet Elijah taken up into Heaven in a fiery chariot. XXIV, The Prophet Daniel in the lion's den. Trimmer, *A New Series of Prints . . . from the Old Testament*, 1808.

Many devout Protestants who might have been dubbed Puritans (or "precisians") in 1700, but who would be "Evangelicals" by 1800, remained in the established church yet maintained their ties with men and women who had seceded from it. An early example is Robert Nelson, High Churchman and tireless worker in the charity school movement from 1699 to his death in 1715, who is acknowledged to be "a representative of eighteenth-century puritanism at its best."[6] John and Charles Wesley are important examples of the same spirit from the middle to the end of the century. Neither ever disavowed his allegiance to the Church of England, though they were deeply influenced by the Moravians and, in 1729, established a "methodist society" for their fellow students at Christ Church, Oxford.[7] In time, John created Methodism and was personally responsible for its explosive expansion in converts and holdings. Similarly, Hannah More and Robert Raikes, the latter credited with starting the Sunday School movement, applauded, supported, and even emulated innovations in that movement by Wesleyan Methodists and Dissenters led by William Fox. Yet both were staunch Church of England Evangelicals.[8]

Such men and women were not eccentric examples of extreme religious sensibility. Their actions were in fact symptomatic of a widespread disposition which accounts for the fluidity, and even the harmony on certain issues, among groups not otherwise in sympathy. And as surprising as it may be in a nation renowned for its class divisions and religious and political fractiousness, the one issue on which the great majority of Englishmen were of like mind was child rearing. They shared a core of similar though hardly uniform inclinations and assumptions about the nature of children, how they ought to be reared, and especially the kinds of adults they ought to become.

Allowing for minor differences of class and for the gradual delay of the marriage age in the respectable classes as the century progressed, childhood was usually thought to consist of four stages: infancy (to four or five years); early childhood (four to eight); childhood (eight to twelve), and youth or adolescence (twelve or fourteen to financial and/ or social independence of parents; legally twenty-one for females, twenty-five for males). Instruction for the middle and upper classes and the fortunate poor began at three or four and continued ideally until twelve or fourteen, at which point the lower orders were apprenticed or found jobs and their betters were given further education.[9]

Childhood was the preparatory period used by wise parents (and a moral society) to plant the seeds of religious training, schooling, and whatever social forms or occupational skills the child was destined to by birth. A *nursery* (applied to many spheres of life) meant a place or set of conditions that nurtured what was needed and deemed right. And what was applicable to seamen or fledgling curates was certainly true for infants. Most adults still subscribed to the venerable notion of the child as an unformed or incomplete, diminutive adult, much like the finished product in essence and quality, differing only in quantity of experience or fixity of character and habit. These needs, education and training were meant to fulfill. And so the thousands of charity schools in Wales, Ireland, Scotland, and England generally agreed on what to study: the Bible, primers, catechisms, and often portions of *The Whole Duty of Man*, Richard Allestree's devotional and domestic conduct guide, published in 1658 and in print well into the late 1800s.[10]

It seems clear that the reason such agreement could exist for two difficult centuries and on so crucial a matter is that the population shared some vital, ingrained leaning that outweighed lesser differences. M. G. Jones has identified this as an "essentially puritan character," and she succinctly diagnoses this aspect of the complex English disposition: "The ambiguities arising from the use of the word puritanism tend to obscure its character in the eighteenth century. If puritanism be regarded as the exposition of theological dogma, the eighteenth century was little interested in it, but if it be regarded . . . as the expression of *an austere and devout religious temper*, apart from any particular dogmatic implications, *then it dominated the social life of the age to an extent not commonly recognized*." Further support of this illuminating insight comes from the late-nineteenth-century scholar Louise F. Field, commenting on a slightly different issue: "It has been said . . . that had the English nation been by nature frivolous, [John] Bunyan might have written his great work [*Pilgrim's Progress*] and yet have remained obscure. The intense earnestness of the Elstow tinker appeals to that stratum of seriousness which is the foundation of the English character."[11]

These critics explain a basic element in the English people of that age and help us to understand how the very classes and religious groups that

16. An American abridged *Pilgrim's Progress.* [John Bunyan], *The Christian Pilgrim,* 2 vols., 1798.

might have shied away from avowedly Puritan books as being not quite socially acceptable for their children in 1720, 1750, or even 1770, came to embrace, by the last decade of the century, fundamentally puritan or evangelical principles in every aspect of child life, including choice of literature.

Three phases of Puritan, Godly, or Evangelical literature exist for the period under study. The first, longest and most harrowing, has bequeathed to the others a stigma that is not entirely just. It lasted roughly from 1600 to the 1730s. The second ran from about 1740 to the 1770s; and the last from thence into the nineteenth century.

As strange as Puritan books of the first phase may seem, we must remember that they are less aberrant in the context of their time than they may seem to us. For the devout people who wrote the books and for much of England, an inner, subjective reality conspired with appalling circumstances to produce a state very like mass hysteria or psychosis. From 1640 on, England suffered the alarms and upsets of bloody civil war and recurring waves of religious oppression; and just as these began to abate, England was threatened with plague. At first it struck

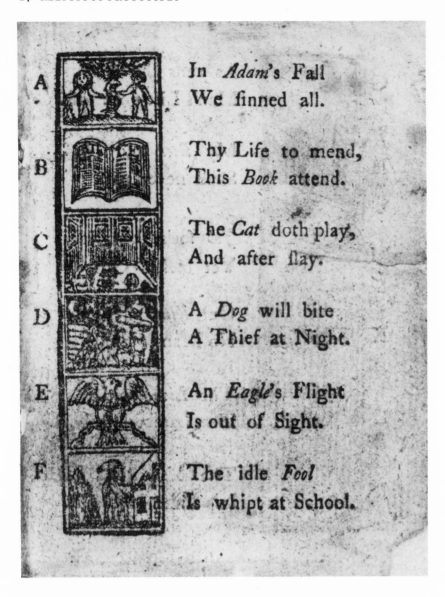

In *Adam's* Fall
We finned all.

Thy Life to mend,
This *Book* attend.

The *Cat* doth play,
And after flay.

A *Dog* will bite
A Thief at Night.

An *Eagle's* Flight
Is out of Sight.

The idle *Fool*
Is whipt at School.

17. "In Adam's Fall / We
sinned all." [Benjamin
Harris?], *The New-England
Primer Enlarged*, 1763.

with misleading mildness, claiming two foreigners and a few others in December 1664. Then it seemed to relent, perhaps due to the unusually severe winter. But with the spring, the plague broke out again with devastating virulence.[12]

In a short time, London became a charnel house; many provincial towns and villages were similarly decimated. With men, women, and children dropping dead in the streets or being boarded up in houses branded with the dreaded red cross to die of plague or starve, with the dead carts pursuing their grisly labors week after week, it is no wonder so many people became mentally unhinged. Some blamed the king's ungodliness for their sufferings. Many more were persuaded that the Last Judgment was at hand, "the fire next time" upon them. And when surely enough the plague began to abate and London timidly to breathe and hope again, in 1666 the Great Fire broke forth and much of London was consumed. The total loss of human life was as incalculable as the impact on the human psyche.[13]

To people already convinced that all mortal existence was a snare of the devil to lure the soul from God, such scenes acted powerfully to harden their resolve to sue for salvation for themselves and their surviving loved ones with utmost fervor. Only in the context of such harrowing ordeals can we glimpse with compassion the state of mind that could produce Janeway's *Token* and offer it to children, as a comfort and consolation in their lives.

Even before the disasters of plague and fire, however, the somberness of Puritan tales and poems stemmed directly from the radical Protestant emphasis on the solitariness of the individual or soul. Having demolished the traditional role of church and clergy as "divinely appointed" mediators between man and God in the matter of the soul's exculpation from Original Sin and personal transgressions, "Puritans" saw it as each person's responsibility to plead for mercy before the Seat of Judgment—no matter how tender his or her years. Even infants had to be examined for and guarded from sin. Consequently parents stood in unique relation to their offspring, ordinary human affection for many being second to their spiritual stewardship. Predictably these parents welcomed a literature to monitor those devil-haunted "idle hours," one that taught "little souls" to read and that focused their sights firmly on the word of God.

A variety of books was created to provide such safeguards. The prim-

18. The first (?) miniature
or "Thumb" Bible. *Biblia;
or, A Practical Summary,*
1727.

19. Job 30:28, 29; Psalm
27:20, 21. *A New
Hieroglyphical Bible,* 1842.

ers or Puritan ABC books taught the rudiments of reading through adaptations of biblical verses mixed with moral maxims and followed by
the catechism. Most such books were somber in tone: "A—In Adam's
Fall / We sinned all" and "B—Thy Life to mend / This *Book* attend." But
F. J. Harvey Darton describes one early Puritan ABC, *A Little Book for
Little Children* (*c.* 1702–12), which has glimmers of the lightheartedness
we associate with post-Newbery books—thus suggesting, if only by the
rule of exceptions, that even Puritan or Godly literature was by no
means monolithic, despite its dominant seriousness.[14]

The earliest Bibles likely to have had special appeal for the young
were at first produced for adults, miniatures of three of four centimeters
with Old and New Testament texts and fine copper-plate engravings.
Among these were John Weever's *Agnus Dei* (1601) and John Taylor's
Verbum sempiternum (1614). Gerald Gottlieb suggests that the first miniature or "Thumb" Bible for children may have been R. Wilkin's *Biblia;
or, A Practical Summary of Ye Old and New Testaments* (1727), measuring
four square centimeters, 278 pages long, and illustrated. These miniatures were much imitated later in the century by trade publishers and
came to be known as "Newbery Bibles." And in an excellent discussion
of the literary impact of the King James Bible on young readers, Mary
F. Thwaite mentions an even earlier version, Elisha Coles's *Youth's Visible Bible* (1675), containing twenty-four illustrations, though this may
have been published with another work.[15]

In addition to Bibles abridged, versified, and later in hieroglyphs,
young Puritans were offered stories based on scriptures, tales of martyrs
and other pious historical figures, and assorted volumes from parents or
other well-wishers offering sage advice. A rather engaging example of
this last is William Jole's *Father's Blessing Penn'd for the Instruction of his
CHILDREN. Containing Godly and Delightful Verses, Riddles, Fables,
Jests, Stories, Proverbs, Rules of Behaviour; And other useful Matter to allure
Children to Read. Adorn'd with 24 Cuts. By* W.J.A.M. (London: G. Conyers, 1674). Jole anticipates Locke's influential dictum, that the child be
enticed to learn (*Concerning Education,* 1693), and is both gentle in his
spiritual guidance and notably tolerant of playful childish pursuits, making this another exception to the prevailing mood of grim spiritual ur-
gency.

Nathaniel Crouch is an interesting example of a professional writer
in the early phase of Godly books, one who was prolific and highly es-

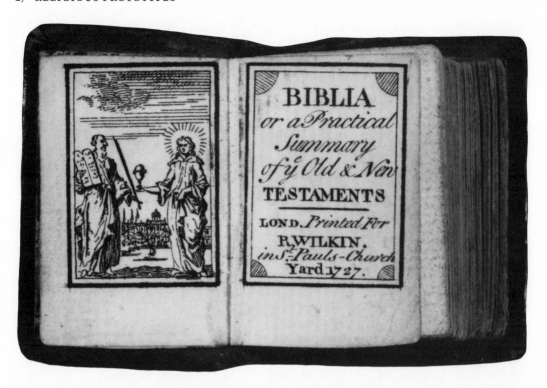

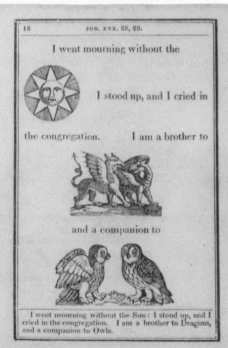

I went mourning without the

I stood up, and I cried in

the congregation.   I am a brother to

and a companion to

I went mourning without the Sun: I stood up, and I cried in the congregation.   I am a brother to Dragons, and a companion to Owls.

Deliver my soul from the

my darling from the

power of the   Save me

from the   's mouth: for

thou hast heard me from the

of the

Deliver my soul from the Sword, my darling from the power of the Dog.   Save me from the Lion's mouth: for thou hast heard me from the Horns of the Unicorns.

HUSH! my dear,

HUSH! my dear, lie ftill and flumber,
Holy angels guard thy bed !
Heavenly bleffings without number
Gently falling on thy head.

32. *The Whipping Top.*

1 SEE the tops on the pavement, they
   twirl and they bound,
And fwift is the circuit they take on the
   ground ;
The lads all purfuing, each doubles his
   blow,
And the fafter they fcourge them, the
   better they go.
x 3

20. "Hush! my dear."
Isaac Watts, *Celebrated
Cradle Hymn,* 1812.

21. "The Whipping Top."
John Oakman et al., *Moral
Songs,* [*c.* 1802].

teemed by his contemporaries and conservative parents through the next century. He published as "R. B." and Richard and Robert Burton. His very popular *The Young Man's Calling; or, The Whole Duty of Youth* (1678) is a revision of Samuel Crossman's *Young Man's Monitor* (1644). In his work—most of it derivative, some of it poor—Crouch used illustrations and exciting historical data woven into the (sometimes thin) moral fabric of the work to broaden his appeal. He also published "secular" histories, *England's Monarchs* (1685), *History of the Nine Worthies of the World* (1687), with accounts of Hector of Troy and Alexander the Great, and abridgements of travelogues of all the continents and major island groups, with good line engravings of native flora and fauna and rather rudimentary anthropological data (intermixed with tales of trade and military encounters), thus anticipating important trends in trade books toward the end of the eighteenth century and the first half of the nineteenth.

By far the most influential first-phase Puritan books were Janeway's *Tokens* (1672), Bunyan's *Pilgrim's Progress* (1678), and Dr. Isaac Watts's *Divine Songs Attempted in Easy Language for the Use of Children* (1715).

All are stamped with the high seriousness we expect of Puritan works, yet they offer very different experiences. The *Tokens*, with their grisly, detailed accounts of children suffering and dying, are macabre. The equally earnest and sometimes frightening *Pilgrim's Progress*, a thrilling adventure, follows Christian through his perilous trials to triumph. And Dr. Watts's *Songs* was especially important because it indicated a slight softening of the stark spirit epitomized in Janeway. The songs are by no means great poetry, but they represent one of the earliest efforts to write verse for the young, and they were long and widely read and recited.

Although certain examples of the grim-warning school of Puritan books continued to find an audience during the eighteenth century, most of what was written after the 1740s reveals a continued lightening of mood and after the 1770s, a growing secularism. Clearly Locke's ideas about luring the child to new understanding and better behavior were taking hold even among the very devout. In fact, children's Bibles that advertised a "lively and striking" approach to revealed truth confirm the general trend away from the mysticism of the Passion of the New Testament toward the Godly but also more worldly tales of the Old.[16] Insensibly, the stark Puritan perceptions of 1700 gave way to the intense but more mundane, worldly "Evangelicalism" of 1800. In a spirit in no way inconsistent with Evangelical *or* Enlightenment ideals, a popular work like Newbery's *Mosaic Creation* (1749) gloried in the new view, emphasizing the miracles of the natural world, God's handiwork, and the great love that engendered it. And when mortality was dealt with, as in Nathaniel Cotton's popular *Visions in Verse* (1757; 7th ed., 1767; new ed., 1808), death itself seems relieved of its sting. There is no evocation of fear and trembling over the aftermath: Cotton, reinforced by a kindly Seraph, assures young readers that reason, which leads them to a good life, and faith will secure them places in Heaven.

No coherent body of literature other than the Puritans' existed for publishers of the 1760s to tap, but there were individual types that had been or would soon be adapted to the ever growing demands of young readers, and among the most lucrative were the archetypes of the eighteenth-century alphabetories.

The earliest ABCs and hornbooks were very little like the engaging child-pleasers of the eighteenth century. They were utilitarian tools with origins in religious life, which gradually were secularized. ABC books are important to the rise of literacy in England, for as was indicated, the wide readership of the eighteenth and nineteenth centuries, which made possible the careers of a Newbery or a Charles Dickens, had its beginning in the nation's religious life. The uneven contents of early ABC books, elementary reading lessons combined with relatively complex religious selections, attest to the concerns that formed them. In particular, the belief that individuals must be able to read for themselves the documents of salvation made Bible reading among even the lowliest acceptable, at least to many.

Originally, many of the readings were in Latin, but by 1549, two years after the death of Henry VIII, the litanies of the Anglican service, parts of Holy Communion, prayers, and the Commandments were "Englished." Over the next century the evolution of the ABCs, or "primers," reflected developments in the new state church; and after the civil war (1642–46) ABCs came under Puritan control. As their formal churchly function diminished toward the end of the seventeenth century, their secular content was enlarged.[17] As early as 1671 this nursery alphabet song was generally familiar:

A is for Apple-pasty [pie],
B baked it,
C cut it,
D divided it,
E eat it . . .
T took it . . .
X, Y, Z, and ampersand
All wished for a piece in hand.[18]

By 1780, entertaining alphabets were a staple of the trade: ABCs of animals, of occupations, of temperament and virtue; German and French ABCs for the affluent; and later (1850) alphabets of trains ("F is for FOG, that in winter we find / Often causes the train to be hours behind"), nations, music making and singing (*The Merry Cobbler* [Glasgow: J. Lumsden, *c.* 1815]), and history. *The Historical Alphabet* (London: John Harris, 1811–12) ends with the bloody Mary Tudor of evergreen memory as "Zealot Mary, a wretched bigot and cruel Queen," shown warming her hands at a fire fueled by a martyr.[19] Of course, the fanciful alphabet books of Newbery and Cooper had led the way from the 1740s.

Related to abecedaria, hornbooks and battledores teach the same ba-

22."O, since the Crop
depends on you, / Give
them the culture which is
due." [Nathaniel Cotton],
Visions in Verse, 1808.

23. "Bringing the Word to
Mohawk youngsters." *A
Primer, for the Use of the
Mohawk Children*, 1786.

Cotton's
VISIONS
IN
VERSE,
For the
ENTERTAINMENT AND INSTRUCTION
OF
YOUNGER MINDS.

Virginibus puerisque canto.   *Hor.*

A NEW EDITION.

LONDON:
PRINTED FOR VERNOR, HOOD, AND SHARPE;
CUTHELL AND MARTIN; J. WALKER; LACK-
INGTON, ALLEN, AND CO.; R. LEA; J. NUNN;
DARTON AND HARVEY; SCATCHARD AND
LETTERMAN; LONGMAN, HURST, REES, AND
ORME; AND J. MURRAY.

1808.

"Osince the Crop depends on you,
Give them the culture which is due."
Vision 2 Page 33.

A
PRIMER,
FOR THE USE OF THE
MOHAWK CHILDREN,
To acquire the SPELLING and READING of their
OWN, as well as to get acquainted with the
ENGLISH, Tongue; which for that Purpose is put
on the opposite Page.

WAERIGHWAGHSAWE
IKSAONGOENWA

Tsiwaondad-derighhonny Kaghyadoghfera; Nayon-
deweyeftaghk ayeweanaghnodon ayeghyadow Ka-
niyenkehaga Kaweanondaghkouh; Dyorheaf-haga
oni tsinihadiweanotea.

LONDON,
PRINTED BY C. BUCKTON, GREAT PULTNEY-STREET.
1786.

Jones Rockey Sculp. 1786

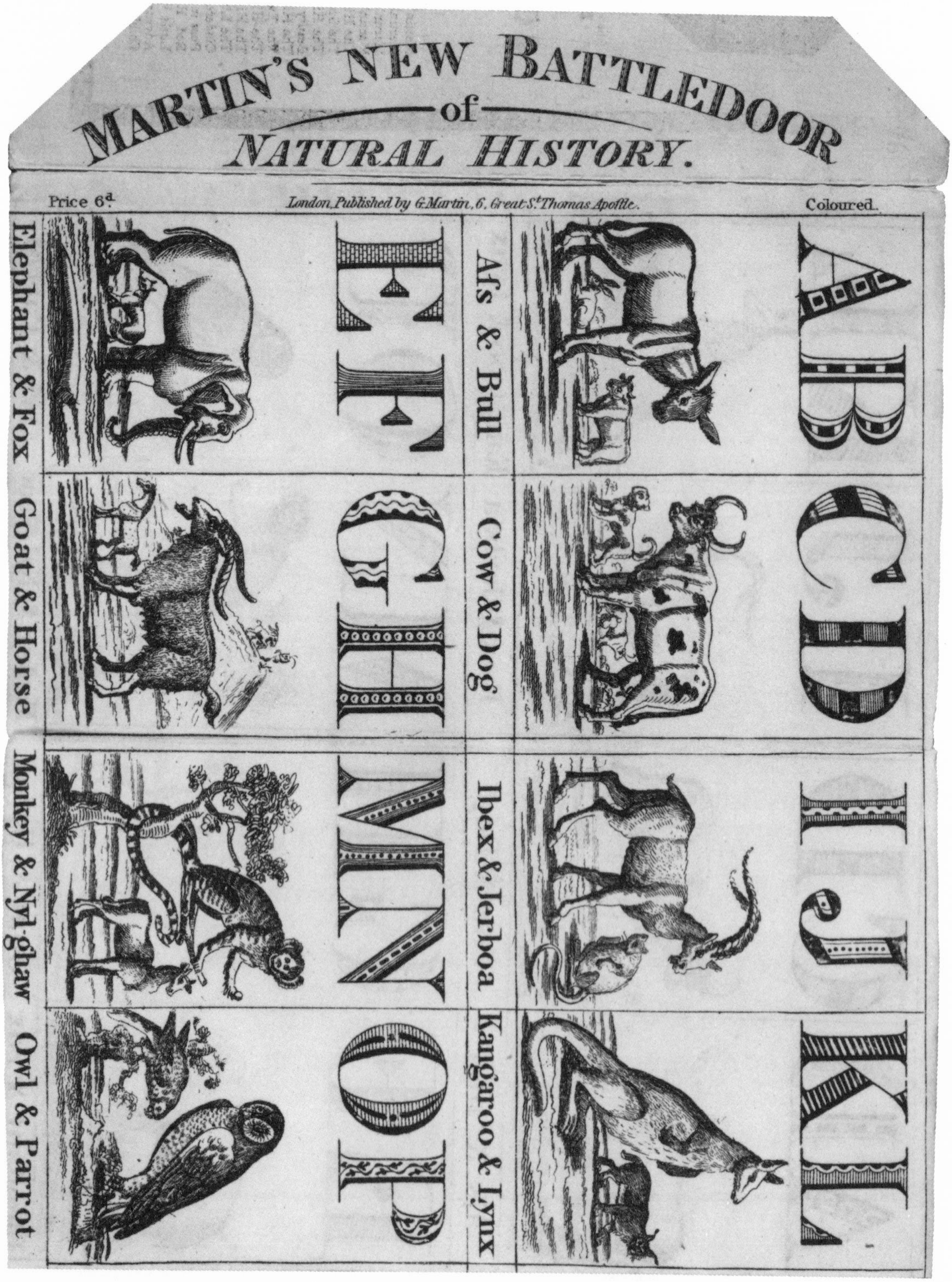

MARTIN'S NEW BATTLEDOOR

of

NATURAL HISTORY.

Price 6.ᵈ   London, Published by G. Martin, 6, Great St Thomas Apostle.   Coloured.

A B

C D

I J

K L

Afs & Bull

Cow & Dog

Ibex & Jerboa

Kangaroo & Lynx

E F

G H

M N O P

Elephant & Fox

Goat & Horse

Monkey & Nyl-ghaw

Owl & Parrot

sic lessons but were not originally books. Invented possibly in the fifteenth century to preserve costly, perishable paper from the depredations of small boys and others, the child's hornbook was usually constructed of a sheet of paper printed on one side, glued to a short-handled wooden rectangle that resembled a paddle. In some the handle had a hole cut in it through which a cord passed to tie about a child's waist. The paper was covered with translucent horn, fixed to the wood with a metal trim and nailed in place. The hornbook's nickname, battledore, came from the irreverent use boys put it to batting shuttlecocks. Early hornbooks contained alphabets in roman, italic, and black letter (a thick, ugly type found in early chapbooks) print, a list of vowels, and a syllabarium (standard table of syllables) to be memorized.[20]

24. "Ass & Bull . . . Owl & Parrot." *Martin's New Battledoor of Natural History*, [c. 1810].

From this schoolroom tool developed fanciful hornbooks, pleasing to the eye and even to the palate. In 1718 Matthew Prior described an inducement to learning that Newbery would make famous:

To Master John the ENGLISH Maid
A Horn-book gives of Ginger-bread:
And that the Child may learn the better,
As He can name, He eats the letter:
Proceeding thus with vast Delight,
He spells, and gnaws, from Left to Right.[21]

This was exactly the program Gaffer Gingerbread set up to start the famed Giles on the road to wealth and position.

Less perishable, for many have survived, were the whimsical paper hornbooks and battledores covered with floral designs called Dutch paper, hand-colored by child laborers. Some folded like a triptych, with flaps to seal them. Like the ABC books, these hornbooks soon added pictures to the alphabets, organized on a theme. A fine example is George Martin's *New Battledoor of Natural History* (1810), in which English children inspected excellent engravings of common creatures like the *a*ss and *b*ull and the more exotic *i*bex and *j*erboa. Pretty covers, pictures, and amusing bits and pieces transformed the starkly functional fare of the original battledore into a favorite of small children that sold briskly into the late nineteenth century.

Other borrowings from religious sources that found their way into children's literature are bestiaries and animal fables. In their earliest forms both were controlled by medieval monks, jealous guardians of

learning, who added their levy of religious and moral freight. Their moralizing penchant in bestiaries was consistent with the source, the *Physiologus* or *Naturalist*, in a tenth-century Greek manuscript of an earlier treatise. This collection of over forty sketches purportedly from natural history describes fabulous animals whose behavior and nature are vehicles for religious and moral lessons. From this source came the earliest bestiaries, extremely beautiful illuminated manuscripts made by the age's best artists and copiers for monasteries and the great nobility. Early printed bestiaries or natural histories were also very costly and were accessible chiefly to the privileged, seldom to the ordinary adult or child. Although in Europe there were surprisingly early efforts (1493) to make inexpensive pamphlet versions of these widely available, I am aware of no such popular developments in England until just before 1700.[22] Only gradually between 1600 and 1770 did printed natural histories become accessible to a wide audience.

One early example stands out because it was written for children, perhaps for classroom use: Edward Topsell's *Historie of Foure-Footed Beasts* (vol. 1, 1607; vol. 2, 1608). This is thought to have influenced the first "modern" children's natural histories: Thomas Boreman's *Description of Three Hundred Animals; viz. Beasts, Birds, Fishes, Serpents and Insects* (1730) and *Description of a Great Variety of Animals and Vegetables; viz. Beasts . . . Plants, Fruits, and Flowers* (1736), which remained in print throughout the century.

Like the bestiaries and moralized natural histories, Topsell's and Boreman's books preserved and helped canonize a wealth of dubious "data." Cheek by jowl, beak, or fang with the lizard, dog, asp, cock, and porcupine may be found the seven-headed hydra, the griffin (half eagle, half lion), the manticore (human face, lion's body, scorpion's tail), the mermaid, and of course the unicorn.

Lore on even the most mundane animals was permeated by the fabulous, as Brian Alderson explains delightfully.[23] Moreover, there are accounts of morally upright storks who, with fine Old Testament spirit, punish females suspected of infidelity (evidenced by foreign eggs in the nest) with death; of pious elephant sun- and moon-worshippers who look to the east on the rare occasions when they copulate, perhaps in remembrance of Eden, their paradise lost; and of pelican martyr-mothers who rend their breasts, offering their very life's blood to their starving young, a favorite symbol of Christian selflessness in emblem

25. The Pelican feeds her young with her life's blood. *Les Dictz Des Oiseaux* [sic] *et Des Bestes,* [c. 1493].

26. The Hydra. Edward Topsell, *The Historie of Foure-Footed Beasts and Serpents,* 1658.

books. There are reports of the efficacy of crocodile dung to cure baldness; and of wolves and even tigers that can be destroyed, "if you look at them back-wards between your legs." Less marvelous but equally doubtful information abounded, about the ostrich's head-hiding, the porcupine's quill-throwing, or the bear's cub-licking tricks. Predictably, lore of this sort is not easily dislodged by reason or science. And even when such venerated fictions were punctured, the more hardy of the creatures simply moved with swift and sure grace from the province of science to the universe of fantasy.

Between Topsell's *Historie* (combined ed., 1658) and Boreman's *Descriptions* (1730, 1736), only one other major work of natural history for children seems to have been published. *A Short and Easie Method to give Children an Idea or True Notion of Celestial and Terrestrial Beings* (1710), described as a "very early science book," aimed "to teach the names of most things that are useful and necessary to human life; as also of arts and sciences, plants, fruits and living creatures." [24] In addition to these encyclopedic goals, this early book of information has two features that link it to pioneering schoolbooks: It is a French-language text and also a picture book, like many of the works inspired by Johann Amos Comenius's famous *Orbis Sensualium Pictus* (1658; 1st English ed., 1659). The format for the engravings in *A Short . . . Method*—numerous miniature figures on each of its thirty-eight copper plates—is anticipatory of that in popular children's emblem books and several eighteenth-century Aesops.

Clearly there was much copying, of whatever was likely to rivet the eye and prove "taking to" young minds (as John Locke put it) and was convenient for the printer's layout, among authors of such books. We find, for example, pictorial Aesops that are also language texts; emblem works that might have been used as encyclopedic books of knowledge; language books that serve up both proverbs and pictures of the world's visible and *in*visible aspects; and at least one polyglot emblem book that could have doubled, and probably did, as an introductory reader for Latin, English, French, and German, with smatterings of Italian and Spanish—*Emblems for the Entertainment and Improvement of Youth* (1733, 1750, 1769, 1787, 1788). [25] Indeed, much of the improvement in the illustrations of texts like *Orbis Sensualium Pictus* in the late seventeenth century, especially the multiple miniature vignette format, may have been owed to emblem books, in particular to the "Cabinets" of numer-

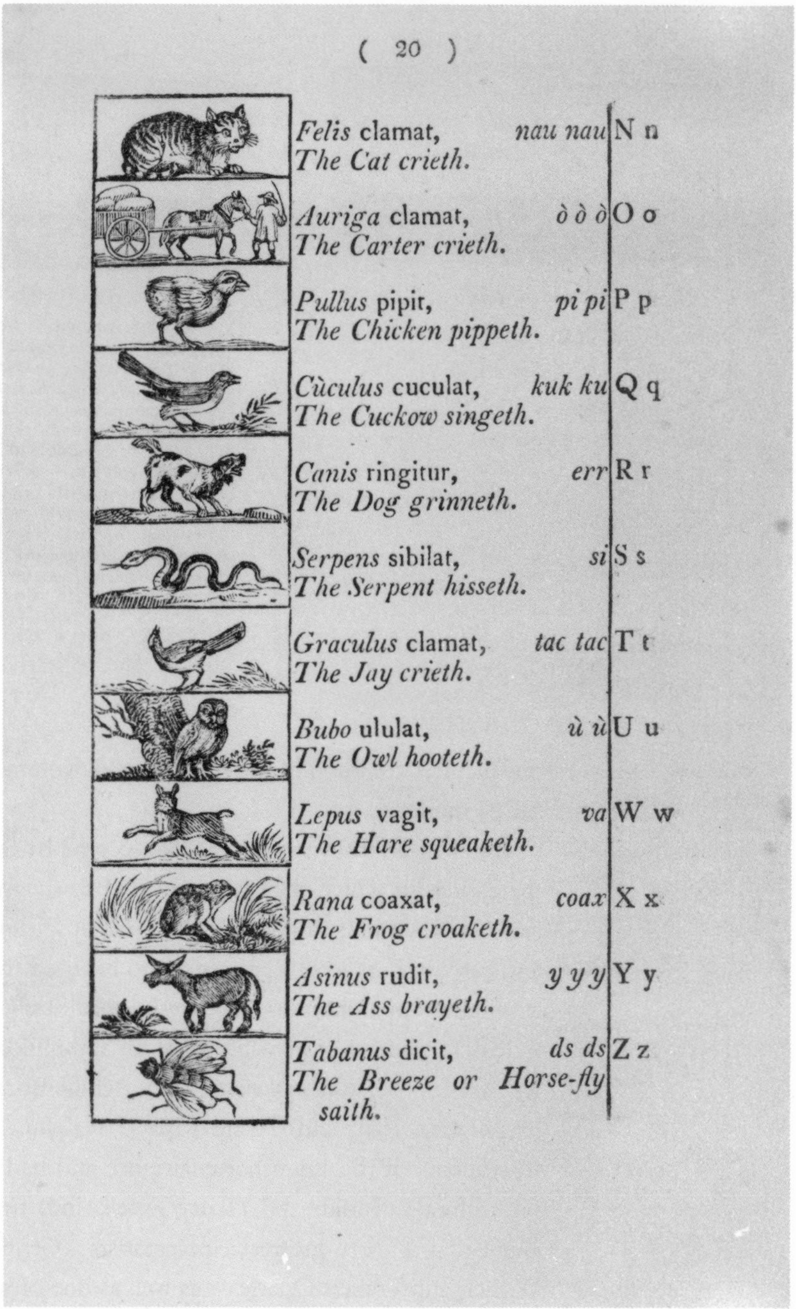

(20)

Felis clamat,	*nau nau*	N n
The Cat crieth.		
Auriga clamat,	*ò ò ò*	O o
The Carter crieth.		
Pullus pipit,	*pi pi*	P p
The Chicken pippeth.		
Cùculus cuculat,	*kuk ku*	Q q
The Cuckow singeth.		
Canis ringitur,	*err*	R r
The Dog grinneth.		
Serpens sibilat,	*si*	S s
The Serpent hisseth.		
Graculus clamat,	*tac tac*	T t
The Jay crieth.		
Bubo ululat,	*ù ù*	U u
The Owl hooteth.		
Lepus vagit,	*va*	W w
The Hare squeaketh.		
Rana coaxat,	*coax*	X x
The Frog croaketh.		
Asinus rudit,	*y y y*	Y y
The Ass brayeth.		
Tabanus dicit,	*ds ds*	Z z
The Breeze or Horse-fly saith.		

27. "*Felis* clamat /
The Cat crieth." Johann
Amos Comenius, *Orbis
Sensualiam Pictus,* 1810.

84   Mr. JOHN BUNYAN's

Of Man by Nature.

FROM God he's a back-flider,
Of ways he loves the wider;
With wickednefs a fider,
More venom than a fpider.
    In fin he's a confider,
A make-bate and divider;
Blind reafon is his guider,
The devil is his rider.

DIVINE EMBLEMS.   85

Upon the Difobedient Child.

CHILDREN, when little, how do they delight us!
When they grow bigger, they begin to fright us.
Their finful nature prompts them to rebel,
And to delight in paths that lead to hell.
Their parents love and care they overlook,
As if relation had them quite forfook.
They take the counfels of the wanton, rather
Than the moft grave inftructions of a father,
They reckon parents ought to do for them,
Though they the fifth commandment do contemn.
They fnap, and fnarl, if parents them controul,
Although in things moft hurtful to the foul,
They reckon they are mafters, and that we
Who parents are, fhould to them fubject be.
If parents fain would have a hand in chufing,
The children have a heart ftill in refufing.
                    G

28. "Of Man by Nature."
John Bunyan, *Divine
Emblems*, [*c.* 1790].

ous pictures common to the small, homely volumes from Germany and the Netherlands.

Emblem books were universally accepted by the English because of the ease with which they were adapted to didactic ends and also the appeal of their illustrations. This was perhaps fitting, since their creators and early writers were Platonists who believed that visual imagery, including all apparent mundane physical realities, was a mere vehicle and a cloak for hidden or invisible religious and philosophic eternal mysteries. Andrea Alciati (*Emblemata*, 1531), Achille Bocchi (*Symbolicarum . . . de uniuerso*, 1555), and Cesare Ripa (*Iconologia*, 1593) are well known to students of the English Renaissance and had their followers (e.g., Sir Joshua Reynolds and Henry Fuseli) into the nineteenth century. But Britain's three greatest emblematists—Geoffrey Whitney, George Wither, and Francis Quarles—as well as one of her greatest Romantic poet-artists, William Blake, were influenced as well by men like Nicholas Reusner, Johannes Sambucus, Martin de Vos, Jan Van Vianen, Claude Paradin, and Hans Holbein, all of whose illustrations are reflected in children's emblem books.[26]

Oddly enough, however, one of the earliest "emblemaria" for children, John Bunyan's *Book for Boys and Girls; or, Country Rhimes for Children* (1686), first appeared without pictures. It featured poems as emblems with "applications" to limn their symbolic meaning—"A Penny Loaf" (No. 44), "Candles" (13, 42), "A Pair of Spectacles" (63), "The Snail" (57), and anticipating the spirit of Locke's famed analogy, a "Sheet of White Paper" (70). Bunyan's workmanlike verse was revised and renamed *Divine Emblems; or, Temporal Things Spiritualized* in 1701, and joined to pictures in 1707. Unlike most later juvenile emblemaria, Bunyan's was outside the mainstream of the larger tradition. But in a short time appeared works borrowing heavily from the best of the verbal and visual tradition of the Europeans, like *Delights for the Ingenious, in above Fifty Selected and Choice Emblems* (1684) and *Choice Emblems, Divine and Moral* (1721), both by R. B. [Nathaniel Crouch], the prolific compiler of Puritan children's books. The second was understandably popular, since it was lifted from George Wither's *Collection of Emblems* (1635). And it seems on internal evidence that Wither was greatly influenced by the Latin text *Occulum animumque . . . emblematum* (Amsterdam, 1718), from which that later, very esteemed work *Emblems for the Entertainment and Improvement of Youth* (1733) was taken almost verbatim and with identical pictures and format.

The special charm and enormous appeal of these little books can be experienced only at first hand. On the whole, the earlier they are the better, for the genre became horribly overloaded with didacticism as the century progressed. This perhaps hastened the genre's decline, though it was comparatively long-lived, selling successfully into the nineteenth century and retaining a small following to its end. Certainly emblemaria were an important part of the more affluent trade in early children's books, as J. H. Wynne's *Choice Emblems, Natural, Historical, Fabulous, Moral and Divine; For the Improvement and Amusement of Youth* illustrates. It may have been "Written for . . . a Young Nobleman," but it was published by Elizabeth Newbery, and from that we may deduce that it was meant for ordinary readers and volume sales. Even Thomas and John Bewick's more somber *Emblems of Mortality* (1789) found an audience, as did revivals of the works of Quarles and Wither (1736, 1766, *ca.* 1790, 1816, 1866).

These diverse forms associated with England's religious life were all adapted for the entertainment and instruction of children once juvenile literature became a viable trade and ceased to be only an occasional pro-

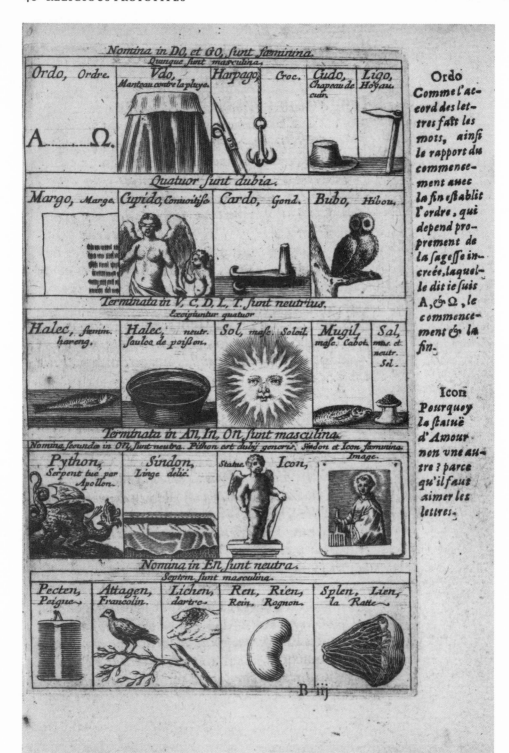

29. "Ordo, Ordre [order] ... Bubo, Hibou [owl]." [Louis Couvay], *Méthode Nouvelle et Très-Exacte,* 1649.

30. "He cometh forth like a Flower, and is cut down." [Hans Holbein], *Emblems of Mortality,* engraved by T. and J. Bewick, 1789.

[39]

The CHILD.

Man that is born of a Woman, is of few Days, and full of Trouble. He cometh forth like a Flower, and is cut down: He fleeth also as a Shadow, and continueth not.

JOB xiv. 1.

Man, who conceiv'd in the dark Womb,
Into the World is brought,
Is born to Times with Misery,
And various Evil fraught.

And as the Flow'r soon fades and dies,
However fair it be,
So sinks he also to the Grave,
And like a Shade does flee.

E 2

duction or the concern chiefly of the Puritans. Yet it was this group that was most influential in the industry that developed after 1740. Puritan values and concerns were transformed or secularized and widely disseminated during the sixties, seventies, and eighties and, in the new guise of Methodism created by John and Charles Wesley, were spread via a network of outdoor revivals and, later, of churches and schools at an astonishing rate throughout the lower and lower-middle and artisan classes in England. These were the especial targets for sales of the first entrepreneurs—Newbery, Baldwin, and Cluer Dicey. And these classes remained an essential and growing portion of the book-buying public even after tradesmen, themselves often partial to Puritan or Methodist ideals, had been (temporarily) relegated to a secondary role by conservative, establishmentarian writers and propagandists.

3. Secular Adult Forerunners of Juvenile Books, and Early Audiences

By the late eighteenth century, emblem books shed many of the qualities they once shared with school and language texts, early Aesops, and books of knowledge. Greater specialization within the last, a response to the explosion of scientific information from the final decades of the century on, in part effected the divergence of the types. But this also reflected or perhaps actually foreshadowed larger intellectual developments: Technically severed in the late seventeenth and early eighteenth centuries, science and religion in fact became independent, if not yet openly antagonistic, by the beginning of the nineteenth. Yet before the divergence of trade genres, considerable overlapping and cross-fertilizing occurred in emblemaria, books of knowledge, language texts, and Aesops.[1]

One such multipurpose book, whose author may have been influenced by Comenius and the emblematists or may merely have expressed the spirit of the times, deserves special mention: *Aesop's Fables In English And Latin, Interlineary, For The Benefit Of Those Who Not Having A Master Would Learn Either Of Those Tongues* (1703). The title page of the 1723 edition states, "By John Locke, Gent." It was issued by his publishers, A. and J. Churchil [*sic*] of London, and may actually have been connected with Locke (1632–1704) in some way, but there is no conclusive proof of this. *Aesop's Fables* was certainly one book Locke endorsed enthusiastically for children; and his views on methods to teach languages and on the use of pictures (here, sixteen tidy little cuts to a plate, mostly of animals) are consistent with that of the work. Yet Locke's book or not, it seems to have had limited success or influence on early children's books.[2] Although this *Aesop* is rare and a bit of a curiosity, Aesop's animals have for so long been staunch habitués of the nursery that we must remind ourselves that they too were transplants.

A Lion was Entangled in a Snare,
Nor could his teeth or paws y.e ambush teare
Since his wilde Struglings more engag'd him
The treacherous foldings of y.e ruder Gin.

Doe not y.e humble w.th neglect dispise.

When a kinde Mouse by gnawing did vntwine
The Snarled Cordage of the raveld line
So did the Lion Life and freedome gett,
Infranchis'd from y.e Prison of his Nett.

A Mouse a Lion rescu'd from Surprize.

FAB. XXIII. *De Leone & Mure.*

LEO *æstu, cursuq; defessus in umbra quiescebat, Murinum autem grege tergum ejus percurrente expergefactus unum è multis comprehendit, Supplicat misellus, clamitans Indignum se esse cui irascatur; Leo reputans nihil laudis esse in Nece tantillæ bestiolæ captivum dimittit; Non multo post, Leo dum per segetes currit incidit in plagas, rugire licet, exire non licet, Rugientem Leonem Mus audit, vocem agnoscit, repit in cuniculos, & quæsitos laqueorum nodos invenit, corroditque, quo facto Leo è plagis evadit.*

MORALE.

INTERDUM *& ipsi potentes egent ope servorum humilimorum, Vir prudens igitur etiamsi potest, timebit tamen, vel vilissimo homuncioni nocere; Nihil est quod magis commendat Reges quam clementia, & annexa potestati Moderatio.*

R 2

FAB.

31. "A Lion was Entangled in a Snare." *Aesop's Fables With His Life,* illustrated by Francis Barlow, 1666.

32. "An Ape . . . a Weesell." *Aesop's Fables, In English and Latin* [ed. John Locke?], 1703.

Of the many English editions between Caxton's of 1484 and 1760, I will discuss six that were vital to the establishment of Aesop as a denizen of the nursery, independent of the existence of the many schooltexts of the fables printed between 1600 and 1760. The first, *Aesop's Fables With His Life: In English, French & Latin. The English by Tho. Phillipott . . . The French and Latin by Rob. Codrington . . . Illustrated with one hundred and twelve sculptures by Francis Barlow* (1666), is known as the Barlow edition. Barlow, a master of book illustration, was also a painter of some note in his day for his scenes of sports and depictions of animals. His illustrations, not the text, influenced developments in children's literature. Shortly after this edition appeared, the bulk fell victim to the Great

Fire of London in 1666, and Barlow issued a second version in 1687, with Phillipott's rhymed English replaced by that of Aphra Behn, playwright, poet, and novelist. Barlow intended both versions for children, and his illustrations must have delighted their audience as surely as they inspired their numerous imitators.

Despite Barlow's and the many school Aesops available, not until 1692 did there appear one for children's leisure that combined light-heartedness with the lively colloquialisms likely to appeal to them. Moreover, like Henry Peacham's prose *Aesop's Fables* (1639) and John Ogilby's *Aesop, Paraphras'd in Verse* (1651) for adults, Roger L'Estrange's version was not a polyglot (in the schoolbook tradition) and was thus more clearly devoted to entertainment. The contrast between L'Estrange's style and that of earlier children's translations is important.

Behn's language in the 1687 Barlow edition is courtly, but many of the plots are pared to near incomprehensibility, very likely on the assumption that readers might fill in, from the fuller French and Latin prose accounts, details omitted from her crabbed, elliptical English verse. In "The Nurse and Wolf," for example, Behn sacrifices much for economy and rhyme:

> A Nurse, to make her Bantling cease to cry
> Told it, the Wolf should eat it instantly,
>
> This heard, the Wolf, and for his prey he waits,
> But the Child slept, and all his hopes defeats.
>
> Morall: Trust not a womans [*sic*] vows, her fickle mind,
> Is far less constant than the seas, and wind.

In contrast, L'Estrange's "A Nurse and a Wolfe," is compact but lively: "As a Wolfe was Hunting up and down for his Supper, he pass'd by a Door when a Little Child was Bawling, and an Old Woman chiding it. *Leave your Vixen-Tricks,* says the *Woman, or I'll throw ye to the Wolfe.*" Hearing this, the wolf waits hopefully for his free meal, tires of waiting, leaves, and returns, only to find that matters altered, and not in his favor: "The Nurse he found had Chang'd her Note[:] for she was Then Muzzling and Cokesing of it. *That's a Good Dear,* says she, *If the Wolfe comes for My Child, We'll e'en Beat his Brains out.* The *Wolfe* went Muttering away upon't. There's No Meddling with People, says he, that say One Thing and Mean Another." The moral, says L'Estrange, is that frail

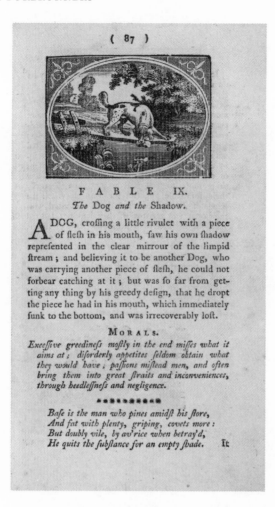

(87)

FABLE IX.
The Dog *and the* Shadow.

A DOG, crossing a little rivulet with a piece of flesh in his mouth, saw his own shadow represented in the clear mirrour of the limpid stream ; and believing it to be another Dog, who was carrying another piece of flesh, he could not forbear catching at it ; but was so far from getting any thing by his greedy design, that he dropt the piece he had in his mouth, which immediately sunk to the bottom, and was irrecoverably lost.

MORALS.

Excessive greediness mostly in the end misses what it aims at ; disorderly appetites seldom obtain what they would have ; passions mislead men, and often bring them into great straits and inconveniences, through heedlessness and negligence.

❋◆❋◆❋◆❋◆❋

*Base is the man who pines amidst his store,
And fat with plenty, griping, covets more :
But doubly vile, by av'rice when betray'd,
He quits the substance for an empty shade.* It

33. "The Dog and the Shadow." [Aesop], *Select Fables, In Three Parts,* illustrated by T. and J. Bewick, 1784.

humans must, like the babe, be frightened into doing their duty when all else fails.[3] For youthful audiences, this was more like the thing. Indeed, the colloquial vigor, humor, and ease of L'Estrange's style gained him a great following and influenced many later versions of Aesop.

Whether or not L'Estrange's *Fables of Aesop and other Eminent Mythologists; With Morals and Reflexions* (1692) was actually perused by great numbers of children, however, is a question. It is a mammoth work, perhaps the largest English collection of fables of the time, with five hundred narratives drawn from ancients like Aesop, Barlandus, Anianus, Abstemius, Phaedrus, and Babrius, and from moderns like La Fontaine. No doubt the cost restricted the class of children who could or would resort to it. Furthermore, it was not illustrated. Yet some scholars argue, rightly I think, that it was at least in part intended for

Page 42.

37 Sick-man and Sons.

38 Lion & Gnat.

39 Miser & his Treasure.

40 Minerva and the Olive.

41 The Mimicks.

42 Dog & Crocodile.

43 Wolf in disguise.

44 Bee and Spider.

45 Ass and his Master.

46 Cock and Fox.

47 The Eagle and Crow.

48 The Farmer and Stag.

Page 42.

37 Sick-man and Sons.   38 Lion & Gnat.   39 Miser & his Treasure.

40 Minerva and the Olive.   41 The 2 Mimicks.   42 Dog & Crocodile.

43 Wolf in disguise.   44 Bee and Spider.   45 Ass and his Master.

46 Cock and Fox.   47 The Eagle and Crow.   48 The Farmer and Stag.

ANCIENT FABLES.   43

their lands yielded a far more *plentiful crop* than those of their neighbours. At the end of the year, when they were settling their accounts, and computing their extraordinary profits, I would venture a wager, said one of the brothers more acute than the rest, that this was the *concealed wealth* my father meant. I am sure, at least, we have found by experience, that " *Industry is itself a treasure.*"

FABLE XXXVIII.

The Lion and the Gnat.

AVAUNT! thou paltry, contemptible insect! said a proud Lion one day to a Gnat that was frisking about in the air near his den. The Gnat, enraged at this unprovoked insult, vowed revenge, and immediately settled upon the Lion's neck. After having sufficiently teized him in that quarter, she quitted her station and retired under his belly; and from thence made her last and most formidable attack in his nostrils, where stinging him almost to madness, the Lion at length fell down, utterly spent with rage, vexation, and pain. The Gnat having thus abundantly

34. "Sick-man and Sons. . . ." [Robert Dodsley], *Select Fables of Esop,* 1761.

34a. Pages 42 and 43. *Select Fables of Esop,* 1761.

youngsters and was read by many of them over the next thirty or forty years. At least two points support this view: The second edition appeared in 1694 and another in 1714, an indication that it sold well; and, more tellingly, L'Estrange was vehemently attacked for his influence on children by the next prominent editor of Aesop.[4]

The Rev. Samuel Croxall found L'Estrange's edition offensive because of the author's militant Roman Catholic views, especially as these were elaborated in the lengthy "Reflexions" that followed the brief "Morals." A translator of some note, Croxall obviously had no quarrel with the style of the fables, to which his own is similar. But the learned doctor, soon to be Chancellor of Hereford Cathedral, found L'Estrange's fulminations on rebellion against Rome and British tyranny intolerable. He set out to counteract their contaminating influence on the nation's young and literally to drive that work from the bookshelves with his own *Fables of Aesop and Others. Newly done into English with an Application to each Fable. Illustrated with Cutts* (1722). Doubtless he knew the value of those "cutts" in his campaign against L'Estrange.

Although few moderns would consider L'Estrange's moral reflections suitable for the young, few would like any better those of other writers of the age, including Behn, Croxall, or later Richardson. Early literature for the young has a worldly, adult quality many moderns find odd and unsettling, a matter we will later explore. But Croxall's sermonizing was free of what he considered "the Catholic taint," and it was mercifully brief. His work was as prized as he had hoped, for it fulfilled a special need. It had illustrations influenced by Barlow's splendid designs, engraved by Elisha Kirkall in relief on metal in what would come to be known as the white-line technique, which was later popularized by Thomas Bewick.

Croxall achieved his goal. His book was enthusiastically welcomed by children and parents, as evidenced by the many reprintings it had throughout the century. Its vogue was not seriously challenged for nearly four decades, despite the appearance in 1740 of Samuel Richardson's *Aesop's Fables*, which relies heavily on L'Estrange's version, is charmingly illustrated, and is consequently an appealing edition. Though this competed well and had its own following, it did not oust the divine's translation, which remained preeminent until the appearance of writer, publisher, and bookseller Robert Dodsley's *Select Fables of Esop [sic] and Other Eminent Fabulists* in 1761.

Dodsley's edition was done by the printer John Baskerville of Birmingham and was illustrated with splendid engravings by Reynolds Grignion, after the art of Samuel Wale, and since its text is rather lively, it not surprisingly rivalled Croxall's. Its format resembles the supposed "Locke" Aesop (1703, 1723), each plate having twelve very fine miniature vignettes in circular cuts set in square frames, under which are numbers and titles corresponding to the text. Considering its quality, the edition was reasonably priced at 5*s*., as one scholar observes.[5]

Understandably, *Select Fables of Esop* was in vogue to the end of the century, when it was gradually superseded by the Newcastle publisher Thomas Saint's *Select Fables, In Three Parts* (1784). The importance of this edition is that it was illustrated by the great Thomas Bewick, using the white-line engraving technique that revolutionized children's book illustrations. With the publication of the editions of Barlow, L'Estrange,

Croxall, Richardson, Dodsley, and Bewick (Saint), the fables of Aesop were firmly ensconced in the child's world of leisure reading.

To be sure, the appearance of the famed Bewick edition hardly marked the end of the publishing story of Aesop for children. For in the nineteenth century, as now, not a Christmas passed that did not bring at least one new edition to the bookshops, and a new generation of youngsters entered that fanciful world where foxes covet grapes and are bested by clever cocks; where brave mice succor lions and foolish ones are eaten by weasels; and boys cry "Wolf!" and a wolf outwitted by a cunning jackass cries uncle.

Another minor category in children's books that became important is books of courtesy. The history of the English branch of these is complicated and need not be parsed here. It suffices to note that its three lines of development were pertinent to the field. Like its Italian and French prototypes of the fourteenth century, the English courtesy book evolved in response to changes in the world of the nobility partly stimulated by courtly romance and chivalric literature. In England such books were meant for the sons of the highest classes and were often unpretentious, even colloquial, and consequently much liked. Two of the best-known examples are *The Babees Book* (*c.* 1475) and *Stans puer ad mensam (The Boy is standing at the table)*. The latter appeared simultaneously in Latin and in English verse with translation ascribed to John Lydgate, its earliest known printing by Caxton (*c.* 1479). Both works taught the rules of the table, courtly manners, and comportment, intermixed with lessons in piety.

A second kind of courtesy book also for the young was a more modern sort, a training manual for workers. It was aimed not at the leisured wealthy but at the lowly-born ambitious youths whose ignorance of the manners obtaining in upper-class households barred their procuring coveted posts as servants. There were many "books of nurture," a common title, but John Russell's "Boke of Nurture" (*c.* 1460–70) was inspired by an encounter with a boy whose ignorance frustrated his ambition. Russell's "Boke" was designed to help such boys bridge the gulf between their world and that of the wealthy.[6] As Louise F. Field has noted, small tracts and pamphlets first in manuscript and later in print were abundant from the fifteenth century, which seems likely to have enlarged the impact of these training manuals on the lower classes.[7] They must have been relatively inexpensive and, like the seventeenth-

35. "When the loud laugh prevails, at your expence. . . ." "Solomon Winlove" [Oliver Goldsmith?], *Moral Lectures,* 1769.

36. "I must not ugly faces scrawl." [R. Ransome], *The Good Boy's Soliloquy,* 1811.

36a. "I must not . . . spoil a lock." [R. Ransome], *The Good Boy's Soliloquy,* 1811.

century tracts and eighteenth-century chapbooks, probably reached many of the poor, furthering Russell's generous wish to improve the lot of the deserving among them.

Yet a third type of book of courtesy or nurture appeared in the sixteenth century; this was in no ordinary sense directed to children, but rather to "Men, Seruantes and Children." Hugh Rhodes's *Boke of Nurture (c.* 1545) is in fact more a book of domestic conduct than a true book of courtesy and is a forerunner of the type that flourished during the seventeenth century, continued to be written throughout the eighteenth, and enjoyed a lively and lucrative publishing career into the second half of the nineteenth. Although commonly addressed to parents, servants, and children, the books were meant for the heads of households and were relied on to clarify parental and employer responsibilities and reciprocal filial and servant duties. They were often read to the entire household by the father, along with family devotions. And many a copy was offered as a wedding gift to inexperienced brides, as in the

historical case of George Savile, first marquis of Halifax, who wrote and presented *The Lady's New-Year's Gift; or, Advice to a Daughter* (1688) to the newly married Elizabeth, and in the fictional case where Henry Fielding waggishly implies that Samuel Richardson's Pamela (*Pamela,* 1740) ought to have been given *The Whole Duty of Man,* though that might have irreparably altered the course of "virtue's reward."[8] Although these manuals of domestic conduct had little direct effect on children's books, they were powerful molders of adult attitudes on child rearing and influenced even Locke's views on education.

In children's literature two quite different types of courtesy books were religious and secular works on moral and social comportment, the former chiefly among Puritans, the latter among those possessing or aspiring to gentility. The Puritan courtesy book was typified by predictably solemn and detailed Dos and Don'ts, a protracted list of Thoushalt-nots. *The Schoole of Good Manners* (London, 1609) by William Fiston (or Phiston) is a useful example of the kind both for its contents and its publishing history. The 1609 edition, based on a lost 1595 version, was refurbished and reprinted in London in 1685 by John Garretson. It crossed the Atlantic, appeared in its first Boston edition (1715), and then was published in twenty editions and reprints in New England up to 1799. Its title page lays bare its quality and design:

The Schoole of Good Manners, Containing I. Twenty Precepts. II. One Hundred and Sixty Three Rules for Childrens Behaviour. III. Good Advice for the Ordering of their Lives . . . IV. Eight wholesome Cautions. V. A . . . Catechism. VI. Principles of the Christian Religion. VII. Eleven short Exhortations. VIII. Good Thoughts for Children. . . . The Fifth Edition . . . , 1754.[9]

In clear contrast to such leaden fare are the secular books of courtesy, epitomized by the urbane, elegant, and sensible advice of Philip Dormer Stanhope, fourth earl of Chesterfield, to his natural son, Philip Stanhope. Of course the letters were meant to remain private, but with both the earl and his son deceased, Stanhope's widow sold them. *Letters Written by the Earl of Chesterfield to his Son, Philip Stanhope, together with several other Pieces on Various Subjects, published by Mrs. Eugenia Stanhope*, 2 vols. (London: J[ames] Dodsley, 1774) was immediately fashionable and profitable and remained in vogue for many decades. Not surprisingly, the enterprising Francis Newbery, John's nephew, came out with an abridged, child-sized version in "Dutch flowered boards" that same year, *Lord Chesterfield's Maxims . . . Being the Substance of the Earl of Chesterfield's Letters*.

Though the most spectacular courtesy book among trade works, the earl's was neither first nor entirely typical. Those honors go to a volume published by John Newbery's compeers, Baldwin of London and Collins of Salisbury: *The Polite Academy; or, School of Behaviour for Young Gentlemen and Ladies; Intended as a Foundation for good Manners and polite Address, in Masters and Misses* (1762, 1771, c. 1790; and thereafter by Darton and Harvey from 1800). Intermixed with instruction on achieving a genteel demeanor in the parlor, at table, at the dance, or "on the strut" (walking) are comic poetry, the fairy tale, "Beauty and the Beast," and scenes from Robert Dodsley's social satire *The Toy Shop*, a play. After 1762 no serious publisher in the trade neglected courtesy or social conduct books, a practice that has continued through our own century beginning with Gelett Burgess's ironic and delightful *Goops and How to Be Them. A Manual of Manners for Polite Infants Inculcating Many Juvenile Virtues both by Precept and Example* (London and New York, 1900).

In addition to the amusement and instruction that post-Newbery books of polite conduct and courtesy provided, they also purveyed both

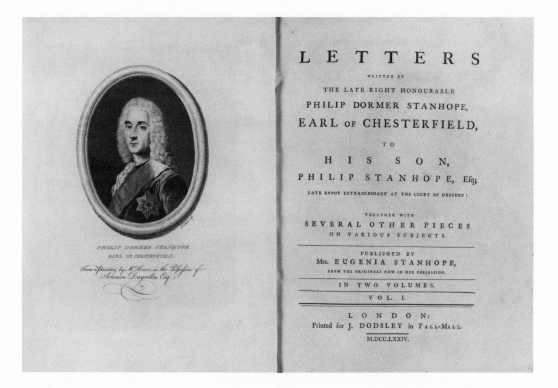

LETTERS
WRITTEN BY
THE LATE RIGHT HONOURABLE
PHILIP DORMER STANHOPE,
EARL of CHESTERFIELD,
TO
HIS SON,
PHILIP STANHOPE, Esq;
LATE ENVOY EXTRAORDINARY AT THE COURT OF DRESDEN:

TOGETHER WITH
SEVERAL OTHER PIECES
ON VARIOUS SUBJECTS.

PUBLISHED BY
Mrs. EUGENIA STANHOPE,
FROM THE ORIGINALS NOW IN HER POSSESSION.

IN TWO VOLUMES.
VOL. I.

LONDON:
Printed for J. DODSLEY in PALL-MALL.
M.DCC.LXXIV.

37. Frontispiece: The Earl of Chesterfield. Philip Dormer Stanhope, *Letters Written By the . . . Earl of Chesterfield, to His Son*, 1774.

the idea and to an extent the wherewithal for lower-middle-class readers to shed habits deemed vulgar and to emulate or at least mimic the genteel manners of their social superiors, the middle and upper-middle classes.[10] Clearly, such books aided—and later critics charged they abetted—what many considered the improper social pretensions of the "lower orders." In varying degrees, most children's books published between 1740 and 1790 inadvertently undercut faith in the inviolability of class distinctions by encouraging aspirations and by heightening economic or social expectations. Indeed, during this period Britain's class system was somewhat more fluid than after the outbreak of the French Revolution and the Napoleonic Wars (1789–1815), when fears of Jacobin (French Revolutionary) influences on the poor and even the artisans of the lower-middle class both widened and intensified class conservatism.[11] Simultaneously, however, economic and religious forces were steadily enlarging England's middle classes and stimulating the spread of bourgeois social values.[12]

To this complex process children's books contributed, for they helped to promulgate ideals of polite social usage as surely as they sharpened worldly ambition. Thus, just as we can chart a shift in the literature from otherworldly *piety* to pious social *propriety,* so also can we trace the diffusion of ideals of social refinement—this notwithstanding the fact that the class system not only remained intact but became more rigid after 1790. The potential for tragedy, but even more for that unique brand of English social comedy, created by these contradictory trends was to be chronicled in the fictional worlds of Jane Austen and Charles Dickens. But the homely juvenile literature of the eighteenth and early nineteenth centuries played its part in the creation of that rich and intricate world. Maria Edgeworth's tales for children and young people were among the first to tap this fertile source of social comedy.[13]

By the time books of courtesy were blossoming as a social force in the seventeenth century, medieval romances, legends, and heroic adventures had already deteriorated esthetically as higher art forms and socially and politically in the tide of nationalism and the reformist fervor generated by the Reformation. England had in fact repudiated the supremacy of "Rome's bishop," the pope, over any other bishop—in particular Canterbury's—but she did not reject either the structure of the episcopacy or the idea of a catholic or universal church. To many, the pope became the symbol of all that was corrupt in the religious and secular spheres in the medieval world, including its aristocratic literature.

Courtly romance and chivalric adventure were increasingly attacked by numerous and diverse enemies from the mid-sixteenth through the seventeenth and early eighteenth centuries. Indeed one branch of courtesy books, forerunners of books of domestic conduct, from the outset set itself squarely against such medieval works on the grounds that they corrupted the morals of the young and ignorant, children and servants. Hugh Rhodes's *Boke of Nurture* included prescriptions "to teche vertew," to encourage Bible reading and "Godly Books," and to ban fables, fantasies, romances, and "fylthy" songs, that is, ballads.

An even more vehement attack along the same lines came from Roger Ascham (1515–68) in *Toxophilus* (1545), a treatise in English on archery and the value of what is today called physical education, and in his most influential work, the *Scholemaster* (1570). Ascham, who had amazingly enough been appointed tutor to Princess Elizabeth (1548), Latin secretary to Queen Mary I (1553), and again private tutor to Elizabeth upon her ascension to the throne (1558), was a confirmed Protestant and, after Mary's passing, a voluble antipapist. He blamed Roman Catholicism, or "popery," for the lewdness and depravity spread through tales of romance and adventure, and he indicted "Morte Arthure," whose "whole pleasure" is in "open manslaughter and bold bawdry."[14] These were charges the Puritans would press relentlessly in the next two centuries. But such charges stemmed as much from an ingrained distrust of all fancifulness as from the loathing and fear of the powers an openly Catholic monarch might be pressured to grant the pope. For fictive tales and even the use of metaphors and similes were rejected because they were seen as distortions of language and were believed to undermine truth, and thus to let Satan's cloven hoof in the door.

Yet not everyone who thought the tales of romance and chivalry reprehensible was motivated by religious fanaticism. To some extent the widespread censure of these by more worldly persons proceeded from momentous changes in England's perception of herself, which began to crystallize in the late fourteenth century with the demise of feudalism and villeinage or serfdom and with the official replacement of French by English as the nation's first vernacular tongue. Latin and English were used in the courts, among the aristocracy and upper classes, and, by 1385, in all grammar schools. From the late fourteenth century, these were the languages of the land. For the first time since the Norman Conquest, the polyglot that was English shed all vestiges of the stigma that had attached to it as the language of the conquered, the socially inferior, and the powerless.[15]

Still, during the transition period in which the new Protestant England evolved, medieval lore continued to be popular with many groups, as the successful sales of William Caxton (c. 1421–91), England's first printer, and Wynkyn de Worde (Jan van Wynkyn, active in England 1477–1535), his assistant, indicate. But the deep-seated trends set in motion were irreversible. And as England, further liberated by the Reformation, flowered during the reign of Elizabeth I, a crucial aspect of her rebirth was the creation of new aristocratic literary forms.

This matter went far deeper than the mere discovery and establishment of definitive Greek and Latin texts. The artistic ferment leading to an explosion of literary genius in the Renaissance affirmed, indeed authenticated, English as a fully mature language worthy to take up where the glories of classical literature and the more recent new Italian forms left off.[16] In this spirit, courtiers and diplomats, who in the fashion of the age were often also supremely accomplished artists, set out quite deliberately to create new literary modes to reflect and elevate the tastes of the English ruling classes that developed out of the Norman (French) feudal aristocracy. Thus, criticisms of medieval romances from such quarters focused less on morality, if at all, than on esthetics and class distinctions.

As the new aristocratic literature cloaked itself in ever more intricate and exalted conventions and arcane symbolism—developments defended by Sir Philip Sidney in *An Apologie for Poetrie; or, The Defence of Poesie* (*c.* 1580; pub. 1595)—the once highest adornments of feudal Roman Catholic culture degenerated into common entertainment for lesser folk. The gulf between the two was widened by the very means of the latter's transmission to "children and servants," or the quasiliterate. As the romances passed from the dignity of the legitimate press (Caxton and de Worde, for instance) to the seediness of the cheapest printing mode—*chap*books (both *cheap* and *chopped* or short)—their literary embellishments were lopped off, eventually leaving the bare bones of plot and character.[17] These, however, were quite enough for their audience. For not the Puritans' aggressive piety, not the upper classes' disdain, and not later the middle classes' sneers ever sufficed to cool the ardor of the young and lowly for those marvelous tales and audacious adventures.

Only a fraction of the vast repository of medieval lore circulated through the seventeenth and eighteenth centuries, but it preserved and disseminated an important part of the nation's heritage. Moreover, in it the inventive faculty was allowed free reign—heroes and heroines ranged the entire known world on hair-raising quests; great empires fell, and rose; the great array of human suffering and triumph was chronicled; and seemingly quite ordinary affairs developed in a twinkling into bewitching ordeals simply stiff with marvels—potent stuff all, and no more welcome to the Enlightenment's priests of reason than to the apostles of blind evangelical faith.

Medieval tales of chivalry, love, and the supernatural in prose or verse are still today divided into the three categories first suggested by the twelfth-century troubadour or minstrel, Jean Bodel: "The Matter of France," which heavily emphasized courtly love elements; "The Matter of Britain," which stressed action and adventure; and "The Matter of Rome the Great," which delineated the remainder of the known world in ancient times, with stories of the siege of Troy, Alexander the Great, the Eastern world, and the "classical" worlds of Greece and Rome as well.[18] Relatively few of these numerous tales were adopted by early children's literature, though they were increasingly revived after 1775 and were much in vogue by 1850.

Among the French romances, *Chanson de Roland (The Song of Roland)* was favored by English audiences, for it suited their taste for action over sentiment or passion. Greatly loved among the "Matter of Britain" romances were *Arthur and Merlin*, the alliterative *Morte Arthur*, *Sir Gawain and the Green Knight*, and two others that had a more religious cast. The very important *Joseph of Arimathie*, a chapbook favorite as late as 1800, and *Sir Percyvelle of Galles* (Percival, Parsifal) tell how the Holy Grail, the communal wine cup at the Last Supper, was brought to Britain by Joseph, was secreted away, and was rediscovered after long years of quest. Such tales linked Britain's Arthurian legends to the very roots of Christianity, just as others in the "Matter of Rome" traced Trojan civilization (deemed morally superior to the Greek in the Middle Ages) from Ilium to England or Albion, through Brut (Brutus) Aeneas's grandson, who renamed the isle for himself. The dispersion of such lore through all levels in the land helped to hammer out a coherent national consciousness in a disparate, often fractious people.

Much of the material in even the "Matter of Britain" was written in French, tongue of both English and Norman nobility, and had to be "Englished." William Caxton, one of the earliest translators, completed his *Recuyell of the Historyes of Troye* in 1471 (pub. Bruges, 1475), *Godfrey of Boloyne* (London, 1481), Malory's *Morte Darthur,* which he helped to translate (1485), *The Four Sons of Aymon* (*c.* 1489), and many others. Wynkyn de Worde continued Caxton's work, printing *Guy of Warwick* and *Bevis of Hampton* (1491), *Valentine and Orson* (1510), and such fare. Native texts on many of these subjects existed in various early dialects and Middle English verse, but except for a few tales of Viking invasions and *Gawain and the Green Knight,* most romances were translations.

A second source of similar lore was the great medieval storybook, the *Gesta Romanorum, Deeds*, or *Acts of the Romans*, a collection of "sermon stories," whose appeal was not obscured by the weighty overlay of priestly moralizing. The origin of the *Gesta* is uncertain, but its earliest appearance in England was about 1326 in a Latin manuscript compiled by monks, who in time produced many copies. It was first printed early in the fifteenth century, and the first illustrated, vernacular (Dutch) version was published in 1481. Its most popular tales were issued separately

A Pleasant Song of the valiant Deeds of Chivalry, Atchieved by that Noble Knight Sir *GUY* of *Warwick*; Who for the Love of fair *Phillis*, became a Hermit, and dy'd in a Cave of a Craggy Rock, a Mile distant from *Warwick*.   Tune was ever Man, &c.

WAS ever Knight for Lady's fake,
    fo toft in Love as I Sir Guy?
For *Phillis* fair that Lady bright,
    as ever Man beheld with Eye.
She gave me leave my felf to try,
    the valiant Knight with Shield and Spear,
E'er that her Love fhe would grant me,
    Which made me venture far and near,
The proud Sir *Guy* a Baron bold,
    in deeds of Arms the doubtful Knight,
That every Day in *England* was
    with Sword and Spear in Field to fight.
An Englifh-man I was by Birth,
    in Faith of Chrift a Chriftian true,
The wicked Laws of Infidels,
    I fought by Power to fubdue.
Two hundred twenty Years and odd,
    after our Saviour Chrift his Birth,
When King *Athelfton* wore the Crown,
    I lived hereupon the Earth,
Sometimes I was of *Warwick* Earl,
    and as I faid on very Truth,
A Lady's love did me conftrain,
    to feek ftrange Ventures in my Youth,
To try my Fame by feats of Arms,
    in ftrange and fundry Heathen Lands,

Where I atchieved for her fake,
    right dangerous Conquefts with my hands
For firft I fail'd to *Normandy*,
    and there I ftoutly won in Fight,
The Emperor's Daughter of *Almain*,
    from many a valiant worthy Knight.
Then paffed I the Seas of *Greece*,
    to help the Emperor to his Right,
Againft the mighty Souldan's Hoft,
    of puiffant *Perfians* for to fight.
where I did flay of *Sarazens*,
    and Heathen Pagans many a Man,
And flew the Souldan's Coufin dear,
    who had to Name Doughty *Colbryn*.
Ezeldered, that famous Knight,
    to Death likewife I did purfue;
And *Almain*, King of *Tyre* alfo,
    moft terrible too in height to view.
I went into the Souldan's Hoft,
    being thither on Ambaffage fent,
And brought away his Head with me,
    I having flain him in his Tent.
There was a Dragon in the Land,
    which I alfo my felf did flay,
As he a Lion did purfue,
    moft fiercely met me by the way.

From thence I paft the Seas of *Greece*,
    and came to *Pavyland* aright,
where *I* the Duke of *Pavy* kill'd,
    his heinous Treafon to requite,
And after that came into this Land,
    towards fair *Phillis* Lady bright,
For love of whom I travell'd far,
    to try my Manhood and my might.
But when I had efpoufed her,
    I ftaid with her but forty Days;
But there I left this Lady fair,
    and then I went beyond the Seas,
All clad in Gray in Pilgrim fort,
    my Voyage from her, I did take
Unto that bleffed holy Land,
    for *Jefus Chrift* my Saviour's fake:
where I Earl *Jonas* did redeem,
    and all his Sons, which were Fifteen;
who with the cruel *Sarazens*,
    in Prifon for long Time had been,
I flew the Giant *Amarant*,
    in Battle fiercely Hard to Hand:
And Doughty *Barknard* killed I,
    the Mighty Duke of the fame Land.
Then I to England came again,
    and here with *Colbren* ftill I fought,

from the 1500s into the 1900s. Between 1600 and 1703 at least fifteen editions appeared, a large number for the age.

To all moderns except perhaps antiquarians, the *Gesta* is as dust. But to medieval and early Renaissance audiences of all classes, and to the young and lowly into the early nineteenth century, it was a fount of delight and wonder. A motley of jostling cultures and eras, it contains ac-

38. "Was ever Knight for Lady's sake / So tost in love as I Sir Guy?" *A Pleasant Song of the Valiant . . . Sir Guy of Warwick* [a broadside, *c.* 1700].

An Only Giant which the *Danes*,
   had for their Champion hither brought,
I overcame him in the Field,
   and slew him Dead right valiantly;
where I the Land did then redeem,
   from *Danish* Tribute utterly:
And afterwards I offered up
   the use of weapons solemnly,
At *Winchester*, whereas I fought,
   in fight of many far and near.
In *Windsor Forrest* I did slay
   a *Boar* of passing might and strength,
The like in England never was,
   for hugeness both in Bredth and Length.
Some of his Bones in *Warwick* yet,
   within the Castle there doth lie;
One of his Shield Bores to this Day,
   hangs in the City of *Coventry*.
On *Dunsmore Heath* I also slew,
   a monstrous wild and cruel Beast,
Call'd the *Dun-Cow* of *Dunsmore Heath*,
   which many People had opprest.
Some of her Bones in *Warwick* yet,
   still for a Monument doth lye,
which unto every Looker's view,
   as wondrous strange they may espy.
And the *Dragon* in the Land,
   I also did in Fight destroy,
which did both Men and Beasts oppress,

and all the Country sore annoy,
   And then to *Warwick* came again,
like Pilgrim poor, and was not known;
   And there I liv'd a *Hermet's* Life,
a Mile and more out of the Town,
   where with my Hand I hew'd a House
out of a Craggy Rock of Stone;
   And lived like a *Palmer* poor,
within that Cave my self alone:
   And daily came to beg my Food
of *Phillis* at my Castle-Gate.
   Nor known unto my loving wife,
who daily mourned for her Mate,
   Till at the last I fell sore sick,
ye, Sick so sore that I must die,
   I sent to her a Ring of Gold,
by which she knew me presently.
   Then she repaired to the Cave,
before that I gave up the Ghost,
   Her self clos'd up my dying Eyes,
my *Phillis* fair whom I lov'd most,
   Thus dreadful Death did me arrest,
to bring my Corps unto the Grave,
   And like a *Palmer* died I,
whereby I hope my Soul to save.
   My Body in *Warwick* yet doth lye,
though now it is consum'd to Mould,
   My Statute was engraven in Stone,
this present Day you may behold.

counts of saints and martyrs, adventures of various European nobility, and tales "by Bidpai," a corruption of *bidbah,* title of the court scholar in ancient Indian princedoms. Such tales originated in the Sanskrit *Panchatranta* and eventually found their way into Arabic as *The Fables of Pilpay.* So remarkable a cross-fertilization of Far Eastern, Arabic, and European cultures and folklore is less startling if one recalls that the first

39. "The Courtly Valentine and Orson, reared by bears." *The History of Valentine and Orson,* [*c.* 1790].

40. "Deeds of the Romans." B. P., *Gesta Romanorum; or, Fifty-eight Histories . . . from The Roman Records,* [*c.* 1720].

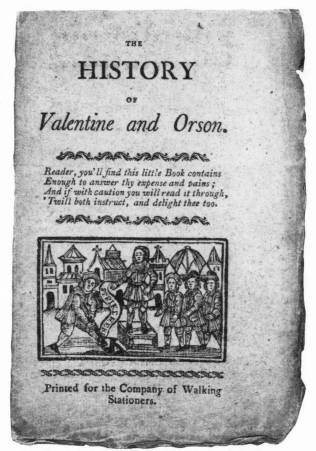

THE
HISTORY
OF
Valentine and Orson.

Reader, you'll find this little Book contains
Enough to answer thy expense and pains;
And if with caution you will read it through,
'Twill both instruct, and delight thee too.

Printed for the Company of Walking
Stationers.

three major crusades occurred between 1095 and 1192. By the time the lore reached the solid form of monks' manuscript around 1300, it had doubtless been assimilated and had become "native" to its audiences.[19]

A very popular example, *The Seven Wise Masters,* or *The Seven Sages of Rome,* has the frame story that was originally considered distinctive of Arabic tales, familiar to moderns in *The Arabian Nights* and probably borrowed from the Sanskrit. In *The Seven Sages*, the son of the emperor Diocletian is accused of attempted seduction by his jealous stepmother, who to ensure the success of her lie casts a spell that renders him mute for seven days. Thus left defenseless before his father's fury, he is condemned to be executed. This, however, is cleverly forestalled by the youth's seven wise tutors, who engage the would-be Phaedra in a contest of fictional disputations, legally or morally suasive in intent but studded with thrilling events and magical contrivances.[20] Each night the queen tells a tale to remind Diocletian of youth's ambition, treachery,

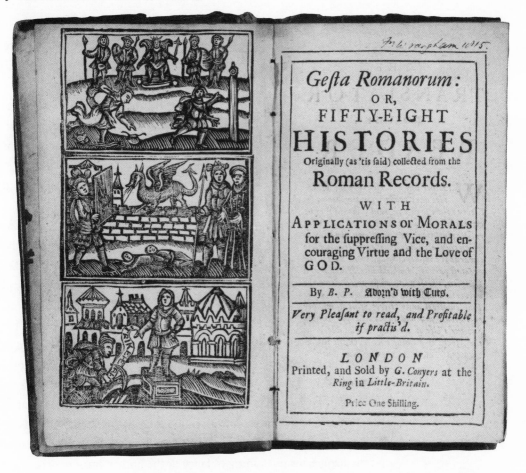

and hot blood; each morning, one of the tutors pelts him with a coun-
terfiction on the theme of woman's perfidy, a perennial medieval favorite. Thus the seven days' enforced silence pass. The prince, released, reveals the queen's schemes to his till-then-vacillating father. And another
of Eve's daughters is chastened, this one burnt at the stake.

A tale like *The Seven Sages of Rome* obviously offered monks plenty of
scope for "pointing a moral," but they were no less diligent with what
may seem to be less malleable stuff. *Guy of Warwick* is a dashing mixture
of sanctimonious mayhem (in the Crusades), dragon and beast slaying,
and maiden wooing, though typically the wooing is swift and chaste
and the bliss extremely vague and brief. Yet into this are tucked many
monkly harangues on moral duty to God and Church and worldly duty
to King and Lord. An even less likely vehicle, at first glance, is *Valentine
and Orson,* the wildly improbable, hugely popular tale of royal twins
separated in infancy, one raised as a knight at court, the other suckled

and bred by bears. Of course, the brothers meet and fight, but the chivalrous Valentine spares the defeated wildman Orson and even tries to civilize him, with mixed results. The two enjoy numerous adventures, going intrepidly against giants and sorcerers and rescuing their own mother and the loved character Pacolet, a dwarf, as well as his magic wooden horse which can transport one anywhere. The training of Orson, who is very ethical and upright though rough and graceless, was turned to good account by the monks.

After the Reformation, as learning passed into secular hands and Catholic doctrine was rejected, the outmoded homilies of the *Gesta* fell away. This meant that anything that smacked of Rome and popery was ruthlessly cut out. Yet never in their printing history, even when the tales dwindled into chapbook fare, did *all* of their ethical elements disappear. The crudest, most truncated versions of *Guy of Warwick, Bevis of Southampton,* and *Valentine and Orson,* to cite just three examples, always included avowals of moral purpose and often also prayers for God's aid, forgiveness, and salvation, if only brief, obligatory, and relegated to the final death scenes. It is rather important to stress this moral aspect of *Gesta Romanorum* tales, even if it is merely vestigial, because that book, like romances and the fairy tales that flourished a bit later, came in for much vilification from both religious conservatives and enlightened men of reason chiefly on the score of questionable morality and the dangerous unleashing of fancy or the human imagination.

Tales with supernatural beings or magical contrivances were not of course new to England. And in the *Gesta Romanorum* and oral folk tradition they had clear moral purpose. But the new tales that arrived at the end of the seventeenth and the start of the eighteenth centuries were, in the eyes of the devout, wholly given over to fancy and had no redeeming value. They came from two sources chiefly. The Eastern tales in *The Arabian Nights* were first translated into English from Antoine Galland's French version, *Mille et une nuits (A Thousand and One Nights),* 12 vols. (1704–17). Translations from this were in the press by 1705 and 1708, long before Galland completed his oeuvre. Thereafter, *Sinbad* and *Aladdin,* for example, were in constant demand in respectable volumes and chapbooks.

At roughly the same time, French fairy tales, possibly inspired as Gottlieb suggests by the tales of the Italian Straparola,[21] came into vogue as entertainments for the nobility. Two authors were best known

41. "The Genie appears; Aladdin's Mother swoons." "Aladdin," *Popular Tales of the Olden Time,* [*c.* 1830].

42. "Contes de ma Mere Loye" or "Tales of Mother Goose." [Charles Perrault], *Contes du Temps Passé,* 1700.

The Genie of the Lamp.

Page 18.

in England: Marie Catherine La Mothe, Countess d'Aulnoy, whose tales appeared as *Diverting Works* in 1707, and Charles Perrault, whose work first appeared in a journal (1696) and then as *Histoires ou contes de temps passé* (1697). In the frontispiece scene of this is a plaque that reads, "Contes de ma mere l'Oye," source of the immortal soubriquet, "Mother Goose's Tales."

The two authors differ greatly in style and tone. D'Aulnoy's tales are literary productions for a courtly audience. They include "Graciosa," "The Yellow Dwarf," "The White Cat," "The Bluebird," and some actually written by Jean de Mailly, like "Fortunio."[22] Perhaps they were too elevated in style for "new" or semiliterate readers. They were printed first as the tales of "Queen Mab" (1752) and later as "Tales of Mother Bunch." Under the latter alias they appeared far into the nineteenth century, when they evidently found their audience and were in vogue. In contrast, Perrault's simpler tales are enlivened by the rhythms of human speech and are more accessible to all readers. Robert Samber first translated them in *Histories; or, Tales of Past Times. Told by Mother Goose* (1729). Many of them are familiar today: "The Sleeping Beauty," "Red Riding-Hood," "Puss-in-Boots," "Hop o' my Thumb," and "Cinderella, or the Glass Slipper." Except for "Beauty and the Beast" (1756), the one enduring tale among several published by and usually credited to Jeanne Marie le Prince de Beaumont, no "immortals" were added to this group until the translation of the Grimms' tales in 1823.[23]

A late entry into children's literature was the very mixed bag of adult prose fiction. It included *Pilgrim's Progress; Robinson Crusoe* (1719); *Gulliver's Travels* (1726) (usually the voyages to Lilliput and Brobdingnag); and *Don Quixote* (trans. Pt. I, 1605; Pt. II, 1615); but also *Moll Flanders* (1722); Richardson's *Pamela, Clarissa Harlowe* (1747–48) and *Sir Charles Grandison* (1754); and Smollett's *Roderick Random* (1748). In all these works the sexual elements are simply omitted and the adventurous or psychologically thrilling aspects highlighted. The three Richardson novels were the earliest bona fide children's abridgments, appearing in 1756 as *The Paths of Virtue Delineated*. Francis Newbery, Samuel Crowder, Richard Baldwin, and others in the trade brought out their own editions of such novels, and ruthlessly shortened but illustrated versions of many of these works were printed in chapbooks, especially after 1760.

Chapbooks are a rather problematic aspect of the history of the field chiefly because they had a scandalous reputation from the start of the

43. "The Magic Ring turns the base Teressa cumbersome and fat." *Fat and Lean; or, The Fairy Queen,* [*c.* 1815].

century, one they partly deserved. They have been vilified as repositories of smut; manuals of profligate and shiftless conduct; traducers of rationality and promoters of perilous delusions; and, by those of nice tastes and esthetic leanings, breeders of ugliness and pictorial crudity.

Those who might have pled for some tolerance for the motley trade were undercut by the simple fact that, for every conceivable accusation launched against chapbooks, at least one unarguably damning example was ready at hand. But that was in part because every imaginable subject was to be found in chapbook pedlars' packs: historical and political sketches; moral and devotional manuals; scripture tales and hagiographies; descriptions of the major phases of Christ's life, especially His death and resurrection; geographical descriptions and local history; abridged fictions and dramas, including Shakespeare; songbooks, metrical tales, and ballads; "cookery" books; tales of kings, queens, and "lemans," like fair Rosamond and Jane Grey; tales of Hector of Troy and Charles of Sweden; medieval romances, fairy stories, and tales from England's "folk" tradition; vilely coarse jestbooks and indecent stories; ABCs; books on the occult, dreams, fortune telling, and other prophecies; accounts of demonology and witchcraft; the adventures of Robin Hood, Dick Whittington, and Tom Hickathrift; timeless "cryes" (songs to advertise wares and services) of London; ghost stories; accounts of

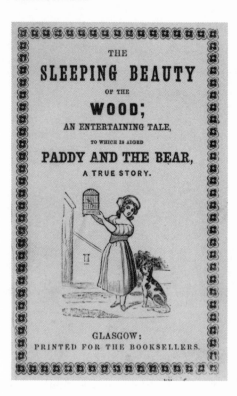

44. A chapbook cover. *The Sleeping Beauty of the Wood*, [*c*. 1840–55].

great criminals, lurid crimes, and satisfyingly grisly punishments; and herbals and books on infallible cures of every sort. Moreover, the booklets were indeed ugly and the illustrations crude and often inapposite, affixed willy-nilly to any text in need of sprucing up.[24]

Yet whatever the religious and respectable said, chapbooks sold, very well indeed. To children at all levels, some of whom were necessarily surreptitious patrons, to the lower-middle class and the poor in London, to people in every major provincial town and every village and hamlet to which the chapmen—"peripatic vendors"—wandered, they sold. Their enormous vogue demonstrates the hunger of ordinary folk for entertainment, particularly for reading matter. It also supports M. G. Jones's evidence that a surprisingly large portion of the population was in some sense literate.

Of course this was not the sort of literacy accepted as such by the truly educated or cultured, who assumed literacy included the arts of reading and writing in English and also in Latin.[25] But among the lowly, those skills were separated; even if reading was taught, writing might in fact not be. Many a man and woman who had difficulty writing the simplest note could read the King James Bible, no mean feat. And others who could barely sign their names could nonetheless decipher the contents of their treasured chapbooks, whose very popularity helps to explain the thread of a common cultural heritage in the nation, however elevated or debased may have been the source of those historical, religious, and (to a far lesser extent) literary elements.

Victor Neuburg deserves great credit for his pioneering research into these matters[26] and for the consequent shift in recent scholarship away from the long-unquestioned class prejudice against all chapbooks. Such prejudice lurked even in the splendid, indispensible *Children's Books in England,* by F. J. Harvey Darton, until its recent revision by Brian Alderson. The true value of chapbooks in preserving much that might otherwise have been lost or long obscured and in fueling and satisfying England's growing desire to read is now clear—despite the accuracy of many of the charges against them. Moreover, the magnitude of nationwide chapbook purchases, which grew astonishingly until 1800, explains in part the base on which the market for bona fide children's books rested.

Chapbooks swiftly evolved from their disreputable origins into decent and even attractive wares. They were in a sense England's first paperbacks. Their publishers were astute businesswomen and -men, as ready as Newbery and his rivals to adapt their goods to prevailing tastes. Thus, though it is true that chapbooks read by the young before 1760 might contain vulgar humor and frank references to bodily functions or sexuality, by 1770–80 most such works had been cleaned up greatly. By the simple expediencies of deleting crude episodes and of substituting decent language for the openly profane or slyly risque, once dubious popular heroes were reclaimed. No longer did young Tom Thumb, accidentally swallowed by a cow, exit through the digestive tract terminus: He was genteelly and tidily regurgitated. And the bellicose Tom Hickathrift's history simply skips over the incident in which he unchivalrously pokes an insulting old woman in the posterior with his sword. Where chapbooks were still strenuously opposed after the 1790s, the reason was more often political than purely moral or esthetic.

As the century advanced, chapbooks became an important catalyst in the growth of children's literature. Sometimes they were the chief, if not only, sanctuary for stories and poems temporarily out of favor in the "legitimate" press because of pressures from certain interest groups. Al-

45. "Tom coughed up by the Cow." *Park's Entertaining History of Tom Thumb,* [c. 1830s].

Tom to the fields with his mother went,
To milk the cow was her intent;
The wind blew high as they did walk,
So she tied him to a thistle stalk;
The cow the thistle view'd and cropp'd,
In her mouth, with Tom, it soon was popp'd!

ways, they were a source of healthy competition to that press, particularly with their illustrations after 1810.[27] By the early nineteenth century, the vast majority of English chapbooks were produced almost entirely for children and ranged in quality from the gorgeous works of W. Belch to the cheap and crude (but highly prized) products of John Pitts and James [Jemmy] Catnach. Tellingly, many respectable publishers of hardcover volumes for the more affluent also issued paper-cover versions of these and other works, offered at prices to compete with and in forms generally indistinguishable from the better sort of chapbook.

4. The First Innovators and Their Creations

Today three publishers are generally credited with the developments that firmly established children's books as a separate branch of the trade: Thomas Boreman, Mary Cooper, and John Newbery, though four short decades ago only the contributions of the last were widely known. Our understanding of the history and wider social and literary implications of the field increases as we reassess complicated aspects of it: changing concepts of childhood, new patterns of familial interaction created by urbanization and emerging modes of labor in an industrialized society, the impact of major intellectual trends on child life, and considerations of religion, class, and politics. Similarly, our perceptions both of the nuts-and-bolts procedures in the trade and of the literary fashions that substantially affected the production of children's books are being more finely tuned as primary research in the appropriate areas progresses and also as more of the extant literature becomes available in museums, public and private libraries, and private collections in England, Canada, and the United States. Given the ephemeral nature of much of the literature, an astonishing amount has survived. Yet catalogues of some collections have only recently been published, and heretofore unknown editions and printings of books, copies of works recorded but undiscovered, and entirely new books still turn up occasionally among rare book dealers and collectors.[1]

Barely under way is the research on the history of some major and many minor publishers and printers of juvenile books. Comparatively extensive and reliable data exist for firms like Newbery, Darton and Harvey, John Harris, and Lumsden, for example.[2] But similar excavations remain to be completed for dozens of firms. Such data are compiled from surviving business records, advertisements, sales catalogues,

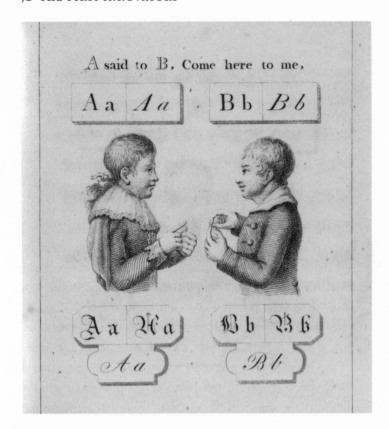

A said to B, Come here to me,

46. An ABC in verse and sign language. R. R[ansome], *The Invited Alphabet*, [*c.* 1804].

47. "The tail of this hideous animal [crocodile] is two-edged." *The Youth's Natural History of Animals,* 1829.

brochures, and editions sighted or rumored. Thus there is sometimes uncertainty about basic matters such as the precise date of publication of even the major works, or their printing history.[3] In the last twenty years, for example, it has become clear that there was considerable printing of children's books from the 1730s to 1760, many of which are important because they were long reprinted or closely imitated. Their authors often remain anonymous, but not their publishers. To the names of Boreman, Cooper, and Newbery, we may add other early innovators: C. Corbett, Richard Ware, R. Owen, Ann Law, John Mein, and Edward Ryland, for example. Doubtless the list will grow.

THOMAS BOREMAN

Thomas Boreman published seven books for children that we know of. His natural histories, forerunners of scientific books of knowledge, were widely read and freely borrowed from by later writers: *A Description of Three Hundred Animals* (1730) and *A Description of a Great Variety of Animals and Vegetables* (1736). His somewhat more adventurous efforts are

18

THE CROCODILE.

The tail of this hideous animal is two-edged; the feet triangular, the fore ones having five, and the hinder feet only four toes. Within the mouth of this beast, are two jaws of numerous sharp-pointed teeth, thirty or more on each side; its eyes are large and fiery, projecting out of its head, but immoveable, so that they can only see as they walk straight forward : they have the largest mouths of almost any other animals. It is reported of them, that they weep over their prey, and send forth a piteous and distressful cry, in order to allure men or beasts to its haunts, that it may seize and devour them. The armour or scales with which the upper part of the

19

body is coated, is most wonderful. In the full grown animal, it is so strong as easily to turn off a musket ball; on the lower part, it is much thinner and more pliable. The whole animal appears as if covered with the most curious carved work. In various parts of Asia and Africa, they exceed twenty feet in length, and chiefly haunt such large rivers as Niger, Ganges, Nile, or near the sea shore : they are exceedingly voracious, yet capable of sustaining abstinence for many weeks together. In the large southern rivers of the United States, Alligators are found of various dimensions, being like the Crocodile in its form and natural propensities. They are sometimes very bold, and will follow the boats which are descending loaded with live stock, and sometimes succeed in taking off a portion.

contained in a series of fat, little, mostly two-volume works which are the earliest known guided-tour books for children. There were four of these pleasing tomes, measuring 1¼ by 2½ inches and bound in stiff boards covered with brightly colored Dutch paper, which like the much-coveted colored book illustrations were hand-painted until the mid-nineteenth century by children as young as four years. As Boreman explained to his youthful clients, the volumes fit either hand or pocket and were quite portable. They seem to have sold reasonably well, most going through at least two editions. They appeared in something of a flurry between 1740 and 1743: *The Gigantick History of the Two Famous Giants, and Other Curiosities in Guildhall,* 2 vols. (1740); *The History and Description of the Famous Cathedral of St. Paul's,* 2 vols. (1741); *Curiosities of the Tower of London,* 2 vols. (1741), and *The History and Description of Westminster Abbey,* 3 vols. (1742–43). Boreman's seventh work, which I have not examined, returns to the engrossing subject of giants, *The History of Cajanus the Swedish Giant* (1742).[4]

In the main, Boreman's books are rather prosaic accounts of scenes

THE WILD BEASTS AT EXETER CHANGE

that, if interesting in themselves, are seldom lightened or enlivened with wit. Giants seem to have fascinated him, and those in Guildhall (town hall of the City of London) sparked his imagination. He confides to his readers that the giants—mythic colossuses associated with the origins of Britain—often come to life at the noon hour to partake of lunch, but—he hurries to assure them—his readers will not likely *see* this because Corineus and Gogmagog, though huge, are shy of publicity and prefer to dine in privacy. His other tours are less sprightly: *Westminster Abbey* doggedly drags its readers past all 103 monuments in the abbey and promises with menacing gaiety to describe equally thoroughly the remaining royal monuments in the later volumes, a promise he kept. His tour of St. Paul's is not noticeably more lively, but *Curiosities of the Tower of London* benefited from much innately interesting material. The Tower housed the royal collection of wild beasts and the mint, where one might actually see coins being struck. His accounts of the animals are prosaic, but the pictures were appealing, poor stuff by today's standards but evidently very welcome to Boreman's customers.

48. "The Wild Beasts at Exeter Change." *A Month's Vacation . . . in London,* n.d.

It should in fairness be noted that Boreman tried to leaven instruction with amusement, as Locke had suggested. He clearly knew the value of offering variety to catch the attention of the young. Perhaps it was this insight that led him to fix on the tour as the main device for his books; moving as it must from place to place, a tour might be thought to be the essence of novelty. Missing, however, was the touch of imagination or wit that might have brought his excursions to life. His tone is avuncular, which is to say it has that unmistakable nuance of an adult trying to be "matey" to little people. Too often the books' merriment was consigned to their whimsical advertisements and to the sometimes partly fictional subscribers' lists appended to them—one of which is headed by the giants Corineus and Gogmagog, for one hundred copies each. Within Boreman's gaily colored covers too often lay the heavy provender of the Giant Instruction's bill of fare.[5]

MRS. MARY COOPER

Mary Cooper, the widow of Thomas Cooper, took over the printing business after her spouse's death to provide for her young family. Little is known about the Coopers' life, but it is clear that they had scented the new trend in children's books, as had Newbery, and were prepared to take advantage of it. *The Child's New Play-Thing: Being A Spelling Book*

K   L

k knocked it down.
l laughed at it.

49. A later version of "A, Apple pie." *The Life and History of A, Apple-Pie,* [c. 1835–40].

50. Oliver Goldsmith, *Dr. Goldsmith's Celebrated Elegy,* 1808.

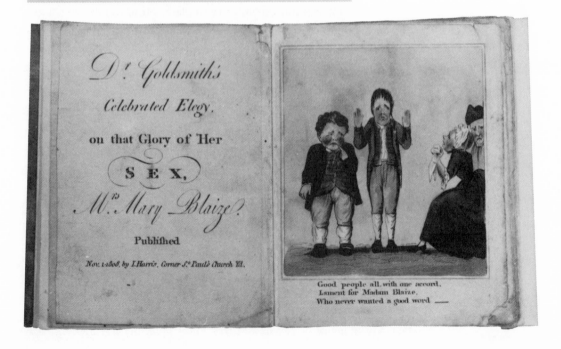

Intended To make Learning to Read a Diversion and not a Task (1742) is quite as competent and appealing as Newbery's legendary first effort, *A Little Pretty Pocket-Book* (1744). It contained two alphabets—one apparently intended to be cut out and used for letter games—and scripture stories in simple language, like *Joseph and his Brethren* (a chapbook favorite), as well as fables, songs, proverbs, and stories, including abridgments of *Guy of Warwick, St. George,* and *Reynard the Fox.* The second edition of *The Child's New Play-Thing* was produced in 1743 by Cooper's widow. And for a few years thereafter she published several juvenile works on her own, though the bulk of her business was printing adult literature and on occasion others' children's books.

Perhaps Mary Cooper's greatest contribution to the field and to posterity was the collecting (with which she is traditionally credited) and printing of nursery songs that were apparently part of the oral culture. Nursery rhymes are today linked to Mother Goose (of French origin), but it seems likely that Cooper's were English children's street songs or games, many of indeterminate and remote, if not ancient, origin. Though some may well have appeared in broadsides now lost to us, it is nevertheless no exaggeration to say that the service Cooper performed in collecting and disseminating them is comparable to that of Thomas Percy, whose *Reliques of Ancient English Poetry* appeared in 1765, years after Cooper's immortal little volumes.

Tommy Thumb's Pretty Song Book "for the Diversion of all Little Masters and Misses" by Nurse Lovechild was advertised in the *London Evening Post* on 22 March 1744. *Nancy Cock's Song Book* was described as the companion "to Tommy Thumb, and Second Vol. of that great and learned Work" and its imminent publication touted in the *Daily Advertiser* on 23 May 1744. Neither work has survived in the first edition, but there is a hand-engraved copy of *Tommy Thumb's Pretty Song Book,* labeled Volume II, in the British Library. There is some uncertainty here because this was clearly advertised as the first volume. However that mix-up came about, the contents of the book were published as *Tommy Thumb's Song Book,* "for all Little Masters and Misses" in 1788 by the American children's book publisher Isaiah Thomas of Worcester, Massachusetts.[6]

The frontispiece of the "Volume II" *Tommy Thumb* in the British Library depicts three figures, two seated young ladies looking at open books on their laps and a boy standing between them playing a flute.

She strove the neighbourhood to please,
With manners wondrous winning';
And never follow'd wicked ways ___

___ Unless when she was sinning'.

51. "She strove the neigh-
bourhood to please."
Goldsmith, *Dr. Goldsmith's
Celebrated Elegy,* 1808.

52. "Mrs. Mary, sinning."
Goldsmith, *Dr. Goldsmith's
Celebrated Elegy,* 1808.

This is clearly a visual reminder of the link between the actual song tradition and the printed (or engraved) rhymes, as are the directions at the
bottom of each page. The charm and whimsy of the work are increased
by the operatic instructions to its simple lyrics, illustrated by cuts of
small children playing accompaniments or singing:

Sing a song of sixpence,
A bag full of Rye,
Four and twenty
Naughty boys,
Bak'd in a Pye.

This is to be sung in the "GRANDE" manner; "The Old Woman who
liv'd under the hill," in "RECITATIVE"; "Robin Red Breast,"
"PRONTO"; and "Robbin and Bobbin," "TIMOROSO."[7] The collection contains forty rhymes, including many that are familiar, like "Lady
Bird, Lady Bird," "Who Did Kill Cock Robin?" "London Bridge,"
"Hickere, Dickere Dock," "Mistress Mary, Quite Contrary," and only
two that are objectionable and are traditionally deleted.[8]

This is a work of unalloyed fun, and its spirit of playfulness is heightened by its truly Lilliputian dimensions: The pages, 1½ by 3 inches, con-

tain illustrations 15/16 inches long by 1⅝ inches wide. Black print alternates at times with red, surely one of the earliest testimonies to the appeal of color in children's books.

In the next few years Mary Cooper published two other books, one influenced perhaps by Boreman's tour guides and both containing the notorious chapbook hero who had figured in the title of her first collection of songs. *The Travels of Tom Thumb Over England and Wales* (1746) and the *History of England* "By TOM THUMB, Esq." (1749), together with *Tommy Thumb's Pretty Song,* are among the earliest attempts to reform and place in decent society that ribald, beloved denizen of chapbooks. Of course, she clearly hoped the waggish, diminutive madcap would add zest to her books, which he does but feebly. *The Travels* provided her with a larger scope of action and variety in a cast of chance-met characters. But though she threw these in with the famed adventurer, who traditionally went over (or through) far less dignified terrain, he is not endowed with the sort of Pickwickian comic spirit that would have raised the work above the ordinary. The straightforward tour guide with topographical, region-by-region descriptions is only rarely lightened by Squire Thumb's anecdotes. The *History* is even less fanciful, being little more than a standard survey of the reigns of selected British monarchs.

Cooper's instincts were entirely correct, however, and had she persisted, her efforts to make amusing chapbook characters serve Locke's formula for luring the young to read and to learn might have succeeded, for soon others were following her lead: Newbery created his own, quite successful "Thumb," one Tommy Trip, Esq. And in the years to follow, Thumb the rapscallion was himself reclaimed and admitted into the select company in respectable parlors, to the delight of his youthful admirers. Moreover, in one later book Cooper revealed herself to be in tune with the trends of the developing trade: She published a collection of Mme. d'Aulnoy's fairy tales, *The Court of Queen Mab* (1752), one of the earliest to link Mab to these tales, which became traditional.[9]

One scholar has recently suggested that Cooper's mysteriously brief foray into children's books may have coincided with her own offsprings' early childhood and that, the phase having passed, she simply returned to her former primary interest, adult publications.[10] Perhaps this is so. In any event, her contributions are notable, however short-lived her involvement. She had all the qualities needed to make a success in the new trade, save one. She was demonstrably capable of creating books of purest fun; she recognized the need for novelty in juvenile books; and she showed herself able, at least potentially, to conscript existing humorous resources in learning's service. The one thing she lacked, which set Newbery apart, was the driving desire to produce and go on producing. As Brian Alderson points out, it was this as much as anything else that made Newbery so important in the field; his ascendancy rested on the realization that his firm *had* to publish, even if not every volume was as novel and edifying as his "puffs" claimed.[11]

JOHN NEWBERY

The crowning accomplishment of John Newbery's career as a publisher was the creation or popularization of a triad of related literary types which were vital to his firm's financial success and, it is perhaps no overstatement to say, to the trade in its infancy. The first of these was, of course, the miscellany that grew directly out of the ABCs of the early part of the century. The last was the children's novel, or novella, a short form of the genre prevailing in the age. The link that closely binds the two has sometimes gone unnoticed; it is Newbery's creation: the children's magazine.

Of course, in exploiting the potential of the early ABCs, Newbery was following the well-worn path of one of the earliest fanciful ABCs, *A Little Book for Little Children,* by "T. W." (*c.* 1702–12), one of at least three works of that title.[12] It contains the famed nursery mnemonics, "A was an Archer and shot at a Frog. / B was a blind Man led by a Dog"; two additional alphabets, including one of games; a number of miniature cuts; and a poem, misprized for its punctuation flaws, which is an eerie vision of apocalyptic events and calls to mind some of Blake's poetry.[13]

Cooper, Corbett, and Newbery followed this—or some now lost ABCs like it—in their productions, expanding on the earlier work's twelve pages by adding riddles, fables, prayers, and newly concocted tales. In short, the ABC miscellany, like the holiday miscellanies that soon followed, was an accommodating catchall, perfectly suited to the needs and limitations of the new trade.

The nature of the miscellany is to offer its mixed delights in a single volume, though a unifying device like the alphabet or Christmas or Twelfth Night might be incorporated into it. Newbery's special contri-

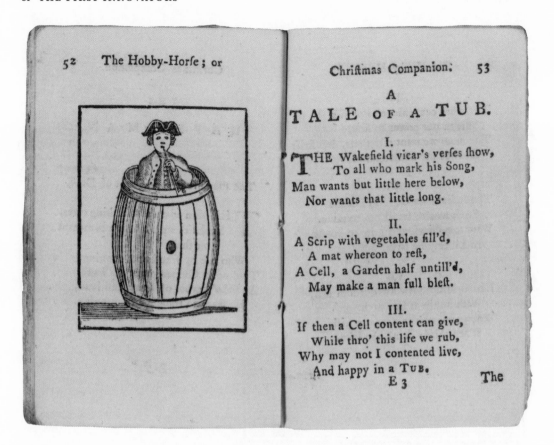

52   The Hobby-Horfe; or

Chriſtmas Companion.   53

A
TALE OF A TUB.

I.
THE Wakefield vicar's verſes ſhow,
    To all who mark his Song,
Man wants but little here below,
    Nor wants that little long.

II.
A Scrip with vegetables fill'd,
    A mat whereon to reſt,
A Cell, a Garden half untill'd,
    May make a man full bleſt.

III.
If then a Cell content can give,
    While thro' this life we rub,
Why may not I contented live,
    And happy in a TUB.

E 3   The

53. "A Tale of a Tub."
"Toby Ticklepitcher," *The
Hobby-Horse; or, Christmas
Companion*, 1784.

bution was to include in his very first work, through the letters of Jack
and of Newbery to Master Tommy and Pretty Miss Polly, cohesive elements that were also links to future works. Tommy and Polly are his
audience personalized as minor characters in the frame device to read
the tale and show enthusiasm for the ball or pincushion that went with
the sixpence book (twopence extra). Newbery suggests that they and all
his readers are very like the two lucky children whose virtue is very
splendidly rewarded, as two appended letters from "Mr. Newbery"
make clear. What began as an advertising gimmick became a unifying
device for his many miscellanies and, in time, the basis of his magazine
stories and novellas.

    This was the story that would be got by heart by generations of
young readers before 1768: Little Master, who Newbery points out is
very like Tommy, was so good and dutiful and "learned his Book" so
well that he soon was noticed by the great people of the realm and was
fitly rewarded by being raised up from a lowly life to one of high estate

54. "Mounted on Jouler, Tommy Trip tames Woglog." *A Pretty Book of Pictures for Little Masters and Misses; or, Tommy Trip's History of Beasts and Birds,* 1767.

as the owner of a coach and six. And a girl no better or prettier than Polly demonstrated such modesty, learning, dutifulness, and charm "in Company" that Lady Meanwell gave her a "fine Gold Watch" and took her for rides in her coach. Coach and six and gold watch were shown in small cuts to cinch the point.

We have here the germ of many a Newbery staple of the coming years. Jack-the-Giant-Killer combined in Newbery's imagination with the renowned Tom Thumb to become tiny Tommy Trip, Esq., who of course does not kill the giant Woglog but chastens and reprograms him solely to do good by rewarding children according to their deeds. Master Tommy reappears as the intimate of a prince in the *Lilliputian Magazine* and is the archetype for many famed characters, including Master Peter Primrose and Master Thoroughgood (*Lilliputian Magazine*), Giles Gingerbread, and Tom Two-Shoes. Polly is the first of Newbery's good, sweet, and learned girls. Florella, whose virtue turns a would-be seducer into a family friend; the penniless but cheerful and sweet Sally Silence, espoused by a duke and made the dutchess of Downright; a second Little Polly Meanwell who becomes queen of the Far Eastern realm of Petula (*Lilliputian Magazine*); and of course Margery Two-Shoes Meanwell—all are stirring examples of the potency of virtue, learning, and hard work in overcoming the disadvantages of fortune and even of birth, as indicated by the frequency with which lowly and penniless boys and girls achieve wealth and high estate.

These loved characters served a multiple purpose for Newbery: They helped to unify and make more familiar the sometimes higgledy-piggledy contents of a miscellany; and they advertised Newbery's other books and boosted sales. They also fed into one another creatively: The lowly miscellany culminated in the particularly fine *Lilliputian Magazine,* first of its kind in English children's books; tales and figures from it eventually flowered into the first trade novels for children, *Giles* and *Goody Two-Shoes.*[14]

We cannot always tell what Newbery himself wrote, what he commissioned others to write, or what he collaborated to produce. But it seems clear that two major figures were involved to some extent in some of his publishings: Christopher Smart (1722–71) and Oliver Goldsmith (1730–74). Goldsmith, who arrived in London in need of work in 1756, published in Newbery's *Public Ledger* a series of "Chinese Letters" now known as *The Citizen of the World* (1760–62); for children he wrote *An History of England, in a Series of Letters from a Nobleman to his Son* (1764), partly edited *Plutarch's Lives* (1762), and perhaps wrote *Goody Two-Shoes* (1765?), as tradition and some internal evidence indicate. Smart, who married Newbery's stepdaughter, Anna Maria Carnan, wrote or co-edited the *Lilliputian Magazine.*[15]

Yet despite Newbery's many different collaborators, the consistent personal and public goals and ideals iterated in his many diverse projects clearly indicate that his was the guiding hand, his the spirit that breathed a characteristic quality into them all. Darton was quite correct when he said it was useless to attribute to John Newbery any systematic psychology or philosophy.[16] We err, however, if we take this to mean that he had no coherent, discerning ideals and that he merely endorsed, chameleonlike, anything that was popular or profitable.

With a fine impartiality, Newbery's publications chide the idle or profligate rich, smug middle-class cruelty, waste and folly in politics, pa-

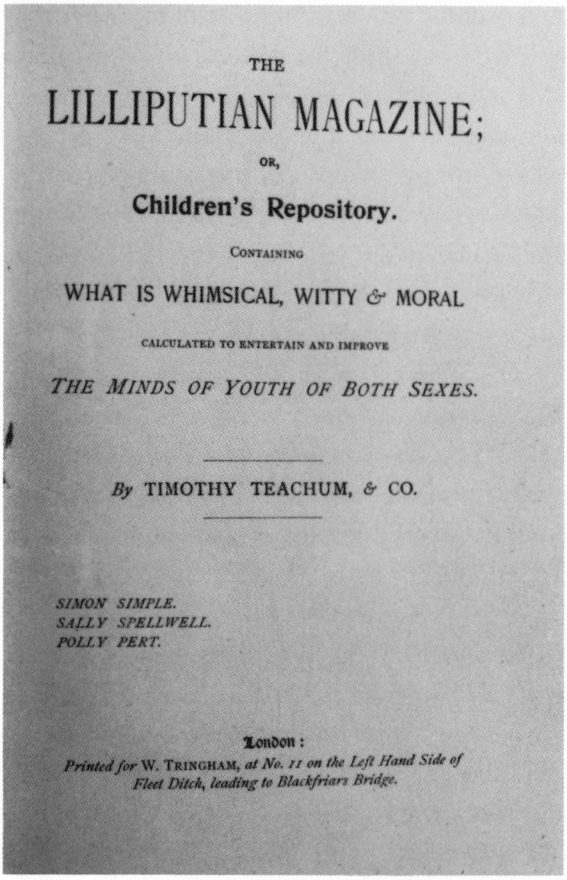

THE

LILLIPUTIAN MAGAZINE;

OR,

Children's Repository.

CONTAINING

WHAT IS WHIMSICAL, WITTY & MORAL

CALCULATED TO ENTERTAIN AND IMPROVE

THE MINDS OF YOUTH OF BOTH SEXES.

By TIMOTHY TEACHUM, & CO.

SIMON SIMPLE.
SALLY SPELLWELL.
POLLY PERT.

London :
Printed for W. TRINGHAM, *at No. 11 on the Left Hand Side of*
Fleet Ditch, leading to Blackfriars Bridge.

55. An imitation of Newbery's *Lilliputian Magazine.* "Timothy Teachem, & Co.," *The Lilliputian Magazine; or, Children's Repository,* [*c.* 1800s].

56. "Labourers in the farm yard." Jefferys Taylor, *The Farm,* 1834.

rental folly in careless child rearing, and anything that seemed in his view likely to diminish rather than to build the British nation—a particular obsession of his—anything from the small vices of children, like stoning birds or cats, to the largest sin, where those blest with position and wealth failed to set a proper moral example for their countrymen. Instances of these in his book intended clearly for adults, *A Collection of Pretty Poems For the Amusement of Children Six Foot High . . . Calculated . . . to do Good,* are uncompromising, sometimes scathing.[17]

Newbery's view of the public consequences of private laxity or probity was that the nation's moral health and economic prosperity resulted from the collective character *and* efforts of the British. Standards applicable to adults were even more vital for children, who could be trained away from vice, to good. With a freedom and lack of place-consciousness that would have been punished as Jacobin presumption in 1789, Newbery's *For Children Six Foot High* (1757), the *Lilliputian Magazine*

Drawn by J. Williams.   page 85.

The Farm Yard

Pub.d June 1.1835. by John Harris, St Paul's Church Y.d

(1751), and miscellanies like *The Twelfth-Day Gift* (*c.* 1767) offered advice to young and old, high and low, on their roles in what he correctly foresaw as European competition for economic predominance in new, world markets. In *Twelfth-Day* the Marquis of Setstar argues forcefully that tradesmen and farmers are as necessary to the nation as "Gentlemen" and that men of fortune who do no active good in fact harm society (pp. 6–8). The narrator ends with a panegyric on the contributions to British well-being of labor at home and of trade in the far corners of the world.

Taking quite literally the Enlightenment concept of the tabula rasa and the focus on the means of acquiring knowledge and values (as opposed to the emphasis on the innate or inherited), and following them to their logical conclusion—always the danger of untutored, which is to say unconditioned, reaction to ideas—Newbery arrived unwittingly at a brand of ardent nationalism as revolutionary in its threat to oligarchy as any hatched in the American colonies or France, though devoid of malice or even envy, so sure was he of the inevitability and benign efficacy of it. In short, he believed passionately in the meritocracy he thought Britain was becoming. Understandably, he could not imagine (who could have?) what in fact would develop: Ruling classes fearful for ancient privilege would ruthlessly trample the social and economic aspirations of countless Britons, strictly limit or even discourage learning among the poor, enforce self-serving laws carrying harsh penalties, and manipulate the revolution in industry to the disadvantage of the working poor, whose numbers would grow and whose condition worsen between 1800 and 1840, as we shall see.[18]

These were hopeful times, before uprisings and terrors like the Gordon Riots (1780) or the Peterloo Massacre (1819, when troops ended a political rally at St. Peter's Fields, Manchester) or the bloody government retaliations against starving field laborers' riots in the south of England (1830). In 1760, the crude but kindly, astute, and optimistic Newbery could see only that many might better their condition, as had he. *Concerning Education* seemed to him and numerous others of his class to support this dream and detail the means to effect it for all classes and both sexes. Locke's treatise shaped his ideas about the kinds of books children needed, the proper themes to stress, the best methods to use, and even what toys to devise, which Newbery did as adjuncts to his books, in his efforts to make his fortune and to aid English youngsters.[19] But setting aside practical suggestions, the most important thing Newbery got from Locke was reinforcement for his own optimism about human nature, especially child nature: The great philosopher and he agreed that a good character, a sound mind, and the capacity for hard work (all teachable) shaped a fragile twig into that hardy plant, the useful, successful, and happy man or woman, provided that all was seasoned with good nature and that laughter was not banished even from this serious business, as Newbery often implied and openly maintained in *The Midwife*, coedited with Smart.[20]

If Newbery's beliefs were homely, though stamped with shrewdness and generosity, his literary antecedents were even homelier. To be sure, he owed to Swift the literary legitimacy of the term *Lilliputian* and the idea of miniature and Brobdingnagian worlds in conflict. But his greatest debt was to chapbook characters and motifs. Duly purified, Tom Thumb and Jack-the-Giant-Killer are his little people, and the giants

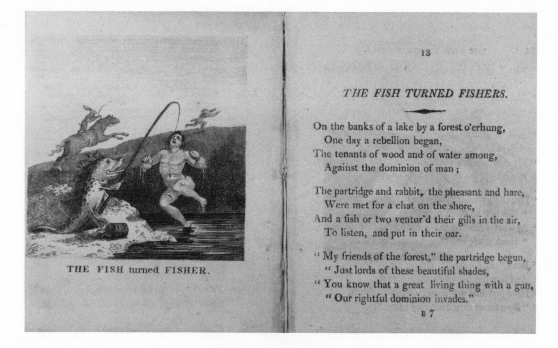

13

THE FISH TURNED FISHERS.

On the banks of a lake by a forest o'erhung,
　　One day a rebellion began,
The tenants of wood and of water among,
　　Against the dominion of man ;

The partridge and rabbit, the pheasant and hare,
　　Were met for a chat on the shore,
And a fish or two ventur'd their gills in the air,
　　To listen, and put in their oar.

" My friends of the forest," the partridge begun,
　　" Just lords of these beautiful shades,
" You know that a great living thing with a gun,
　　" Our rightful dominion invades."

B 7

THE FISH turned FISHER.

57. "The Fish turned Fishers." [Ann Taylor], *Signor Topsy-Turvy's Wonderful Magic Lantern,* [1810].

they outwit and tame are his specially tailored foes—ignorance, sloth, and profligacy. Yet apparently he had no Swiftian cynicism, perhaps because he had no doubt his opponents *could* be reclaimed, and, once done, they were conscripted into Newbery's schemes for "Bettering."

At the core of many of the chapbook tales alluded to is a basic motif Newbery interpreted characteristically, that is, socially and economically. He metamorphosed the chapbook favorite *The World Turn'd Upside Down* into the mite rendered mighty, the bully beaten, the deserving pauper made rich, and the Nobody made mayor. Certainly, some realities of London life justified such expectations: Shortly before Newbery opened his London firm, Sir John Barnard's *Present for an Apprentice; or, A Sure Guide to gain both Esteem and Estate by the late Lord Mayor of London* appeared. A boy who started as an apprentice in a counting house, Sir John, knighted in 1732, rose to become mayor of London. Editions of this memoir and handbook for humble, ambitious lads appeared in 1740, 1741, and 1742. Idealistic yet businesslike, and replete with all manner of tips for shrewd dealings, it could have been a model for Newbery's social and economic bettering schemes written for worthy youngsters over the next two decades.[21]

Newbery must have enjoyed *Fortunatus, Valentine and Orson,* and

58. *Whittington and His Cat,* [1827].

Friar Bacon, all of which are mentioned in his books on occasion. But the true heroes for him were Thumb cured of naughtiness, Jack dedicated to moral and educational pursuits, and, most of all, Dick Whittington. A farmer's son, self-educated, "self-made," having left home at sixteen "to seek his fortune," Newbery may simply have been too practical to offer magical solutions as serious examples for his young readers. Goody Two-Shoes, his Cinderella, works hard and long for her reward, which is no glass slipper but instead the position and means to do even more good in her parish. Giles Gingerbread, his Dick Whittington, is still working for that coach and six when we last meet him in *The Fairing.* Tom Trip and Tom Telescope, Esq., quite different social permutations of the chapbook Thumb, go about the world unmasking evil or ignorance, aiding the good, and spreading knowledge.

Given a choice between enchanters' gimmicks and enlightened human solutions, Newbery the pragmatist always chose the latter. There is a revealing comparison in *Goody Two-Shoes* when the narrator tells us of Margery Meanwell's "Considering Cap." The cap's exotic look transforms a staid gathering of lawyers or divines or an ordinary English family into an apparent "Synod of Egyptian Priests," but its value is no laughing matter. It is a cure for wrongheadedness, a preventer of quarrels between husbands and wives, between parents and children. "What was Fortunatus's Wishing Cap when compared to this?" asks the narrator. Conveying people from one place to another is useless, he stoutly avers, as they simply take their defects with them. Similarly, the ever full purse, though a pleasant possession for Fortunatus, is less valuable than Goody Two-Shoes's cap, for it could not "purchase Peace." He ends, in a neat puff, by alluding to Friar Bacon's lost opportunity to perform a great feat of magic due to his assistant's being too stupid to awaken him as ordered as soon as the Brazen Head spoke: "Now the *Time is*, therefore buy the Cap immediately, and make proper Use of it, and be happy before the *Time is Past*, *Yours*, Roger Bacon."[22]

Newbery's use of chapbook and fairy tale motifs is most important: He frequently invites his young readers to enjoy a "time out" from the serious business of life, but neither they nor his reformed and transformed chapbook heroes and heroines are allowed to indulge endlessly in playfulness and jollity or to forget that they have a crucial goal and mission—to achieve their moral, educational, and social maturity.

In children's stories by the reformers of the 1780s (Thomas Day, Sarah Trimmer, Mary Ann and Dorothy Kilner) and for at least sixty years more, most of the children do not grow up by the story's end. In many of Newbery's tales, however, be they 5 pages or 150, the small children who start an adventure are often adults at its end. We *see* them reap the happy rewards or the just misery of the seeds they sow in their childhood. They grow up quickly. So did their audience.

It is in part this inescapable reality in child life of the age that accounts for an odd quality of worldliness, or adult wariness and awareness, that many present-day readers find exceedingly unsettling in these books. By twelve or fourteen all but the well-to-do or indigent paupers were working or learning a trade. Their success depended on their performance, perspicacity, and good character. Consequently, we should not be startled that books written for four- or five-year-olds offer max-

p.115

Chariot fired by Motion

ims we associate with graybeards; or that a child in a tale swiftly matures into a beautiful maiden who, her virtue assaulted, resists temptation; or that a child bully and bird torturer is plunged, in three pages, into an adult life of woe. Given the nature of child life then, none of this is peculiar or inappropriate. If it seems so to us, it is only because we have a strikingly different concept of childhood and its relation to the adult world.

59. "Chariot fired by Motion." Tom Telescope [Oliver Goldsmith?], *The Newtonian System of Philosophy*, 1761.

Once we understand and allow for this profound difference in perspective, many things that critics have puzzled over make sound sense. Newbery's *Pocket-Book* is a fine example. Most moderns find nothing seriously amiss with its alphabets, fables, riddles, and poems. But the forty-five "Select Proverbs For the Use of Children" evoke at best doubt. One of our ablest scholars in the field implies they were neither fit nor selected for children but perhaps were put in as moral placators for parents.[23]

Such aphorisms were definitely meant for the young, whose lives and immediate concerns were at all levels far closer to those of adults than we can easily realize today. The proverbs deal with discerning the real from the fake, the trustworthy from the not, the possible from the impossible, and with finding joy in one's life while still keeping an eye open for opportunity. Bearing in mind the world Newbery's readers had to face and conquer, we can understand the points made: "A Fool's Bolt is soon shot," "First come, first served," "Enough's as good as a feast," "Try your Friend before you trust him," "When the Fox preaches beware the Geese," "Fair and softly goes far," "Tell the Truth and shame the Devil," "Faint Heart never won Fair Lady," "It's a good Horse that never stumbles. / It's a good Wife that never grumbles," "The weakest goes to the Wall," "Make Hay while the Sun shines," "Nothing's so certain as Death," or "A Bird in the hand. . . ."

Newbery's plans to help ambitious youngsters or to improve lazy ones—and, to be sure, to sell lots of books—developed in two directions after his early ABC miscellany, *Pocket-Book*. The first was his grand scheme to put into children's hands most of the basic information they might be expected to need. This was to result in *The Circle of the Sciences*, variously projected as seven, ten, and even twelve volumes.[24] In fact, between 1745 and 1748 eight volumes of *The Circle* appeared—Grammar, Writing, Arithmetic, Rhetoric, Poetry, Logic, Geography, and Chronology. Two others were advertised as part of it but there is some

Emma and Jemima stopp'd
by the Robber in the Wood.

60. "Emma and Jemima
Stopp'd by the Robber in
the Wood." *Rainsford
Villa; or, Juvenile Independence,* 1823.

doubt they appeared: Spelling and a Dictionary. Projected but apparently not published were those on Criticism, History, and Philosophy.[25]

The second direction Newbery took was with a different sort of venture but one entirely in accord with the larger aims of *The Circle*. This was Newbery's plan, with Christopher Smart as coeditor/writer, to provide through the *Lilliputian Magazine* a moral and esthetic education complementary to that given in volumes of solid instruction. Through fables, tales, and *histories,* that term long used to fend off foes of fiction, they would mold the tastes, sensitivities, and morals of young readers. This they announce boldly in the Preface and in "A Dialogue" between "the Author" and a "Gentleman," insisting here, as Newbery had firmly in advertisements for *The Circle*, that the moral improvement of each child was of the greatest import to the nation's well-being.

The subtitle of the *Lilliputian Magazine* combines whimsy and purposefulness: "The Young Gentleman & Lady's Golden Library, being An Attempt to Amend the World, to render the Society of Man more Amiable, & and to establish the Plainness, Simplicity, Virtue & Wisdom of the Golden Age." It was impossible for "MAB, Queen of the Fairies" to resist so noble, so select a society, and from her court at a "Corner of Harnsey Wood" "in a Bean Blossom," she urged—in a puff in the *General Evening Post*, 22 January 1750—those of like mind to join her: "All [her] little Friends . . . who would be wise, happy and never want Money."[26] England's first children's magazine has a charm that can still be felt; but for all the drollery and jesting, it has a clear moral point. The stories of Florella, Polly, Peter, Billy, Sally, and others do not merely illustrate virtue personally rewarded but reveal it to have far-reaching social effects and the power to change others' lives.

The exciting adventures of boys and girls growing up successfully are not without touches of humor, often created by insights into the vagaries of human nature: Miss Biddy Johnson, because of her vanity and willfulness, finds herself in urgent need of rescue from two murderers. Having got a new coat and earrings and to show them off to her greatest rival, "away she run forsooth without any body with her to see miss *Fanny Tinsel*. Miss *Fanny* was as proud a little girl as any in *London*, she hated every body that was finer than herself, and because miss *Biddy* was dressed out so, she would not play with her: upon which miss *Biddy* huffed, and left her," promptly falling in with her captors. This is the humor of gentle but pointed malice at human foibles. Neither this nor any of the jests or riddles are childish. The wit is wry, the targets fools or dullards.

Many of the themes, characters, and even bits of plot from the *Lilliputian* found their way into later holiday miscellanies and, more important, into the new trade genre—novels, or novellas. We can see the origin of *Giles Gingerbread* in the stories of Master Thoroughgood, the faithful apprentice; in Billy Hiron, who was so learned that he reformed, and became a counselor to, young King Miram of Lilliput; in Master Peter Primrose, whose learning (at first) brought estate and esteem; and finally in Master Meanwell, made speaker of the Lilliputian Society by its permanent president, the Young Prince. Like the ragged Giles, many start in lowly circumstances, but, says the prince, *merit* is what the *Society* (surrogate for Britain) rewards, not wealth or *position, even when inherited*. Similarly, we can trace the beginnings of the saga of Goody-Two Shoes to this magazine, as I have suggested.

Although the *Lilliputian Magazine*, no financial success, was discontinued after three issues, it came out in book form in 1752 and appeared with regularity from then until 1783.[27] The title was kept alive in many imitations thereafter. Newbery's venture was far ahead of its time. His audience had not formed the reading and buying habits that in six decades would make possible the support of periodical literature. Yet in attempting to raise the quality of the miscellany's instruction and entertainment and to organize it more effectively, Newbery set an example for future magazines and paved the way for children's trade novels.

The Renowned History of Giles Gingerbread and *The Renowned History of Little Goody Two-Shoes* share many themes and a similarity in plot but are different types. *Giles* is an episodic tale, with casually strung together adventures and lessons of the urchin who was "ragged as a colt." Like the picaresque eighteenth-century novel, it employs digressions for variety and to offer Giles more opportunities to observe and learn. Unlike Goody Two-Shoes and many of the characters in the *Lilliputian*, Giles is still a child at the story's end, still working to earn his coach and six, but he is progressing steadily.

Goody Two-Shoes, though it too has digressions, is a novel of development, a homely Bildungsroman, in which a newly orphaned child must bear all the responsibility for her own support and maturation. The Meanwell family is ruined by the financial skullduggery of Sir Timothy Gripe and his tool, Farmer Graspall. Young Margery and her brother,

61. "Giles . . . was as
ragged as a Colt." [John
Newbery?], *The Renowned
History of Giles
Gingerbread,* [*c.* 1766].

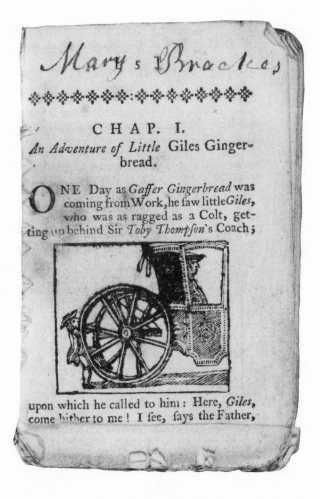

Tom, are "thrown on the parish," or charity, after their parents die of grief and privation. Tom is soon rescued by a benevolent stranger who arranges for him to start a career as a sailor. Left alone, Margery has only one shoe and is ragged and hungry. Kindly neighbors are prevented from helping her as much as they would by the vindictive Gripe; so she sets out to work and help herself.

From the children going to and from the local dame school, she learns her letters so well that she soon becomes a "trotting tutoress" and earns her bread teaching others. Industry and probity eventually win her the post as school mistress, at which she is remarkably successful. She distinguishes herself throughout the parish by her kindness and practical help. She has several birds for companions and tells the farmers when to gather hay by consulting a barometer, leading to her trial for witchcraft. A jealous farmer from the next parish brings the charge, but she is acquitted when she explains her enlightened methods to the court, much to Goosecap's discomfiture. Thus, she comes to the attention of Sir Charles Jones, who soon wishes to marry her. Margery is rescued from playing the beggar-maid married to King Cophetua by the lucky return of her brother at the start of the ceremony. Now wealthy, he settles a handsome dowry upon Two-Shoes so that Sir Charles marries a lady, an heiress, and a paragon of virtue and learning.

Prominent in this tale of personal triumph are several social concerns, such as better means of aiding the deserving poor and of controlling the rapacious rich, and Newbery/Goody offers pointed suggestions for their correction. Indeed, the point of Margery's life is that it is not merely personal but is always lived in full consciousness of the larger social and spiritual contexts. Goody Two-Shoes is a British heroine. She is a model, literally, for those who would ameliorate England's evils: Her Sunday School, in which she provides food for body, mind, and soul, was operating to the glory of God and England years before Raikes and Hannah More got started. Today she bears a soubriquet tainted by connotations of the self-congratulatory and meddlesome, but the character in Newbery's book lacks these flaws. She matter-of-factly does what is right and needful and moves on to the next task, asking no thanks, seeking no glory.

Indeed, matter-of-factness is a constant in the complex tonal quality of this and most other Newbery fictions. It corresponds to a remarkable absence of self-pity in the characters, or of sentimentality in the narrators, and stems clearly from that adult wariness and awareness we noted earlier. Along with these, which distinguish the serious aspect of tone, went a type of humor that is also quite worldly, and rare after 1790. Customarily in Newbery, wit and satire, seldom pointless buffoonery, form the essence of the humor. And a misstep can bring anyone or anything under its revealing light.

Such qualities, and the spontaneity with which they are expressed, far more than any alleged excess of levity, made Newbery's books undesirable to many respectable adults by the last decade of the century. This was so for very good reasons. When children spontaneously laugh at something or, especially, someone, they demonstrate a degree of social parity with those around them. Humor or laughter is license, freedom, an entitlement of sorts. Ironic or satiric laughter is a more emphatic manifestation of social enfranchisement. Therefore, humor or

62. "See here's little Giles, / With his Gingerbread Book." [Newbery?], *Giles Gingerbread*, [*c.* 1766].

Little *Giles Gingerbread.*

See here's little *Giles,*
     With his Gingerbread Book,
For which he doth long,
     And at which he doth look ;
Till by longing and looking,
     He gets it by Heart,
And then eats it up,
     As we eat up a Tart.

                                   TOM TAGS.

irony occasioned between social unequals is governed by complex laws. Except for the servant-master relation, the most unequal is that between children and (most) adults. And since much laughter and all irony is judgmental, sometimes harshly so, stated rules as well as unspoken shibboleths control what is seen as funny, whom a child (especially a preadolescent) may laugh at, and when. In short, the dynamics of humor and satire in children's books tell much about how the young are trained to see themselves in relation to the adults around them.

Honest error was never the butt of a joke, but fools were ever fair game, for Newbery used satire as a potent corrective. The wayward boy trampled by a bull in *Giles Gingerbread*; the silly, obstinate Wilful Wat banged up in the dangerous Up-and-Down, and simpleton Dick Sudbury "choused" of all his money by slick gamblers in *The Fairing*; Goosecap and his troop of "gabies" trying to get Two-Shoes convicted of witchcraft—all are Simple Simons held up to ridicule because they were warned or, *at their age,* should have known better. There are many such examples. Adults who are fooled and heedless children who were warned of danger suffer the consequences and are admonished to take their medicine stoically, and to remember next time. They are spared no further sympathy or attention.

Many childhood transgressions and painful retributions that would be long, earnestly, and even lovingly dwelt upon in books after 1790 were washed away with humor before 1768. Laughter—sometimes scornful and painful but always swift, clean, and forthrightly pointed at the real heart of the matter—was Newbery's way.

His laughter was not reserved for children's errors or for poor or lowly adults like Goosecap and his credulous crew. *The Fairing* (1765?, 1767) contains a funny account of a dog show in which the canine cast, dressed as fops, dandies, and spoiled beauties, mime their human targets' favorite parlor games, ending with a zany dance. A very mixed audience—young and old, and those of high and low birth—join in laughter at the folly of such vain and useless people. Although Newbery certainly never encouraged children to rebel against or to ridicule their parents or decent, sensible adults, simply *being* an adult did not provide imbecility with a special shield. Newbery encouraged children to observe closely and to assess prudently and likewise allowed them to join in the hilarity created by a puffed-up poseur's discomfiture.

Profound changes in the code regulating children's laughter greatly altered their books in the final decade of the eighteenth century. The child's world shown in early trade books was shaped by the values of small businesswomen and -men and artisans of the lower-middle classes, like Mary Cooper and John Newbery. Even the renowned Goody Two-Shoes, though born a lady, braved crises usually faced by children who were lower in the social hierarchy and had to make their own way in the world. She and they display remarkable self-reliance and discernment because their dependent, helpless childhood is brief. From their early years, a sense of responsibility, an adult vigilance, and a healthy skepticism were the traits that stamped them or, if lacking, were the flaws that would trip them up in life. Their ABCs gave sage advice, sometimes in cynical proverbs; their stories showed danger and even brutality to be very real possibilities—pitfalls the children themselves had to avoid. Such realities and the temperament they bred were repugnant to respectable conservatives. Like many of us today, the reformers preferred to ban ugly facts from pictures of child life, to soften them, or to feature them as evils that bad youngsters brought on themselves but from which the repentant were rescued by adults. In contrast, Newbery's ironic, instructive laughter tempered the harsh facts of life. Satire and humor were conscripted for his paramount task: to show the young how to become successful adults—honest, shrewd, industrious, and happy.

The child who exposes the folly of adults or unselfconsciously laughs when others do so is on a different footing with those adults than is the docile, dependent child who dares not laugh and more often gives lachrymose evidence of his "proper feelings." Goody Two-Shoes cries when her parents die and her brother disappears. She sheds no tears over her homelessness, hunger, long hours of work, loneliness, or her very uncertain future. Few of Newbery's stalwarts do. She is modest, gentle, and polite; she is also on her own—economically, socially, and morally.

This is the "child's world" that developments in industry and urbanization, as well as systematic propagandizing in children's literature, would soon render obsolete, at least as an acceptable ideal; in other words, would render obsolete in theory if not in fact for the vast majority. What replaced it was a vision of a world where all-powerful, all-knowing parents (increasingly mothers) examined, weighed, and assessed every thought and act in their children's lives. And in return for the means of survival, for the love and approval, as well as for this essential guidance, parents exacted strictest obedience or, in lieu of that, extravagant repentance.

Although *Goody Two-Shoes* was printed less and less as the nineteenth century progressed, it was resurrected for England's children during the bombings of World War II when, perhaps, its virtues were needed and appreciated.[28] But what really had made it and all those "wonderful old Newberys" obsolete in the early 1800s was the newly emerging concept of childhood and the family. The writers who routed the lower-middle-class vision of the child in juvenile books were largely of the respectable classes, actively supported by a few upper-class women, who sought to impose their views on all levels of society. Naturally, their notions of youthful propriety in general and of the decorum of laughter in particular were in profound conflict with Newbery's.

5. Years of Transition: 1768 to 1788

TRADE AND PLUMB-CAKE—FOR A WHILE!

In the two decades after John Newbery's death, no single publisher or group of writers entirely dominated the field as he had
done. The Newbery name was still influential, partly because of
the continued popularity of many of his books and partly because there
were actually two rival establishments bearing that name. The original
business at the Bible and Sun had passed into the hands of John Newbery's son, Francis, who ran it with the help of John's stepson, Thomas
Carnan. They published many new works but also relied heavily on the
old stock created by the founder. Their books appeared under various
imprints: "Newbery & Co.," "F. Newbery and T. Carnan," "Carnan and
Newbery," and "Thomas Carnan." In 1779 Francis retired from publishing to work solely in patent medicines, a lucrative sideline of John's,
leaving Carnan to carry on alone until his death in 1788.[1] At that point,
over twenty of John Newbery's titles and the blocks (masters) for his
woodcuts were purchased by the Quaker publisher William Darton,
who had opened a firm in Gracechurch Street the year before; in a short
time Darton took Joseph Harvey on as a partner and, later, his own son,
Samuel.[2]

The second Newbery establishment "at the corner of St. Paul's
Church-Yard" was opened by a second Francis, John's nephew, in 1767.
This Francis had apparently not worked for his uncle, and there was
some conflict between him and John's heirs.[3] But he had experience at
bookselling and a flair for spotting good material, which was fortunate,
for having no right to the original family stock, he had to create his
own. This he did successfully until his death in 1780, whereafter his wife
Elizabeth operated the business.

It is not known whether Elizabeth actually worked in the firm before

keep them always full. Two simple rules, well obser-
ved, will do the business. 1st Let honesty and industry
be thy constant

companions: 2d Spend one shilling every day, less
than thy clear gains. Then shall thy pockets soon
begin to thrive;

248

LOUIS THE SIXTEENTH.

LOUIS THE SIXTEENTH was grandson to the
late King. He was twenty years of age when
he ascended the throne, and was married to
Marie Antoinette, daughter to the Emperor
of Austria; but his education had by no means
fitted him for ruling over a nation in so per-
turbed a state as France then was. He was
himself a bigot to the Romish faith, while his
people, too plainly perceiving that their ambitious clergy were even greater lovers of the
world than themselves, became inclined to
reject all religion. Infidelity grew to an
alarming height, and it can be no matter of
surprise, that those who refused to submit to
God, soon cast off all other control.

On the accession of Louis, a difficulty arose

Louis XVI.

Reigned from 1774 to 1793.

In contests with England this reign first begun,
And America's Isles were lost and were won.
But troubles at home, and discords arose,
Which Turgot and Necker found vain to oppose.
Though gentle and good, too unstable to guide
A nation now bursting with infidel pride,
Poor Louis, alas! on that scaffold has bled,
Where the blood of his wife and his sister was shed.

LITTLE LIBRARY.

Francis's death, or how deeply she was involved in its day-to-day work-
ings afterwards, because she employed managers during her entire own-
ership. The first was Thomas Badcock, who worked for her until 1797.
Sometime in the early 1790s, she added to her staff John Harris, who
assumed full management from 1797 to 1802, when he bought the firm
from Elizabeth, who retired.[4] For over twenty years, an extensive and
varied collection of books had appeared under the imprint of E. Newbery. Indeed, this firm, rival of Newbery's heirs, was in fact and spirit
more his successor, and the same would be said—indeed advertised
constantly—of the firm under John Harris's brilliant guidance.

63. Honesty and Industry.
Benjamin Franklin,
*The Art of Making Money
Plenty,* 1817.

64. "Poor Louis, alas! on
that scaffold has bled."
The French History, 1833.

Elizabeth Newbery published most of her books independently, but
she entered into joint ventures with a number of firms over the years, a
common practice, apparently much favored by new firms or those with
a partial interest in juvenile books. The outlay in time and cash (and
intelligence and ingenuity, carped critics) for children's books was considerably less than that needed for the adult market. But even this fairly
comfortable margin for success was enlarged by such alliances. Several
of these sometime associates became exceedingly prominent in their
own right after 1790: Vernor and Hood (all types of books), John Wallis
(originally maps, later also dissected maps or jigsaw puzzles, and
books), and Darton & Harvey (moral/cautionary tomes), to cite a few.[5]

These years, like the era before them, were a time of trade domi-
nance, and most—but by no means all—of the books that were printed
were produced by anonymous hack writers guided by their publishers'
needs. A few of these deserved the modest attention they eventually received, probably the best known being Richard Johnson, who wrote for
Carnan and Newbery and many others. He did his finest work for Elizabeth Newbery under the pseudonym "The Rev. Mr. Cooper."[6]

But other writers also gained prominence as the 1780s progressed,
like Thomas Day, who wrote the enormously popular *Sandford and
Merton* (Pt. I, 1783; Pt. II, 1786; Pt. III, 1789); R. E. Raspe, who wrote
Baron Munchausen's Narrative of his marvellous Travels and Campaigns
(1785); and Anna Barbauld, author of the much-loved *Hymns in Prose for
Children* (1781). Raspe's delightful work, although often excerpted in
chapbooks, was something of a sport, for its unbridled, whimsical nonsense belongs to a far later phase of children's books. Day and Barbauld
were the advance guard of a growing tribe of writers who had a philosophical ax to grind. Harbingers of developments to come, they did not

65. Frontispiece: The Baron. [Rudolf Eric Raspe], *The Travels and Surprising Adventures of Baron Munchausen,* illustrated by George Cruikshank, 1868.

enter into the spirit of the trade dealings. For the time, however, the mighty outflow of new books and new editions of the old was still perceived as the handiwork and commodity of a prospering trade: In London and many provincial towns new firms opened; some firms established provincial branches, and many added juvenalia to their stock.

Most of these businessmen would have endorsed Newbery's motto, "Trade and Plumb-Cake for ever, Huzza!" (*The Twelfth-Day Gift, c.* 1767), but to most it meant something quite vague or superficial. They routinely seconded the prevailing values—learning, self-improvement, moral conduct, and innocent mirth—and seldom opposed anything except blatant transgressions and, of course, books that did not sell. No publisher had the obsessive nationalistic concerns or the coherent view of the individual's relation to society that was reflected even in Newbery's catchpennies. Consequently, their books lacked the integrity of purpose that had touched his homeliest ABCs and miscellanies. Ironically, this lack may actually have delayed the Lilliputian battle of the books, between the vested interests of the higher orders and the growing aspirations of the lower, until 1787 or '88. But when the inevitable pressure from the top was exerted to purge the trade of "unsuitable" wares, the tradesmen abandoned what their "betters" contemned and adopted, at least ostensibly or temporarily, what they sanctioned.[7]

Transitional publishers bid, as had Newbery and his colleagues, for the children's market of the respectable, or middling, classes as well as for that of the lower-middle class and working poor. But Newbery had been the nursery world's apostle of what today is called "upward mobility," which he believed would strengthen and enrich the "body politic" (inseparable to him from the "body economic"), and he had championed the interests of those at the lower end of the scale. Had he lived to express this between 1776–96, and stuck to it, he would have landed in the black books of Trimmer, More, and the conservative establishment, and perhaps indeed among those indicted or tried for sedition, as were Thomas Paine and William Blake, respectively.[8] But since later publishers mainly paid lip service to such ideals, they avoided controversy longer than might have been expected.

If the books of the transitional years lacked substance, they succeeded often enough in merriment, if not wit, to sustain the phenomenal growth of the new trade branch. If their laxity of vision bred a degree of license in decorum (not in morality), then it was of the sort that came unthinkingly, not from deliberate indelicacy. Because of the severe criticism and even loathing trade books would face by the century's end, the precise nature of their failings must be made clear: Transitional books increased elements of fantasy, especially fairies and magical contrivances, and tolerated a resurgence of chapbook figures and a growing frivolity and "levity." But though their lapses in taste might shock modern readers, they were within the boundaries of prevailing standards of nicety, yet not within those that would be forged in the late 1780s and enforced in juvenile books in the nineties by the reformers. Because of the standards and, even more, the class biases of these reformers trade publications would soon come under a cloud not fully deserved.

Juvenile libraries offered a great mixture of books, including moral and devotional, as had the chapman's pack of yore. And none, not even major chapbook firms like the prolific Cluer, Dicey, and Marshall of London, supplied only "empty" entertainments to the young.[9] For one thing, given the dual strain of jollity and puritan seriousness in the English character, that would not have been prudent. For another, there is no reason to assume that publishers of children's books as a group greatly differed from their fellows and did not share their values. As was the case from the birth of the literature, their stock always included religious and devotional books, improving works of all sorts, and imitations of Newbery's amusing tomes. And, as from the start, the competition between firms to corner the lion's share of the market was fierce.

The contending Newbery firms were typical both in the kinds of books offered in these transitional decades and in their ready response to rivals, including each other. But in many firms the rivalry was amicable and included occasional joint ventures. Not with these kinsmen. In the field of history, Francis Newbery and Thomas Carnan continued to offer John's *New and Noble History of England* (*c.* 1763, 1781) and *Short Histories for the Improvement of the Mind* (1764). Francis and Elizabeth's firm brought out *A New History of England* (1773, 1788, 1791), *A New Roman History* (1784), *The History of France . . . comprehending every interesting and remarkable occurrence in the annals of that monarchy* (1784, 1792), and even *The History of North America* (1789), by the prolific Reverend Mr. Cooper, Richard Johnson. And in response to, for instance, the popular Baldwin and Cradock courtesy book, *The Polite Academy* (1761, 1769, 1771, 1773, 1777, *c.* 1780, *c.* 1790), Carnan and Newbery published several books, including *The Polite Lady; or, . . . Female Education. In a Series of Letters* (1775), whereas Elizabeth vied with *Newbery's Familiar Letter Writer, adapted to the Capacities of Young People* (1788). Similarly, when James Dodsley's coup appeared, *Letters Written by the Earl of Chesterfield to his Son,* 2 vols. (1774), Francis and Elizabeth's firm rushed forth that same year with a shortened version of it, *Lord Chesterfield's Maxims . . . Being the Substance of the . . . Letters,* a speedy riposte indeed.

In the field of the sciences there was something of a lull in the creation of new, popularly priced books. Newbery's *Circle of the Sciences* (1745–48) was issued periodically in individual volumes by his son and stepson until 1783; and the widely applauded *Newtonian System of Philosophy,* or Tom Telescope's *Philosophy of Tops and Balls,* was quite regularly printed, Carnan producing the seventh edition in 1787, Ogilvy and Speare another in 1794. But few similarly ambitious or innovative efforts appeared to challenge it. One was adapted with some success from *The*

66. "Ancient Britons." J. Aspin, *Ancient Customs*, 1835.

67. "The Jerboa." *The Children's Cabinet*, 1798.

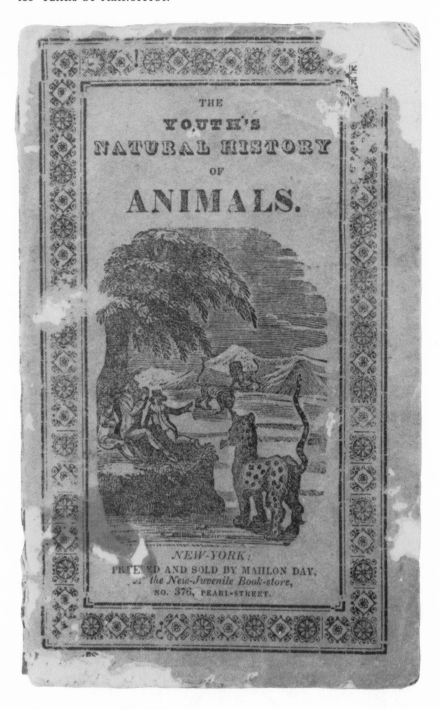

68. An American
chapbook cover. *The
Youth's Natural History*,
1829.

General Magazine of the Arts and Sciences (1755) by Benjamin Martin: *Young Gentleman and Lady's Philosophy, in a continued survey of the Works of Nature and Art; by way of Dialogue,* 3 vols. (London: W. Owen, 1772; vol. 3, 1782). This offered a description of the "Newtonian system for the young" with sections on "the solar system, electrical gadgetry, optical instruments," and the like.[10]

Books of knowledge proliferated in the next century, but prior to such developments, most of the inexpensive scientific children's books were modernized natural histories. Thomas Saint of Newcastle reissued, for example, John Newbery's *Pretty Book of Pictures for Little Masters and Misses; or, Little Tommy Trip's History of Beasts and Birds* (1752; rev. ed., 1779), a particularly fine version. Like Saint's own *New Lottery Book of Birds and Beasts* (1771), it was illustrated by Thomas Bewick, whose beautiful, realistic engravings using the white line technique revolutionized and immensely upgraded the quality of illustrations in juvenile books of moderate price.[11] Bewick soon opened his own firm and published several very fine natural histories, like the *General History of Quadrupeds* (1790, 1792) and *History of British Birds* (1797–1804). Carnan continued to issue the original version of Tommy Trip's *History of Beasts and Birds;* Francis and Elizabeth competed with Samuel Ward's *Natural History of Birds; or, A Complete System of Ornithology* (1775), a fine work with thirty-eight engraved copper plates. In these and in every area of children's books, the two publishers contended with dozens of firms offering similar books, most priced from the very inexpensive to the costly.

During the transition period it was uncommon for juvenile libraries or bookshops to specialize in one sort of work or to select stock by philosophical view. Books of learning, fairy tales, manuals of polite usage, ABCs, chapbook romances, "Newbery" or "Thumb" Bibles (from 1771), humorous miscellanies, juvenile novels, histories, religious and devotional books, and dissected puzzles of maps, of history, of the New Testament, of ABCs, of *The Pilgrim's Progress,* of the Apostle's Creed, of pleasant rural scenes, and of amusing but cautionary city scenes jostled each other on the shelves, to the delight of young patrons.[12]

NEW ENTERTAINMENTS: FUN AND IMPROVEMENT

In some respects, the easiest books to imitate were the alphabet and holiday, or seasonal, miscellanies, relying as they did on a hodgepodge of

69. "The Goose with
Golden Eggs." [Richard
Scrafton Sharpe], *Old
Friends in a New Dress*,
1820.

70. Frontispiece and title
page. Henry Fielding,
*The History of Tom Jones,
A Foundling*, 1784.

material, but they were growing stale with overuse. Although they continued to find a market among new generations of readers into the nineteenth century, the Newbery miscellany and those of the transitional years were gradually rendered obsolete by several trends. To begin with, the urge to specialize produced a uniformity of elements better suited to works centered on a particular activity or social event. Then too the new trade novels, with their comparatively cohesive and faster-paced plots, perhaps made the sprawling medleys seem old-fashioned and dawdling or tedious. The use of ABCs as primary readers was soon to end, as reformers and their imitators captured the market with graded readers fitted to the stages of learning. And the ABC portion was modernized all out of recognition in lavish specialized, pictorial alphabets around 1800.

When in 1788 John Stockdale issued *The Children's Miscellany*, a collection of stories featuring "Philip Quarll" and Thomas Day's "Little Jack," the trend of the future was set. The antiquated hodgepodge of tales, lessons, bits of information, poems, riddles, and the like would survive, if one can call it that, in the pages of respectable children's magazines, like John Marshall's *Children's Magazine*, a monthly which lasted two years; E. Newbery's *Young Gentleman's and Young Lady's Magazine*, which survived a year; Darton's annual, *The Minor's Pocket Book* (1798–1810); the Religious Tract Society's *Child's Companion; or, Sunday Scholar's Reward*; and from 1866 on in journals like the very fine *Aunt Judy's Magazine*, edited by Margaret Gatty.[13] But the transition from the miscellany to the magazine, which Newbery attempted in 1751, took a century to establish.

In the meantime, especially to 1800, the old works were reissued, pirated, and imitated. John Marshall's *Whitsuntide Present* (*c.* 1780), a close copy of Newbery's *Whitsuntide Gift* (1765), is a good example. Except in the characters' names and the choice and magnificence of gifts bestowed, the plots changed little: The good boy who "learned his book," is "noticed" and elevated by some great man; and the lovely, modest, virtuous, handy, and learned young damsel is similarly distinguished by a great lady and her offspring. Newbery's Master Billy and Miss Kitty Smith become Marshall's George and Charlotte Goodchild; and the noble philanthropist, the Duke of Goodwill, Marshall's Duke of Goodmanners, seconded in his benevolence by his wife and noble offspring, Lady Maria Dutiful and the Marquis of Wellbehave.[14] *Gaffer Goose's*

Golden Plaything (*c.* 1780) substitutes a retired tradesman for Newbery's Woglog and sets him off, like an optimistic Diogenes, to seek out and reward the pure in thought and deed with their choice of a bag of gold or a brick of silver.

A host of plots and motifs were hatched to help unify various hopefully improving and entertaining lessons. Groups of children gather for events which they know will be edifying and trust will amuse in *Tom Thumb's Exhibition* (F. & E. Newbery, 1775), *The Lilliputian Auction* (T. Carnan, 1773, 1777), and *The Lilliputian Masquerade. . . . [for] Lilliputians and Tommythumbians* (T. Carnan, 1783). In *The Exhibition,* Tom, now settled and respectable, makes a hobby of education and displays his treasures to all who need them. His mahogany "conjuring box" has "the uncommon property of converting every thing" in it "into the very thing it ought to have been." His Advice-Bird sings charmingly and counsels sagely. And his "Intellectual Perspective glass" lays bare the real dangers of apparent temptations, like sweets and "unwholesome trash," by revealing them to be "swarms of worms" and "devouring reptiles," a more biblical than empirical transformation, but one that works.

Carnan's more appealing *Lilliputian Auction,* by Master Charly Chatter, features the precocious executor of his uncle's estate offering a number of choice items for his circle of friends to bid on. What follows is mildly amusing. Lot 1 is a very special mirror that reveals one's disagreeable traits. Master Affable "jovially" challenges Master Froward to look in and, when Froward rather sensibly refuses, laughs and buys the glass for him as a gift. Lot 2 is an envelope "containing a Receipt to make young Ladies beautiful." Miss Surly successfully bids for the packet, illustrated in a circular frame, but on opening it finds, "If beautiful you wou'd appear, / Always be good humor'd dear"—enough surely to sour a Miss Affable, and the children have a good laugh at her expense.

Games made moral and tasks rendered pleasurable are the staple patterns of many of these medleys. Dr. Hurlothrumbo's *Fortune Teller. By Which Young Gentlemen and Ladies may easily fortel . . . Events that will happen both to themselves and their Acquaintance* (1769) recalls *Hurlothrumbo* (1729), a burlesque associated with dance and frivolity that got into chapbooks by 1730–32 but is here shorn of every vestige of wit. Hurlo is a moral astrologer who does not plan to deliver on the promise in the title but who uses the game to discover flaws and mend characters. Oddly enough, *The Letters between Master Tommy and Miss Nancy*

6   JUVENILE SPECTATOR.

to be made; as at all ages a love of inquiry leads to wisdom; and a habit of thinking correctly is only to be derived from forming our opinions on those principles which experience has sanctioned. Mrs. Argus will not think any question too trivial which shall help to establish the happiness of a young lady, whose well-written note, has impressed her with the most favourable opinion of the juvenile writer.

         ARABELLA ARGUS.

    I soon discovered that my character of Spectator was generally known, and rejoiced that my person was screened from notice. For on going to my daughter's one morning, I was compelled to smile internally, such a scene met my view; but I will describe it for the amusement of my readers. My four grandchildren were seated at a large book-table, each scribbling according to their abilities. " I cannot kiss you just now, grandmamma," said Lucy, " for I am writing to such a funny old woman about my wax doll. Harriet wants me to let her nurse it sometimes, but I am determined she shall not; so I shall ask Mrs. Argus if I have not a right to do what I please with my own doll." I was on the point of replying, when Harriet overturned the ink-stand, which unfortunately defaced the half-finished epistle of William, who, enraged at the accident, turned in great anger to his sister, and in reaching his hand to give her a slight chastisement, threw his elder sister, who was sitting on one corner of

Page. 6.

'I cannot kiss you just now Grandmama.' said Lucy, for I am writing to such a funny old Woman about my wax Doll.'

71. William throws his sister to the floor. Arabella Argus, *The Juvenile Spectator*, Part I, 1813.

Goodwill (Carnan and Newbery, 1770) was more amusing. Their proper but very human exchanges are enlivened by exotic Eastern tales in Miss Nancy's letters. After devouring these, her brother recalls his duty and warns her and her school friends to avoid becoming bluestockings, or "Female Philosophers," a fate deemed worse than a squint and a crooked back, for it insured spinsterhood.

OFFSHOOTS OF FAIRY TALES, CHAPBOOK TALES, AND TRAVELOGUES
Novels, the glory of adult literature in the eighteenth century, were likewise royalty in juvenile books, and tales or short stories were crown prince. Great prose fictions were written before 1700, notably *Don Quixote* (1605; rev. juvenile ed., 1824) and *The Pilgrim's Progress* (1678), both very popular. But the most frequently encountered early prose fiction was the short form—tales and romances preserved in chapbooks. The adult-length novel was of course overwhelming even to the preco-

King Arthur loved good furmenty,—
The cook made a bowl for his majesty;
In conveying it to the palace, hot,
Our hero into the bowl did drop!
The cook was fill'd with great surprise,
For the liquor burnt his nose and eyes.

72. "Our hero into the bowl did drop." *Park's Entertaining History of Tom Thumb,* [*c.* 1830s].

cious, hence the appeal and prevalence of abridgments and the creation of the more manageable novelette. In this as in so many matters, John Newbery led the way with short stories in the *Lilliputian Magazine, Giles Gingerbread,* an episodic tale, and *Goody Two-Shoes,* a homely *roman à clef,* all of which were freely borrowed from by the important and controversial publisher John Marshall.

A number of stories in miscellanies and novelettes between 1768 and 1788 offered the young fresh diversions, but in time they also attracted criticism from parents of the respectable classes, partly because of the greater laxity in the use of traditional fictional devices. Revived were the once banished fairy tale and chapbook characters, for the most part refurbished and decent but no more welcome for that, including several Tom Thumbs whose sagas veer uncomfortably close to their ancestor's. More and more, fairies, magic, and fantasy found their way into the trade wares stocked in the juvenile libraries.

One medley, *Tom Thumb's Folio* (Carnan and Newbery, 1768), contains the story of a hero who, like Tommy Trip, is moral, is nice in his habits and tastes, and is not connected with Merlin or fairies. He even has the bit of the reformer in his teeth; he lurks, however, in a delightful fantasy world. His adventures are truly comic and literally soar above Trip's workaday world. Rather than jumping off his dog Jouler's back or out of his "gig," or small coach, to attack wayward giants, this hero flies to meet his adversary on the back of a talking bird.[15] The giant is the tyrannical ruler of the oppressed "Kingdom of the Cuckows," and the obliging bird, one of his beleaguered subjects, acquaints Tom with the problem.

Tom makes an undignified and dangerous entry into the despot's realm when he accidentally tumbles off the bird's back into Giant Grumbo's bowl of porridge, luckily cooled enough not to end the saga prematurely. Quick of wit and limb, he rescues himself and sneaks into the pocket where Grumbo keeps a supply of bread and his snuff box. From this ambush, Tom conducts the merry games of hide-and-seek and harrowing-and-wracking aimed at preventing Grumbo's committing some new barbarity. Soon realizing that half-measures will not suffice, Tom determines to break his foe. Quickly mastering "the language of the country," he haunts and taunts Grumbo in a ghostly voice, pricks and stabs him with his sword at unexpected moments, and utterly reduces the giant to a shambles with the illusion that Larger Forces are punishing him for his past crimes. The victim thus prepared, Tom appears like an avenging cherub, following up his good work with suitably painful, therapeutic tongue lashings.

Of course, this is a delightful reversal of the child's role as recipient of instruction and chastisement. But Tom has been in that pocket for a goodly time, and through no moral fault of his own, nature has taken its course. Grumbo is not overjoyed at what he finds in the tucks and folds of that pocket, but he lumps that with the rest as part of Providence's plan for his reclamation. All ends well, with Tom owning a fine coach drawn by ten squirrels, marrying Grumbo's daughter, and, mightiest of feats, fathering two "bouncing boys, Nine Hundred Times as big as himself." All of this was harmless enough, perhaps, but closer to the unreformed chapbooks than many could allow; *Folio* seems to have been less frequently printed after the reformers' control was secured.

Discovers the corn.

To my great amazement, I found about ten or twelve ears of green barley appeared the very same shape and make as that in England.

73. Crusoe discovers corn, and a man's footprint. [Daniel Defoe], *The Life and Adventures of Robinson Crusoe of York, Mariner,* 1823.

A second example combines a chapbook favorite with faery: *Robin Goodfellow, a Fairy Tale. Written by a Fairy* (F. & E. Newbery, 1770). Robin is a very puckish fairy who makes friends with young Jacky and, as a prankish treat, transports him to the forbidden kingdom of the elves. The festivities and foods served here recall a scene from *Round About Our Coal-Fire; or, Christmas Entertainments. Containing . . . Stories of Fairies, Ghosts, Hobgoblins, Witches* (1730; 3rd, rev. ed., 1732). Robin has made Jacky invisible so that he may watch the antics of King Fancy, his Consort, Whim, and their son, Imagination. Despite this precaution, the King senses alien presences and uses superior magic to make Jacky visible. Fancy, remembers Jacky, whom he blessed at birth with sound wits. He forgives Jacky's intrusion because he is a good and studious boy, and grants him safe return to London. Back in Newbery's

Discovers the print of a man's foot.

One day it happened, that, going to my boat, I saw the print of a man's naked foot on the shore.

Juvenile Library, Robin and Jacky resume invisibility to play pranks on naughty customers—Billy Bilk gets a halter around his neck and Miss Pert, a padlocked jaw—and to reward the good.

Francis and Elizabeth Newbery printed a number of fairy tales but few that could be considered indelicate, like *Tom Thumb's Folio*. Elizabeth carried *Robin* on her list of 1800, despite intense censure of such stuff at the time. She also carried the new moral tales, graded readers, and the like, but she never entirely bowed to the ban on fancy provided such works had a clear moral point.

Similar imaginative flights and thrills were to be found in the adventures inspired by the fictional travels of Gulliver and Robinson Crusoe and by the historical but no less daring voyages of Captain Cook between 1768 and 1780. Before 1789 there were few original works based directly on Cook's travels,[16] but two abridged "Robinsonnades," as the French dubbed imitations of Defoe's *Crusoe,* filled the gap. *Philip Quarll* (1727) was continually in print far into the nineteenth century and was often viewed more favorably than a later imitation, *Peter Wilkins* (1751), perhaps because it was safely unfanciful and full of stringent moralizing. *Quarll*'s chief variation from *Crusoe* was the substitution of a monkey, Beau Fidele, for Friday, a justifiable and even necessary device, since Longueville makes his hero such a thorough misanthrope that he cannot bear even the presence of his morally corrupt fellow humans. When a ship appears and Quarll is offered escape from the island and his one companion, he rejects it with a shudder and goes placidly back to his life with Beau!

In contrast, it is Peter Wilkins's fate to land on an island where he has a number of adventures and meets his wife, a king's daughter and member of a nation of flying people. Peter, finding her injured, rescues and nurses her, and after a year in which each learns the other's language, she stuns him by demonstrating her wonderful ability to fly. In due course, they are rescued by her family and marry. Elizabeth Newbery published one of many editions of Robert Patlock's *Peter Wilkins* in 1788, with illustrations of the future Mrs. Wilkins adorned only by her magnificent wings.[17]

Rudolf Eric Raspe's *Baron Munchausen's Narrative of his marvellous Travels* (1785), inspired partly by the Robinsonnades, *Gulliver,* and Cook's voyages, is a delightfully zany odyssey that follows its main character, named for an actual Baron Munchausen of Germany, on his voyages overland, across and under seas, and by various means of flight around the globe, as well as on several visits to the moon. With insouciant matter-of-factness, Munchausen recounts various of his and his father's encounters, in which figure the very sling with which David slew Goliath, the site of Noah's Ark, the (reawakened) Sphinx, the giants Gog and Magog, Don Quixote, Lord Whittington, Hermes Trismegistus, Voltaire, Rousseau, Beelzebub—and Marie Antoinette!

In a typical chapter, strung together on the theme of the hunter who runs out of bullets, Munchausen resourcefully shoots a stag with cherrystones; finds it a year or two later with a full-grown, heavily laden tree sprouting from its forehead; brings it down with a shot and so enjoys his venison with cherry sauce; is attacked by a huge bear which he slays by throwing one flint down its throat and another through its "back

74. Inhabitants of
the Dog Star and the
Moon. [Raspe], *Baron
Munchausen,* 1868.

door," whereupon these meet, strike fire, and explode the bear; and, in
the final paragraphs of the adventure, is assailed by a mad dog that he
fends off with his fur coat, which later develops rabies from the dog
bites and tears itself and the rest of his wardrobe to shreds in its death
throes.

The penchant for derring-do runs in the family, as the present baron
shows by relating an experience of his sire's. On a crossing to Holland
undersea, for his marine horse or "salt-water Pegasus" can run only on
the ocean floor, Munchausen's father conquers the discomfort of a restricted air supply with the willpower of a seasoned traveller and takes
note of his surroundings "five hundred fathoms below the surface." He
sees mountains, valleys, deserts, and gardens and is particularly impressed by orchards of oyster-, crab-, and lobster-trees.

Not to be outdone, the son's voyages include two trips to the moon,
casting him into the odd company of its inhabitants and doggy-looking
men from, of course, the Dog-Star. The moon men have removable

75. "I . . . took the proboscis of his elephant, and . . . struck him [the rider]. . . ." [Raspe], *Baron Munchausen*, 1868.

258   ORIGINAL TRAVELS OF

at Tippoo, and shot off his turban. He had a small field-piece mounted with him on his elephant, which he then discharged at me, and the grape-shot coming in a shower, rattled in the laurels that covered and shaded me all over, and remained pendant like berries on the branches. I then advancing, took the proboscis of his ele-

phant, and turning it against the rider, struck him repeatedly with the extremity of it on either side of the head, until I at length dismounted him. Nothing could equal the rage of the barbarian finding himself thrown from his elephant. He rose in a fit of despair, and rushed against my steed and myself: but I scorned to fight him at so great a disadvantage

heads and eyes and leave these vital but vulnerable appendages safely at home when going to war. These accounts of strange places and still stranger people and customs are punctuated by the baron's solemn assurances of his veracity. And the whole is sworn to be "barest truth" in a legal document—copies affixed to each book—registered in the Mansion House of the Lord Mayor of London, signed by those august adventurers Gulliver, Sinbad, and Aladdin and witnessed "in the absence of the Lord Mayor," by a veritable Diogenes, his porter John.

Munchausen was not written for children, though it was swiftly adopted by them. Nothing rivaled its delicious nonsense and tall tales until the appearance of Edward Lear's and Lewis Carroll's diminutive travellers to sea and down rabbit holes. Indeed, the charm of Raspe's yarns is as vital today as at their birth; the book deserved its popularity and was in print throughout the nineteeth century. Naturally, it was pirated in chapbooks as well, but since these almost exclusively recounted the moon voyages, children who had no access to fuller abridgments missed the many wildly comic escapades that every armchair adventurer should be lucky enough to have.

"REALISTIC" NOVELS: HISTORY AND ROMANCE

Although they passed through far tamer, familiar terrain and confronted less fantastic obstacles and less startling persons, the odysseys of Giles Gingerbread and Margery Meanwell, social journeys both, held for children of the age their own special fascination. The Newberys and their successor, John Harris, kept *Giles* and *Goody Two-Shoes* in print continuously far into the 1800s, and the books were also available from other publishers. The themes of rags-to-riches and virtue-rewarded had enormous appeal to young readers, especially those of the lower-middle classes.

Oddly, Newbery's novels and stories from the *Lilliputian Magazine* did not foster as many imitations as one might have expected. Indeed, relatively few exist, though more may in time be discovered. Many of those we have were published by John Marshall, a puzzling figure whose role in the coming clash between free-wheeling tradesmen and socially conscious reformers was murky. However, since his alliance with Trimmer's reformers was apparently important to their eventual predominance, and since we have evidence of his having played a double role in the struggle, what we know of his dealings is best told here, the better to see the full implications of his influential copies of Newbery.

Percy Muir is right to point out that there is uncertainty about the history of the family and the man.[18] His was an old name in publishing in England. The first John Marshall of record seems to have been a bookseller in Gracechurch Street from 1695 to 1726, according to Muir. And a Joseph and William Marshall were licensed as chapbook publishers from 1679 to 1726, states Victor Neuburg (or from 1707 to 1734, according to Muir), at the Bible in Newgate, London.[19] A Richard Marshall is first recorded as partner to Cluer Dicey, chapbook publisher in Aldermary Churchyard, in 1764. Our John may have started his chil-

76. "Lovelace forces
Clarissa to leave her
Father's House." Samuel
Richardson, *Clarissa*,
[*c.* 1780].

dren's book firm around 1770. Darton locates him at No. 4 Aldermary
Churchyard until about 1787, when he moved to 17 Queen Street,
Cheapside. He removed from there around 1806 to a third establishment at 140 Fleet Street, staying here until 1828.[20] From publications I
have examined, it seems that he was joined here by an E. Marshall before 1828, and this Marshall, who issued some books under his own
name and in conjunction with David Carvalho between about 1820 and
1828, carried on after John left the business, putting out children's chapbooks of rather fine quality. Neuburg also locates a firm of a John Marshall in Newcastle, long a center of chapbook production, between 1801
and 1831.[21]

It is quite possible that these are one family's businesses. And it is
very likely that the John Marshall whom an associate of Hannah More's,
Henry Thornton, identified as a partner in the "firm of Cluer, Dicey,
and Marshall" early in 1795 is the same John Marshall whom Sarah Trimmer identified to More as, to her sorrow, her publisher in May 1787, as
M. G. Jones argues. Probably he was in business publishing chapbooks—indeed in more than one business, for he is linked with the firm
of "Marshall and White of London," and "Simpkins and Marshall" with
John Hatchard for the Philanthropic Society. And like others, he probably turned gradually to children's chapbooks as the adult market
dwindled, and thence also to actual books for children.[22]

He was a man at least as talented in business and as clever in his creations as John Newbery. He seems to have lacked completely, however,
Newbery's philanthropic impulse and his noble if homespun vision.
Thornton described him as a worldly man. To Sarah Trimmer he proved
himself a skinflint. Her extremely lucrative *Descriptions* made him all the
richer; he paid her poorly and used her, she complained, like "a mere
bookseller's fag," or slave, even though it seems he owed to her recom-
mendation his access to the gold mine of little books put out by Dorothy and Mary Ann Kilner and Lady Ellenor Fenn. How fairly they were
recompensed is unclear. To secure all this, moreover, he apparently convinced Trimmer and the Kilners of his desire to reform and to quit publishing "chapbook nonsense" perhaps as early as 1780–81, though 1785 is
usually cited as the date of his very public "conversion."[23]

We know Sarah Trimmer looked at Dorothy Kilner's books before
publication, and it now appears that Dorothy's and Mary Ann's books
began to come out before 1783–84, possibly in 1780–81. Marshall

Frontispiece

Lovelace forces Clarissa to leave her Fathers House

avowed in print in 1785, in an advertisement to *The Footstep's to Mrs. Trimmer's Sacred History,* that his books were "entirely divested of that Prejudicial Nonsense (to young Minds) the Tales of *Hobgoblins, Witches, Fairies, Love, Gallantry, etc.,*" and he "implies" that his "books were tools . . . which the 'mighty workmen' of the 1780s would find useful in shaping" young minds.[24]

Meanwhile, he was busy selling a collection of tales calculated to madden any Trimmerite: *Goody Goosecap, Gaffer Goose's Golden Play-Thing, Jack Jingle, Tom Thumb's Play-Thing, Nancy Cock's Pretty Song Book, Cock Robin*—all published about 1780—and *The Renowned History of Primrose Prettyface,* in 1785. His apparent duplicity and sharp tricks are of a piece with his well-documented dealings with Hannah More and the Religious Tract Society. More's associate, Thornton, had chosen him because he hoped Marshall's worldliness would make practicable a seemingly impossible dream, Hannah More's scheme to oust what she judged indecent and radical chapbooks from the lives of the poor and to replace them with her *Cheap Repository Tracts,* entertaining propaganda cleverly disguised to look like its rivals. Amazingly, this woman of modest means and indifferent health brought it off, as we shall see (chapter 6), but not because of Marshall's cooperation.

More had disliked and distrusted Marshall since learning of his treatment of Trimmer, and she soon had cause on her own behalf for those feelings. She accused him of negligence and other faults, clearly despised his trying to winkle and wring out of her religious venture every farthing he could for his own pocket, and declared him "selfish, tricking and disobliging from first to last."[25] In More he had no easy victim, as in Trimmer. After nearly two and a half years of squabbling with him, she got him dismissed as printer of the *Tracts* in 1798; thereafter, Samuel Hazard of Bath was the Society's agent. Marshall threatened suit, an empty salvo which, when it failed, led to his last and meanest blow: He published his own monthly under the usurped title, *Cheap Repository Tracts.* Though not precisely indecent, these tracts were not up to More's standards. She was galled at the "mildly ribald," frivolous stuff he passed off as her tract. Shortly after this, she discontinued *Cheap Repository Tracts* and turned to other work.

Marshall's venal dealings are clear, but what may not be is why such a fuss was made over his frivolous trade tales. What was so bad about them? They lack moral purpose as Newbery conceived it, but today they

77. Jem falsely accuses
Primrose. *The Renowned
History of Primrose
Prettyface,* with cuts by
Bewick, 1804.

PRIMROSE PRETTYFACE.

in mischief, and when he had done any, to screen himself
would tell fibs and lay it on other people.

Squire Homestead had frequently observed to his lady
that the best apple-tree was often robbed, but by whom he
could never discover. Little Jem who stood by, said he
believed Primrose Prettyface did it, for he often saw her in

the garden near that tree. Upon this she was called into the
room, and interrogated concerning it. Prim, who had been
very little used to accusations of this kind, cried very much
when she was asked how she dared to do it. However, drying up her pretty eyes, she declared she had never
taken an apple off any tree in the garden without the knowledge of her fellow-servants; but in particular she had never

48

seem harmless enough. Yet to respectable parents and reformers alike
they were anathema because they threatened class stability at a time
when Jacobin ideals were feared to be infecting the poor.

The problem is less obvious in those tales where the characters are
children, like *Jack Jingle,* published with *The House that Jack Built,* Marshall's *Giles Gingerbread.* Jack and Gaffer Jingle, like Giles and Gaffer
Gingerbread, are humble, poor, hardworking, and virtuous. Young Jack
"comes to the attention" of one of those handy philanthropists who lurk
in such books, Sir Luke Loveall, a composite of Newbery's Sir Toby
Thompson and Mr. Goodwill. Unlike Sir Toby or Giles, who must earn
their "estate and esteem," Jack is awarded his merely for being good. In

a superfluity of philanthropy, Sir Luke adopts him, has him educated as a gentleman, and then hands over to him his "coach and six"—and does not demand he earn them, as Newbery's Toby and Giles were required to. Such pictures of peasant children being raised above their station seemed dangerous to many.

Two long-favored and widely read Marshall novellas were still more offensive, for in them the motif of the lowly exalted socially—not spiritually—was applied to marriageable adolescents. *Goody Goosecap* (*c.* 1780) was inspired by *Goody Two-Shoes* and perhaps by "The History of Little Polly Meanwell. Who was afterwards Queen of Petula" (*Lilliputian Magazine,* 1753, pp. 116–23). "Polly Meanwell" is about an orphan robbed of her inheritance by a wicked uncle, and it and *Two-Shoes* use the motif from *Pamela* of poor girls who make splendid marriages. Marshall's second such work was *The Renowned History of Primrose Prettyface, who by her Sweetness of Temper and Love of Learning was raised from being the Daughter of a Poor Cottager to Great Riches and to the Dignity of the Lady of the Manor. Set forth for the Benefit and Imitation of those Pretty Little Boys and Girls—*

> "Who by learning their Book and obliging Mankind,
>   Would to Beauty of Body add Beauty of Mind" (1785).

Frances Fairchild, heroine of *Goody Goosecap,* is an heiress of gentle birth orphaned at the age of four. Her uncle robs her and absconds to the West Indies. As there is no one else to care for her, Frances is thrown upon the Parish and sent to a charity school where she quickly masters the alphabet and begins to tutor even younger children. She bears her lot cheerfully and distinguishes herself by her kindness, honesty, and industry, so much so that "she is noticed by Lady Bountiful," who takes her in and raises her as a member of the family. Frances's goodness is further rewarded when her uncle repents on his deathbed, sixteen years later, and wills her the remains of her fortune, £10,000, a tidy sum. Her fortune repaired, her grace, beauty, and virtue unimpaired, she is now an ideal match for Lady Bountiful's son, whom she marries with the lady's blessings.

Such a tale has elements likely to rivet the attention of young readers: abandonment, fear and uncertainty, the dangers and pain of vulnerability, then magical good luck and rescue, the mandatory balancing justice of the returned fortune, and finally the joy and romance of marriage to a paragon of high position. Both Frances and Margery Meanwell are subjected to these thrilling turns of fate, though Two-Shoes is far more active in her own rescue than Frances. Significantly, both were of gentle birth, in other words, ladies though poor, and just as important, both recovered their wealth before marriage. These details did not reconcile the books to the reformers, but they lessened the virulence of the attacks on them.

In contrast, Primrose Thompson has more than a pretty face to recommend her—grace, sweetness, virtue, and learning, all commendable, but without fortune and birth, valueless. Worse still, such traits dangerously incite heedless youths to act foolishly, as does her swain in *Primrose Prettyface*.

A penniless peasant, Primrose is sent into service as a maid, where she endures the usual indignities and hardships with sweet fortitude. Like Frances, she patiently bears her trials and continues to smile— which saintly character, combined with her beauty, leads Lady Worthy to befriend her. Had the lady, who has an "eligible son," William, lived anywhere but in the pages of this novella, she would doubtless have taken great care to hide Prettyface from her boy. Instead, driven by love of virtue, she constantly throws them together for the moral benefit of her beloved son, she says, and in time encourages them to marry, for the same reason. The lesson is dangerously clear: Spiritual wealth and learning, especially in a beauty, outweigh earthly wealth and position.

Although it is difficult to be certain because of his involvement in several London firms, Marshall apparently ceased publishing *Primrose Prettyface* after the first edition in 1785; at least his widely touted moral puff implies he did. Yet even if he told the truth, the damage was done, for others brought out versions, possibly pirated, of *Prettyface*. In fact the popular tale continued to appear in books and chapbooks well into the 1800s. An 1804 edition by Wilson and Spence of York is *"Adorned with Cuts by* BEWICK." The frontispiece shows an improbably short Primrose, looking provocatively like iconographs of Britannia, meeting an elegantly attired young gentleman in a rose garden. Cupid hovers just above his fashionable hat, arrow poised to strike home. We need only consider the endurance of such fare into our own world to understand the attractions such books held for ambitious peasants and servant maids. This sort of tale was one most loathed and, more tellingly, feared by political conservatives and reformers like Trimmer, Fenn, and More.

78. Frontispiece:
Prettyface and her Swain.
Primrose Prettyface, 1804.

The periodicals of the age—*Gentleman's Magazine, London Chronicle,* and *Morning Chronicle*—aired subscribers' complaints about inefficient or dishonest servants and "mushroom-men and women," former servants who advanced economically. In 1789 a Society for the Encouragement of Good Servants was founded to keep track of servants' movements and performance records. But clearly the most threatening form of advancement was that depicted in *Prettyface,* intermarriage between "ineligible" classes. The popularity of the idea of servant girls transformed into duchesses or Ladies of the Manor was believed to endanger class distinctions and social stability—by making servants disgruntled and disinclined to do their duty—and thus to undermine respect for and resignation to the rigid social hierarchy. To the extent that trade books of the transitional years indulged in this sort of social fairy tale, they fueled the opposition of middle-class parents and the religious and political establishment.[26]

In children's books, this group's response was deceptively mild at the start. It seemed, and at the outset possibly was, mainly an attempt to provide more suitable readings for the children of their own classes first and then for the "lower orders." Indeed, from about 1778 to the early 1790s, they did in fact concern themselves chiefly with producing books, some of which were very fine indeed, as we shall see.

6. Early Reform Efforts: 1778 to 1795

By the time Anna Barbauld's *Lessons for Children* began to appear in 1778, many interested in the care and education of the young were dissatisfied with the increasingly fanciful and frivolous trends in children's books and with the obviously ineffective religious and elementary reading tools available. Despite John Locke's warning against teaching religion too early, most parents feared more the dangers in a delay, which to them amounted to neglect.[1] They disliked the trade fiction's encouragement of imagination and whimsy at the expense of reason and, even more, its too realistic tales of children, often of the lower-middle class, who were depicted as having a degree of independence that many considered dangerous for the gently nurtured child. Thus, Barbauld's graded readers, featuring refined, obedient youngsters guided by their mothers, were enthusiastically welcomed, as were her unaffected and graceful prose hymns.

Barbauld's books were indispensable to the early phase of the reform movement in children's books, though she was never the leader of the reform, as some have thought.[2] Her *Hymns in Prose for Children* (1781) proved the feasibility of creating religious works for the very young that were pleasing yet elegantly simple and accessible. Equally important was her identification, in four little volumes, of tasks progressively suited to the child's developing skills, for this brought order and purpose to the once haphazard ABCs and primary readers: *Lessons for Children from Two to Three Years Old* (1778), *Lessons for Children Three Years Old*, in 2 Parts (1779), and *Lessons for Children Three and Four Years Old* (1779). Moreover, the simplicity of her books gave many unsure parents the confidence to teach their children.

The active involvement of parents, which by 1780 meant almost ex-

26

The Morning.

....

In Words of Three Letters.

Mamma. Now get up, it is six.

Boy. O me! is it six?

Mamma. Yes, it is: and the dew is off.

27

Boy. I see the sun, it is fit for me to go out.

Mamma. Now it is; but by ten it may be hot; so get up now.

Boy. May I go to day, and buy a top?

Mamma. Yes, you may.

Boy. A peg top? Sam has a peg top. He has let me get his. One day he did.

I met Tom one day, and he had a top so big!

I can hop as far as Tom can.

Tom has a bat too! and Tom is but of my age.

Let us buy a cup and a mug for Bet.

And let us get a gun for Sam, and a pot and an urn for Bet.

35

The Dog.

....

In Words of Four Letters.

Boy. I love the dog. Do not you?

Mamma. Yes, sure.

36

Boy. Wag! do you love me?

Mamma. You see he does: he wags his tail. When he wags his tail, he says, I love you.

Boy. Does his tail tell me so?

Mamma. Yes; it says, I love you; I love you; pray love me.

Boy. When we go out, he wags his tail; what does his tail say then?

Mamma. Pray let me go; I wish to go with you.

Boy. I love to have him go with me.

Mamma. Here is a cake for you.

79. "May I go to day, and buy a top?" [Ellenor Fenn], *Cobwebs to Catch Flies,* 1833.

80. "When he wags his tail, he says, I love you." [Fenn], *Cobwebs to Catch Flies,* 1833.

clusively mothers, in all aspects of their offsprings' early training and education was a prime objective of the reform movement in its first decade. Therefore, Barbauld's books became model and inspiration for the voluminous output of two early authors, who emerged as leaders of the movement—Sarah Trimmer and Ellenor Fenn—and for a legion of writers, mainly women from the respectable classes, who penned the bulk of children's books. Within fifteen years, led by the redoubtable Trimmer, these writers fashioned and made dominant a vision of childhood that was strikingly at odds with that in *Goody Two-Shoes* and many books of the Transitional Years. The "new child" lingered in a fondly sentimentalized state of childishness rooted in material and emotional dependency on adults. This child lapped up lessons hungrily, was eagerly obedient or lavishly repentant, but most important, the new good child seldom made important, real decisions without parental approval. Bad children struck out on their own on some project, erroneously assuming themselves capable of judging what was proper and of having the right to act independently. In short, the new good child was a paragon of dutiful submissiveness, refined virtue, and appropriate sensibility.

In time, the accounts of such pattern cards of virtue became predictably stilted. But in many of the earliest reform books, one finds a genuine liveliness and lack of affectation. Barbauld's dialogues were based on actual experience raising her adopted nephew, Charles, and educating generations of boys at the school she and her husband operated near Palgrave. Mary F. Thwaite has justly labeled her four *Lessons* "a landmark in the approach to the reading of the very young child." The subjects are simple and realistically geared to infant curiosity about the world: what is good to eat, the animals one can touch and feed, color and motion in butterflies and birds, changing seasons, the sun and stars.[3] The reading lessons share the sense of wonder and joy of her *Hymns.* Many imitators quickly mastered the implications of Barbauld's lesson plan; few could recreate the fragile artistry of the unaffected beauty and delight.

Born an Aikin, a family well known for its literary pursuits in the period,[4] Anna Barbauld was well enough educated to be considered a bluestocking, though she did not join that circle. With all her great learning, she bent with ease and sensitivity to the child's level. Indeed it was her sophisticated taste in literature that made her doubt true poetry could or ever should "be lowered to the capacities of children." Her majestic yet natural prose is so close to the spirit of poetry, however, that one is reminded of William Wordsworth's assertion years later that the line between the finest prose and poetry is thin or nonexistent.[5] One can find examples at random throughout the book:

81. "In Words of Six Letters." [Fenn], *Cobwebs to Catch Flies,* 1833.

82. III, The Flood. IV, Lot and his Daughters. Trimmer, *A New Series of Prints . . . from the Old Testament* [Designs by William Blake], 1808.

Come, let us walk abroad; let us talk of the works of God. Take up a handful of the sand; number the grains of it; tell them one by one into your lap. Try if you can count the blades of grass in the field, or the leaves on the trees. You cannot count them, they are innumerable. . . . The daisy enamelleth the meadows, and groweth beneath the foot of the passenger: the tulip asketh a rich soil, and the careful hand of the gardener. . . . The water-lillies grow beneath the stream. . . . The wall-flower takes root in the hard stone. . . . Each leaf is of a different form; every plant hath a *separate inhabitant.* . . . Who causeth them to grow every where . . . and giveth them colours, and smells, and spreadeth out their thin transparent leaves? . . . Lo, these are a part of his works; and a little portion of his wonders. There is little need that I should tell you of God, for everything speaks of Him.[6]

In language worthy of William Blake's *Songs of Innocence* (1789), which they may have influenced, many of her hymns create a Wordsworthian vision of nature illuminated and animated by God's presence. Their beautiful cadences, vivid yet delicate descriptions, and gentle tone convey with clarity and conviction her sense of God's presence. They deserved the love they evoked.

Although no work of this caliber soon appeared, Barbauld's *Hymns* helped to cultivate other spiritual fruit. Very different but quite rightfully welcomed by generations of children was a series of books by Sarah Kirby Trimmer—mother of six sons and six daughters, active in the charity and Sunday School movements, eventually virtual dictator over what was and what was not proper in children's books.

Trimmer was a proficient and prolific writer. Her early books were done in part for her own small children, and they are fine for their kind, though not to everyone's taste. She seems always to have viewed the world through a lens ground between the stones of religious and social orthodoxy, and she was aggressively committed to the "rightness of things as they are." Over the years, the lens grew thicker, but her early conservatism was milder, apparently softened by maternal love, as were her early writings.

Today it is very difficult to discuss "Mrs. Trimmer" impartially, and

66

a book, and write what I have told you.

Boy. I will get all sorts of plants ; and I will mark by each the name, the place, the bloom, the time when it blows, and the use which is made of it.

67

The Baby-House.

......

In Words of Six Letters.

First Girl. My doll's quilt is chintz—What is this ?
Second Girl. Old point.

III

IV

83. XXIX, Israelites Worship the Golden Calf. XXX, Ark of the Covenant. Lesson XLVIII. Sarah Trimmer, *A Series of Prints* and *Scripture Lessons . . . from the Old Testament,* 1829.

114 SCRIPTURE LESSONS:

went before the LORD, to speak with Him, he took the veil off.

LESSON XLVIII.

[NUMBER XXX.]

The Ark of the Covenant.

AND Moses gathered all the people together and commanded them, in the name of the LORD, to bring offerings towards the Tabernacle, or holy tent, which was to be prepared for the Ark of the Covenant; so they brought their offerings, and the Taberna-

OLD TESTAMENT. 115

cle was made, and all its furniture, and the Ark of the Covenant (or chest) to hold the tables of testimony, namely, the Ten Commandments. Holy garments were also made for Aaron the high priest and his sons, to wear when they ministered in the Tabernacle.* And when the Tabernacle was finished, it was set up, and the Ark of the Covenant, containing the Tables, was placed

* Number XIV. of the former Set of Scripture History agrees with this Lesson.

difficult to comprehend how widespread, if not universal, was the warmth with which her books were received. As we shall see (chapter 8), she was often at the center of acrimonious controversy and was characteristically in positions unlikely to gain our sympathy or tolerance. Moreover, as her leading role in the field became assured, she seems to have grown more opinionated, managing, and smug. Perhaps she was always thus. But if so, these unprepossessing qualities did *not* mar (for most) her earliest children's books, the religious-historical descriptions and a fable.

Inspired by Barbauld's *Lessons,* Trimmer commenced as an author with *An Easy Introduction to the Knowledge of Nature, and Reading the Holy Scripture, Adapted to the Capacities of Children* (1780), a blend of natural history with scripture study. As early as 1782, she apparently conceived her scheme of a large-scale study of the scriptures simplified in a series of volumes. The form these actually took owed much to Mme. de Genlis's *Adèle et Théodore (Adelaide and Theodore; or, Letters on Education,* 1782; trans., 1783). In this work Genlis made use of historical illustrations printed separately from the text of descriptions and explanations. Hers were large, lavishly painted, and intended to be hung on the wall. Trimmer imitated her in miniature and acknowledged her debt in her dedication of her first two volumes to the French author: *A Description Of A Set of Prints Of Scripture History: Contained In A Set of Easy Lessons* (1786). One volume contained brief accounts of thirty-two of the more exciting Old Testament stories; the other volume held prints approximately four inches square.

Perhaps from Genlis also came Trimmer's plan to create an outline of "universal history," which she did in an amazingly short time, encouraged no doubt by the very positive response to the first volumes. Thereafter, each in the series of two-volume works was expanded to contain sixty-four lessons and prints: *A Description of a Set of Prints Taken from the New Testament* (1786), *A Description Of A Set Of Prints Of Ancient History* (1787), and "descriptions of" *Roman History* (1789) and *English History* (1792).

It is not possible to realize the appeal of these squat little volumes, nearly four inches square, unless one has the fortune to examine them for oneself. The print is large and spaced for easy readability; the prints are clear, plentiful, well executed—most are pleasing if not imaginative. The books were enormously and enduringly popular and went through numerous reprintings and new editions with their original publishers and others. As is clear from the style and certain characteristic motifs, William Blake either engraved or designed the illustrations for John Harris's "new series of prints" for *Scripture History* (1803, 1808, 1816, 1822), possibly for all or part of the *New Testament (1805, 1811, 1816),* and for *Ancient History* (1804, 1814, 1817, 1820, 1825, 1828, 1831–32).[7] And Marshall continued to print the original volumes, as did Baldwin and Cradock, and Nathaniel Hailes. Had she done no more, Trimmer's place in children's books would have been assured. She was to do much more.

Anna Barbauld's *Lessons* and *Hymns* also inspired another important figure in the reform movement, Lady Ellenor Fenn. She was much involved in the Sunday School movement and, though childless, had nu-

84. IX, The Marriage Feast
at Cana. X, The Mirac-
ulous Draught of Fishes.
Sarah Trimmer, *A New
Series of Prints . . . from
the New Testament*
[Engraved after William
Blake?], 1805.

85. "Ah, Bet! how you are
grown!" "You are as much
grown, miss." [Fenn],
Cobwebs to Catch Flies, 1833.

merous nieces and nephews for whom she wrote. Fenn's first efforts followed the practical improvements of the *Lessons,* but she also wrote
entertaining moral fictions for boys and girls under various pseud-
onyms: "Mrs. Teachwell," "Solomon Lovechild," and "Mrs. Lovechild."
*Cobwebs to Catch Flies; or, Dialogues in Short Sentences, Adapted to Chil-
dren from the Age of Three to Eight Years* (2 vols.); *Fables in Monosyllables
by Mrs. Teachwell; To Which Are Added Morals in Dialogues, Between A
Mother and Children* (for three to five years); *Fables, By Mrs. Teachwell:
In Which The Morals are Drawn . . . In Various Ways* (for five to eight
years); and *Morals to a Set of Fables,* by Mrs. Teachwell, which is very
similar to *Fables in Monosyllables*—were all published in 1783.

Although these books made important additions to Barbauld's improvements in "entertaining" readers, refining on her grading plan and
adding the "split-word" technique ("MAM-MA") to the reformers' repertoire,[8] and although they were widely imitated in England and
France, they are specially noteworthy for two things. First, *Cobwebs* was
one of the earliest children's books to insist on clear-cut class distinctions between characters. Relations are amicable between a servant,
peasant mother and child, and Little Miss, but there is no confusion:
Farm child or servant girl cannot aspire to Miss's place. This disjunction
became rooted and was more urgently exacted by reformers in the 1790s,
as we shall see (chapter 8). Servants became queens only in fairy tales:
The reformers would try to suppress those as well.

The second special feature appears in *Fables in Monosyllables* when
William's mother tries to explain the rationale for Aesop's "The Fox and
the Crow." She easily sorts out the evil of thievery (the fox) and the
silliness of vanity (the crow). It is much harder to explain the paradox
of using a fable in which animals talk, palpably not true, to point a
moral and reveal the "Truth." In effect she fudges, admitting that the
device is not real but insisting it is "just used" to help explain the moral.

The paradox was insoluble for William's mother and for all of the
reform writers: Its root lay in assumptions about psychology and morality that were part of the "Puritan set" of the age. Fenn and her compeers were suspicious of all fictions and metaphors. Because they con-
fused the literal with the Truth they profoundly mistrusted the
imagination, a fear magnified where children were concerned. But although determined to forbid fairy tales and the like, as had "Puritans"
before them, they accepted Aesop and thereby dug their own pit: If

NEW TESTAMENT PRINTS.

Plate II. IX

X

Pub.^d Augt 1805, by J.Harris, St Pauls Church Yard, London.
& the other Proprietors of the Work.

8

The Country Visit.

[A LITTLE lady is supposed to be come to see a tenant's wife.]

Miss. I like to walk in the fields, and to hear all that you can tell me.

9

Woman. I am glad to see you here, miss.

Miss. Pray call me as you did when I came to you to stay; you were so good to me! you soon made me well. I like you should say, My dear: I love you.—I ought to love those who are kind to me, and nursed me.

Woman. I do not think you would have been here now, my dear, if you had staid in town. I did not think you could live.

Miss. Where is my old friend Bet? I want to walk with her.

Woman. She shall come; she longs to see you; I see her; she is just by.

Little Girl. How do you

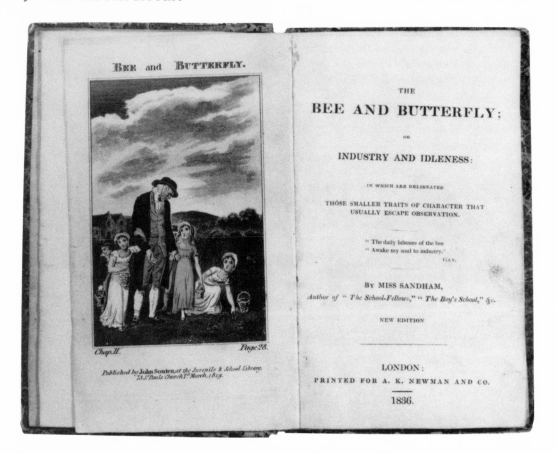

animals talk and display human motives, what cannot happen? Having
opened the door for Aesop, they tried to monitor its use with elaborate
proscriptions based on the equivocation used in *Fables*. At fancy's fee-
blest stirring, they trotted this out, mainly in their prefaces.

FANCY ON THE LEASH: BIOGRAPHIES OF TOPS, CAKES, AND MICE

Biographies of animate and inanimate creatures came into vogue very
early in the history of the novel and were admirable vehicles for the lei-
surely picaresque plot and trenchant social satire so loved in the age.
Four set the fashion and set off a flood of adult and child imitations:
Francis Coventry's *History of Pompey the Little; or, The Life and Adventures of a Lap-Dog* (1751); Charles Johnstone's *Chrysal; or, The Adventures
of a Guinea* (1760); Tobias Smollett's low political satire, *The History and
Adventures of an Atom* (1769); and Thomas Bridges's *Adventures of a
Bank-Note* (1770–71).

Although the episodic structure and opportunities for lesser beings to expose children's folly and sins suited reform writers' needs, their attitudes toward the satiric and humorous effects led to a new element in juvenile fiction: distinctions between propriety in boys and in girls. Mary Ann Kilner, like most of the reform authors and markedly unlike Newbery and the early writers, produced calculatedly different books for girls and for boys.

In these one can trace the foundations of a double, gender standard of conduct in children's fiction. Kilner's preface to *The Adventures of a Pincushion* (*c.* 1780), a fine little work, expressly rejects previously acceptable human conduct for girls and outlines a new, artificially gentle and genteel pattern: Kilner will not "exhibit their superiors in a ridiculous view, . . . present their equals as the objects of contemptuous mirth . . . [or] treat the characters of their inferiors with levity" because that is "inconsistent with the *sacred rights of humanity*" (italics mine).

In other words, females could no longer laugh at fools of any class or stripe but had to preserve a sympathetic countenance. Yet in *The Memoirs of a Peg-Top* (*c.* 1781), when the silly glutton, Tom Swallowell, is tricked into eating, while blindfolded, a custard pie mixed with cow dung, the gleeful laughter of his cronies is unrestrained. But "Young Ladies" were the newly delegated angels ministering to new "sacred rights," to be judged by how assiduously they served. No such restrictions were imposed on young gentlemen. By endorsing so affected a standard for feminine nature, Kilner and the reformers became part of a campaign to "denature" girls and women, to *re*form them in order to render them "truly delicate," as only "walking ghosts" can be. Self-expression heretofore considered appropriate or even becoming was now forbidden respectable females, so as to mold them into guardians and weathervanes of social morality in general and of men's morals in particular, by "soft persuasions" only, however.[9]

Of course, this new school of fiction, created chiefly by Mary Ann ("S. S.") and Dorothy ("M. P.") Kilner,[10] Fenn (Teachwell), and Trimmer, reflected and reinforced, but did not initiate, social trends. And its biases and conventions did not, as it happened, doom all such works to tedious or joyless vapidity, any more than in adult fiction. On the contrary, the engaging *Pincushion,* the funny *Peg-Top,* and others deserved the vogue they enjoyed.

The plot and narrative focus of *Pincushion* became standard for such fictional biographies: The pincushion's life begins quietly in the orderly

87. Women Coal Bearers.
The Rev. Isaac Taylor, *The Mine*, 1832.

home of Martha Airy, who in fact made her. From her position in Martha's pocket, she is privy to a number of lessons a young lady must learn. Her quiet existence ends when Martha gives her to Eliza Meekly, who takes her along to Mrs. Stanley's boarding school. There she is soon carelessly dropped and kicked under a bookcase, from which vantage point she observes a series of morality playlets. But it is Pincushion herself, her feelings and reminiscences, that holds our attention in this delightful book. She is naturally bored with her jail after a bit and chafes to be out and about in the world. Soon an unfortunate pen falls near her, and she confides her woes to her new friend, ending by stoically pointing out that fretting will only make matters worse. They get worse in any case, for in a series of misadventures Pincushion is found, stolen, again given away, borrowed, and lost, and she finally winds up in a poultry yard being pecked by chickens. A rooster mercifully tosses her under a tub where, relatively safe but fast decaying, she reviews her life with the stoicism of a Cardinal Wolsey commenting on the fickleness of fortune.

Comparable adventures and insights are the stuff of Mary Ann's *Peg-Top* and her sister-in-law Dorothy's *Adventures of a Whipping-Top* (1784), both superb miniature sagas. The peg-top lives in a boarding school with a series of owners whose habits and failings he observes with combined acuity and resignation. The whipping-top is purchased by Farmer Clodd for his son and descends slowly and painfully to the ignominy of being a dog's toy. Several accidents free him from this bondage, but he ends up in a river and floats to a shallow spot where he lodges, permanently. Having nothing better to do as he awaits his slow demise, he composes his memoirs and commits them to the stream's current, addressed to Mr. Marshall, as neat a puff as Newbery ever pulled off!

A number of imitations followed, naturally. One, whose author is unknown and which was issued by J. G. Rusher, the chapbook publisher of Banbury, was especially appealing. *The History of a Banbury Cake. An Entertaining Book for Children,* price onepence (*c.* 1803), opens philosophically: "I was born or made (whichever you please, my little reader) at Banbury. Soon after I was made and while still yet warm from the oven, I was sold by my maker's fair daughter to a person on horseback for twopence" to be given to his seven-year-old son. Thereafter, the suspense builds as, by a series of coincidences, he barely escapes being eaten by sets of "sharp white teeth" and is passed along to the next child. We leave him "in imminent expectation of falling prey to Billy," with time only to offer a few last words of advice to his readers.

These little tales were clever and amusing. Although some reform authors handicapped themselves by their insistence on undermining the credibility of their imaginative devices, perhaps their readers wisely ignored that, as we do.

One of the earliest animal biographies, a most un-Aesop-like work, was Dorothy Kilner's exquisite *The Life and Perambulation of a Mouse* (1783–84). Part of the opening is worth quoting, lest we become too dour in our view of reform authors' ideas about children's pleasures: "After the more serious employment of reading each morning . . . , we danced, we sung, we played at blindman's buff, battledore and shuttlecock, and many other games equally diverting and innocent. And when

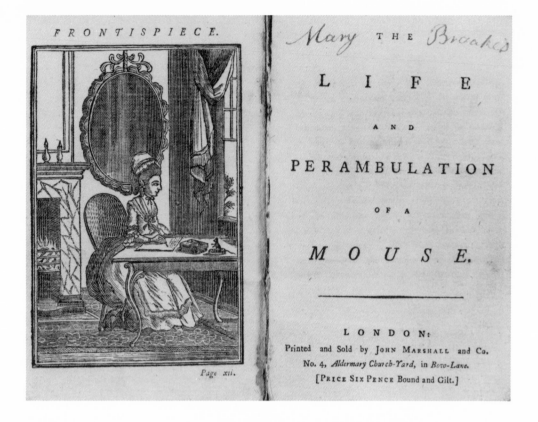

FRONTISPIECE.

Mary THE *Brooke's*

L I F E

A N D

P E R A M B U L A T I O N

O F   A

M O U S E.

———————

L O N D O N:

Printed and Sold by JOHN MARSHALL and Co.
No. 4, *Aldermary Church-Yard,* in *Bow-Lane.*
[PRICE SIX PENCE Bound and Gilt.]

Page xii.

88. Frontispiece and title page. "M.P." [Dorothy Kilner], *The Life and Perambulation of a Mouse,* 1783.

tired of them, drew our seats round the fire, whilst each one in turn told some merry story to divert the company." In keeping with the light-hearted amusement of this opening is the tale that follows. The narrator goes off to her bedroom to write her story but is stumped, for her own life seems dull to her. While bemoaning her attack of writer's block she hears, "Then write mine, which may be more diverting," coming from "a little squeaking voice." Thus begins *Perambulation,* a delightful mixture of whimsy and reality and of pathos too, for a mouse's life is not all cheese.

This voice is that of Nimble, who has returned to Meadow Hall after a long series of adventures during which he has lost his three brothers, Longtail, Softdown, and Brighteyes, forerunners perhaps of certain Potter rodents. The young lady who acts as his amanuensis has her own droll sense of humor, and she first composes herself, lest Nimble mistake her initial surprise for fear.

Nimble's accounts of his and his brothers' rencontres with several savage, prowling cats and with mousetraps, vengeful housewives, and

58   MRS. TRIMMER'S

sented by his god-papa; but Master Jenkins had laid hold of Miss Harriet's dog, and was searching his own pocket for a piece of string, that he might tie him and the cat together, to see, as he said, how nicely they would fight: and so fully was he bent on this cruel purpose, that it was with difficulty he could be prevailed on to relinquish it.

Dear me, said he, if ever I came into such a house in my life, there is no *fun* here. What would you have said to Harry Pritchard and me, the other day, when we made the cats fly?

Made cats fly! said Frederick, how was that?

Why, replied he, *we tied bladders to each side of their necks, and then flung them from the top of the house.* There was an end of their purring and mewing for some time, I assure you, for they lay a long while struggling and gasping for breath; and if they had not had nine lives, I think they must have died; but at last up they jumped, and away they ran scampering. Then out came little Jemmy, crying as if he had flown down himself, because we hurt the poor cats; he had a dog running after him, who, I suppose, meant to call us to task, with his *bow, wow;* but we soon stopped his tongue, for we caught the gentleman, and drove him before us into a narrow lane,

"We tied bladders to each side of their necks, and then flung them from the top of the house."
Page 58

89. "The other day . . . we made cats fly." [Sarah Trimmer], *Fabulous Histories . . . or, The History of the Robins*, 1833.

cruel boys make an exciting tale and offer many opportunities for Kilner to point a moral. But her customary method is to allow the lessons to emerge unaffectedly, and to refrain from refining on these too much. The result is a delightfully fanciful saga, unmatched in the era.

In 1786 Sarah Trimmer published an animal fable that long enjoyed a following, though it lacked illustrations, unlike other fictional biographies. *Fabulous Histories. Designed For The Instruction of Children, Respecting Their Treatment of Animals,* later known as *The History of the Robins,* was so titled to warn parents that it contained a fanciful element, a family of talking birds. To the end of her life, Trimmer always referred to it so and resolutely refused to allow it to be illustrated, in contrast to her historical and scriptural books. She feared pictures attached to such a fiction would unhealthily enflame childish imaginations.

Fabulous Histories, soon shortened to *The Robins,* has amusing moments for all its moralizing. It describes the foibles and follies of a variety of birds and a few eccentric or vicious human beings. There is a good deal of visiting between houses, and as we follow Harriet and Mrs.

Benson on their social jaunts we glimpse genuinely funny situations, as when a monkey invited to tea rips up the table, or a large pride of cats makes the parlor unpleasant and hazardous for visitors. Also, Trimmer briefly forgets her didacticism when describing the antics of fledglings getting acquainted with the world. But return to her lessons she must: Since man is superior to the animal kind, he is obligated not only to use it, judiciously and mercifully, but also to guard against the moral dangers of excessive sentimentality about animals.

90. "He leaped upon the tea-table." [Trimmer], *Fabulous Histories*, 1833.

91. Frontispiece of the second American edition. [Edward Augustus Kendall], *Keeper's Travels in Search of His Master*, 1808.

It was on just this last point that many imitators failed; tales about the plight of animals grew ludicrously maudlin. Trimmer, like Newbery, from whose *Valentine's Gift* (1764) she borrowed the names of two of her robins, Flapsy and Pecksy, was careful to insist on a balance between compassion and common sense on the issue. Many later writers could not perceive the lack or maintain the position.[11]

In the more successful biographies of animals a lack of sentimentality exists, though not a lack of appropriate feeling. Moreover, most of the heroes are creatures of distinctive character and engaging narrative presence. E. A. Kendall wrote a series of bird stories, but his most popular book was *Keeper's Travels in Search of His Master* (1798).[12] Keeper is a realistically doggy hero, whose urge to sniff fowls, when he should keep an eye on his master, gets him lost. His quest to relocate master and home is the stuff of a good picaresque yarn, with variety and excitement. Other works were similarly successful because of the strength of their narrators' personae. Elizabeth Sandham's *Adventures of Poor Puss* (1809) is rather good. Three of the finest are Lucy Peacock's engaging *Life of a Bee. Related By Herself* (c. 1788), little known today; Ludlow's witty, diverting *Felissa; or, The Life and Opinions of a Kitten of Sentiment* (1811); and Arabella Argus's droll *Adventures of a Donkey* (1815). The narrators of these three, with their sharp eyes, clever or satiric tongues, and basic geniality, are among the very best examples of the type.

TALES OF SCHOOL AND VISITS ON HOLIDAY

Sarah Fielding's *Governess* (1749) went through many editions in Britain and was widely imitated during the 1780s and after. Although many educators and parents deplored the book's references to ghosts, witches, and fairies, and the deficiency of self-discipline and "proper feminine delicacy" in its young ladies, they heartily approved of its stern adult character, Mrs. Teachem, who became the model for many fictional

100   MRS. TRIMMER'S

The tea things being set, the footman came in with the urn, which employing both his hands, he left the door open; and was, to the great terror of Miss Harriet, and even of her mamma too, followed by the monkey they saw in the hall, who having broke his chain, came to make a visit to his lady: she, far from being disconcerted, seemed highly pleased with his cleverness. O my sweet dear Pug, said she, are you come to see us? Pray shew how like a gentleman you can behave: just as she had said this, *he leaped upon the tea-table, and took cup after cup, and threw them on the ground*, till he broke half the set; then jumped on the back of his mistress's chair, and tore the cover of it: in short, as soon as he had finished one piece of mischief, he began another, till Mrs. Addis, though vastly diverted with his wit, was obliged to have him caught and confined; after which she began making tea, and quietness was for a short time restored. But Mrs. Benson, though capable of conversing on most subjects, could not engage Mrs. Addis in any discourse, but upon the perfections of her birds and beasts; and a variety of uninteresting particulars were related concerning their wit or misfortunes.

On hearing the clock strike seven, she begged Mrs. Benson's excuse; but said

"He leaped upon the tea table and took cup after cup and threw them on the ground." *Page 100.*

FRONTISPIECE.

KEEPER'S TRAVELS

IN SEARCH OF

His Master.

Ah me! One moment from thy sight,
That thus my truant eye should stray!

Langhorne.

[Edward Augustus Kendall]

Philadelphia:

PUBLISHED BY JOHNSON & WARNER,
No. 147, MARKET STREET.

::::::::::
1808.

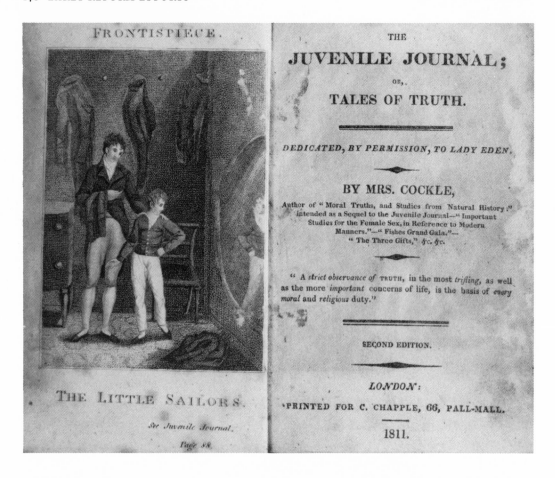

FRONTISPIECE.

THE LITTLE SAILORS.

See Juvenile Journal.

Page 88.

THE

JUVENILE JOURNAL;

OR,

TALES OF TRUTH.

DEDICATED, BY PERMISSION, TO LADY EDEN.

BY MRS. COCKLE,

Author of " Moral Truths, and Studies from Natural History;"
intended as a Sequel to the Juvenile Journal—" Important
Studies for the Female Sex, in Reference to Modern
Manners."—" Fishes Grand Gala."—
" The Three Gifts," &c. &c.

" A *strict observance of* TRUTH, in the most *trifling*, as well
as the more *important* concerns of life, is the basis of *every*
moral and *religious* duty."

SECOND EDITION.

LONDON:

'PRINTED FOR C. CHAPPLE, 66, PALL-MALL.

1811.

92. Frontispiece and title page. *The Juvenile Journal; or, Tales of Truth. By Mrs. Cockle,* 1811.

governesses and headmistresses: Miss Bell, Mrs. Teachwell, Miss Starch, Mrs. Steward, and Mrs. Crabtree, among others. Fielding's book is made lively by some amusingly naughty if unladylike conduct in her characters, a flaw "corrected" when Mary Sherwood issued her revised edition in 1820. But it was precisely the inability or unwillingness of most authors to depict young ladies with livelier natures that weakened their school stories for girls.

Two of the more successful authors of this type were the Kilners, whose ability to give a touch of reality to homely childish activities and to restrain somewhat the moralizing impulse distinguished their efforts above those of many others. But even Dorothy Kilner's skill was strained in *The Village School; A Collection of Entertaining Histories,* 2 vols. (*c.* 1783), an overlong medley of stories about the children who attend Mrs. Bell's school in the village of Rose Green. The institution is like a school of industry, where learning one's book is combined with acquiring practical skills like spinning, sewing, or knitting. Mrs. Bell's pupils are either good or devilish. Jacob Steadfast, Philip Trusty, and Kitty Spruce work hard and are honest and boring. But Betsy Giddy, Roger Riot, Jack Sneak, and several other bad eggs, who seemingly outnumber the good, offer some diversion as they come to grief in manners their names suggest. After many such accounts, Mrs. Bell finally takes in an ill old woman for the night and, due to an accident, both are burned up in the house. It is one real excitement which not even the moral that Kilner draws (to be careful with candles) can dampen.

Her *Anecdotes of a Boarding School; or, An Antidote to the Vice Of Those Useful Seminaries* (1784) is more successful because of its heroine, Martha Beauchamp, an unwilling student in Miss Steward's school while her mother is ill. Martha yearns to return home, and she writes, after several unhappy incidents, requesting her mother's permission to do so. This is refused and her mother urges her to make the best of necessity and learn how to avoid the evil influences, follies, and vice that often go unchecked in such places! And poor Martha does, as she copes with some rather unpleasant young ladies like Miss Creedless and Miss Grumpton. The touches of realism of these characters and incidents give a degree of interest to the tale.

Despite its unpromising title and the saintly temper of its main character, Mary Ann Kilner's *Jemima Placid; or, The Advantages of Good Nature* (c. 1783) is also an engaging work. Jemima visits her London cousins, an unpleasant and overbearing lot whose pretensions are comic and ridiculous, as their uncle insists. But there is poetic justice in the second half of the book, for the cousins pay Jemima a return visit. Though she is too good-natured to take revenge, she fortunately possesses good but refreshingly human brothers who do not scruple to squelch their silly, affected relations.

Two Fenn school tales are more typical in their oppressive discipline and intense moralizing. *School Occurrences: Supposed to have Arisen among A Set of Young Ladies* (1783) and *The Fairy Spectator; or, The Invisible Monitor* (1789) are burdened by both, purveyed with relentless cunning by Mrs. Teachwell, the schoolmistress. In *The Fairy Spectator* she subjects Miss Sprightly to ruthless brainwashing in the form of a mean-spirited anti–fairy tale, till the young lady wistfully agrees that her beautiful dream of a fairy world and magical gifts is false and illusory.

School tales seemed to have brought out the worst in many writers,

Page 434.

Le Sauvage apres sa delivrance se prosterne aux pieds de Robinson.

93. "The savage prostrates himself at Robinson's feet." [Daniel Defoe], *La Vie et Les Avantures Surprenantes de Robinson Crusoe*, 1720–21.

given the number of sinister and dictatorial governesses and teachers they spawned. Mary Wollstonecraft added an incomparable character to this lineup in *Original Stories from Real Life* (1788) in the person of the tutor to young Caroline and Mary, Mrs. Mason, so icy and merciless a soul that William Blake could only depict her ironically in his illustrations for the second edition in 1791. It was the reformers' inflexibility that "did them in." Fortunately for the children whose reading habits they influenced, these writers did balance their repertoire with many extremely appealing creations.

7. English "Rousseauists"

When Rousseau fled France after the publication of *Émile; ou, de l'éducation (Emilius and Sophia; or, A New System of Education,* 1762; trans., 1762–66) and departed from Geneva to England, he must have been pleased to find his work received there as inspired philosophy, key to the thorny problems of social equity (*The Social Contract,* 1762) and child rearing. The widespread acceptance of *Émile,* or at least the forebearance of some who might have been expected to attack it violently, sprang from the growing uncertainties of a society in flux and also from the usefulness of many implicitly contradictory notions to factions and interests otherwise opposed in their ideals. To the fashionable, aristocratic beau monde and to the intellectuals who gathered at the coffeehouses and clubs, Rousseau's daring novelties were stimulating *and* amusing, as Boswell confides to Dr. Johnson.[1]

Émile was many things to many people. It opens, "All things are good when they leave the hands of the Maker, but degenerate in man's hands." Anna Barbauld, impressed by both its optimism and its idea of a world entirely permeated by the divine presence, created her own unique vision of that in *Hymns in Prose* (1781). But *Émile* goes on to argue the essential goodness of human nature, though ruined by "pernicious education and the social environment," an idea worked into Henry Brooke's satiric *The Fool of Quality* (1770) and echoed in Thomas Day's earnest *Sandford and Merton* (1783). Rousseau casuistically insists on Émile's complete freedom from restraints *and* on the absolute necessity of not merely restraining Sophia but of breaking her will with "severe measures," if need be, to suppress her whims and to ensure decorous conduct and submissiveness and her consequent fitness to be Émile's spouse. Day and Richard Edgeworth swallowed this whole. The

FRONTISPIECE.

Page 158. The reconciliation was begun and
completed in a moment.

Publish'd Aug.ᵗ 20 1789 by J. Stockdale

94. "The Reconciliation of Tommy and Harry." [Thomas Day], *The History of Sandford and Merton,* 3 vols., 1783, 1786, 1789.

94 a. "Harry . . . tore [the snake] from Tommy's leg." Day, *Sandford & [sic] Merton,* 1801.

SANDFORD AND MERTON

Harry, who happened to be walking near the place, came running up, and afked what was the matter? Tommy, who was fobbing moft piteoufly, could not find words to tell him, but pointed to his leg, and made Harry fenfible of what had happened. Harry, who though young was a boy of a moft courageous fpirit, told him not to be frightened, and inftantly feizing the fnake by the neck with as much dexterity as refolution, tore him from Tommy's leg and threw him to a great diftance off.

feminine agenda became part of a brisk campaign in adult and children's books to transform English ladies into exaggeratedly anemic and refined guardians of society's virtues—"walking ghosts . . . truly delicate," as the writer for one manual termed it.[2]

Émile supported physical freedom and exercise for boys, as Locke had urged, and physical hardening but heightened sensitivity and feeling. For girls, *Émile* led to near physical tethering to prevent coarsening.[3] It set the fashion in the beau monde for nursing one's own infant, a measure futilely urged by physicians like Walter Harris and William Cadogan.[4] *Émile* was to reinforce in some quarters the wish to involve parents in their offsprings' education; in others, its attacks on books and reading, and its scheme to delay teaching (until seven), ennobled some parents' wish to dodge dreary nursery duties.[5] Whatever the response, however, few saw potential dangers to religion and political stability in Rousseau's books (though Dr. Johnson did); or if they saw, they could not take them seriously—not before the 1770s and '80s, which brought the American Revolution, the Gordon Riots, and the French Revolution.[6]

Except for the general measures suggested above, few English parents seriously considered attempting to rear a child by Rousseau's plan. As an adult, Robert Southey gave thanks that his very fashionable, forgetful aunt never executed her scheme to educate him according to the exact regimen set out for Émile; it had slipped her mind.[7] Three youngsters were not so fortunate, however. Edgeworth's son, Richard, and two girls adopted by the wealthy, stubbornly quixotic Day were rashly subjected to it. The results of Edgeworth's decision to raise his heir as "a child of nature" were disastrous, and the youth who had been presented to Rousseau in Paris as a new Émile was banished to America. So disappointed was Edgeworth with the peevish, gauche, unsteady character he had bred that he thereafter ruthlessly bent Rousseau's philosophy to common sense. Day tried Rousseau's plan for females, taking a pretty blonde from an orphan asylum at Shrewsbury and a likely brunette from the Foundling Hospital of London and grandiloquently renaming them Sabrina and Lucretia. But he also provided honorably for them, legally and unconditionally.[8]

Though well known to scholars, his story is worth repeating. Day set off to live the ideal life, educating his two Sophias in France. Of course, nothing went right. They were neither biddable nor amiable and argued constantly with him and each other. Irritatingly, they got colds and smallpox, and so on, in a comic saga of ideals bruised by reality. He gave up first on Lucretia, apprenticing her and giving her the sum he had settled on her. Sabrina he hoped to salvage, but he never rendered her tractable or achieved unruffled placidity. This he had attempted to instill by unexpectedly firing pistols near her and dropping hot wax on her arm—tests of a lady's delicacy comparable to fairy tale trials of "princessness"! She was packed off to a boarding school. Luckily, Day found his ideal in Miss Esther Milnes, a lady of culture, birth, wealth, and marvelous submissiveness, who in fact made him an excellent wife. But he never wavered in his faith that Rousseau's ideals could work, and he died trying to vindicate them, thrown by a savage, unbroken horse he had "tamed" with kindliness.

French and English "Rousseauist" children's writers were considerably less accurate or unswerving in their application of the master's

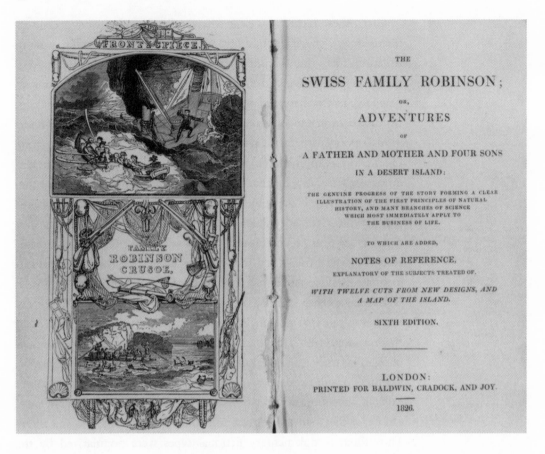

THE

SWISS FAMILY ROBINSON;

OR,

ADVENTURES

OF

A FATHER AND MOTHER AND FOUR SONS

IN A DESERT ISLAND:

THE GENUINE PROGRESS OF THE STORY FORMING A CLEAR
ILLUSTRATION OF THE FIRST PRINCIPLES OF NATURAL
HISTORY, AND MANY BRANCHES OF SCIENCE
WHICH MOST IMMEDIATELY APPLY TO
THE BUSINESS OF LIFE.

TO WHICH ARE ADDED,

NOTES OF REFERENCE,

EXPLANATORY OF THE SUBJECTS TREATED OF.

*WITH TWELVE CUTS FROM NEW DESIGNS, AND
A MAP OF THE ISLAND.*

SIXTH EDITION.

LONDON:
PRINTED FOR BALDWIN, CRADOCK, AND JOY.

1826.

95. Frontispiece. Johann David Wyss, *The Swiss Family Robinson,* 1826.

ideals. They had to be, since his first dictum was "no books" for Émile till he was twelve.

NATURE'S ARISTOCRACY: WILD BOYS AND NOBLE SAVAGES

Rousseau's is a philosophy of feeling. The heart is good until polluted by education (nearly all books) and environment or by contact with corrupt adults and children already infected by these adults—thus the insistence on forbidding reading (except *Crusoe*), on allowing learning to take its course, on providing for practical lessons or experience, and on keeping Émile away from all people except his tutor, Rousseau's surrogate, who has managed to transcend the spiritual staining of the socializing process. Émile's heart (feeling) will infallibly lead his mind to choose aright and to understand truly, for that is his link to the perfection of divinity in the world. Only goodness, truth, and sincere, noble, selfless feelings can proceed from such an education—provided always that contaminating books and people are kept at bay.

Given these ideals, it is clear why the Rousseauists were greatly attracted to any character cut off from society and thrust into full or semi-isolation: He—this is a philosophy based on gender chauvinism—becomes an ideal proving ground for pet theories. Of course, this was no new idea. Its fascination is probably rooted in the human heart as a captivating contrary to our inescapable enmeshing in society. The enormously popular medieval tale *Valentine and Orson* is just such a story. Orson, lost as an infant and suckled by bears, is savage but upright and innocent. When his brother finds and returns him to society, he functions adequately. He is noble, virtuous, and loyal—but always graceless and gauche. His purity would prove the Rousseauist notion in a substantive way; his "social failing" would make their case because it implies that social polish is a meretricious and contaminating embellishment artificially grafted onto the human soul to its detriment.

The eighteenth century found its Orsons in England's "Peter the Wild Boy," in 1724 and in France's *Savage Man . . . Caught . . . near Aveyron in 1798* (1802). Neither personage ever overcame the mental crippling of his early isolation, but Peter grew tame and could speak, barely. Yet these details were really unimportant. For if such creatures had not existed, philosophers and writers would have created them in any case. On paper they had full control and could order "nature" to suit them. Thus three complementary fictional types were popularized by the Rousseauists; examples are Day's Little Jack suckled by a goat, the little African boy in *Sandford and Merton,* and naturally a host of Crusoes.

Two Robinsonnades long in vogue have already been discussed, *Philip Quarll* and *Peter Wilkins*. But others by writers of juvenile books appeared. Joachim Heinrich Campe fathered one, *Robinson the Younger* (Hamburg: n.p., 1781), reissued by Stockdale, publisher of the Rousseauists, as *The New Robinson Crusoe* in 1788. Johann David Wyss's *Der Schweizerische Robinson,* edited and published by his son, Johann Rudolf Wyss (Zurich, 1812–13), was called *The Family Robinson Crusoe* in the first translation (London: M. J. Godwin and Co., 1814). This was extremely popular, appearing in a sixth edition as *The Swiss Family Robinson*—with the original title in the frontispiece, new explanatory notes, twelve new cuts, and a map of the island—by Baldwin, Cradock, and Joy in 1826. That same year Harris brought out *The Rival Crusoes* by Agnes Strickland, which enjoyed some popularity, though it is heavily moralized. Ann Fraser Tytler wrote *Leila; or, The Island,* which I have

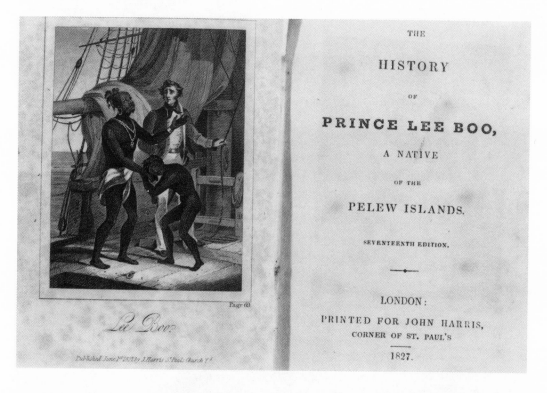

THE

HISTORY

OF

PRINCE LEE BOO,

A NATIVE

OF THE

PELEW ISLANDS.

SEVENTEENTH EDITION.

LONDON:

PRINTED FOR JOHN HARRIS,
CORNER OF ST. PAUL'S

1827.

96. Frontispiece and title page. *The History of Prince Lee Boo,* 1827.

not seen (London: J. Hatchard and Son, 1833). Jefferys Taylor produced *The Young Islanders* (London: Tilt and Bogue, 1842), featuring a troop of mischievous boys whose lark turns very serious. And Catharine Parr Traill, sister to Agnes Strickland, wrote *Canadian Crusoes: A Tale of the Rice Lake Plains* (London: A. Hall, Virtue & Co., 1852). Indeed, over the next century, Robinsonnades rolled off the world's presses, eloquent testimony to the profound fascination of the topic.

Day's "The History of Little Jack" appeared in 1787 in Stockdale's *Children's Miscellany* and separately in 1788, with especially fine illustrations; for long thereafter it was seldom out of print. It is an entertaining story of an abandoned infant nurtured by a goat, Nan, near the home of an aged hermit. It is fortuitous that the hermit who finds him is, like Émile's tutor, a voluntary exile from the world. Being very poor and uncontaminated by corrupt social prejudices, he keeps Nan with them to suckle the babe, who grows strong and vigorous. But after Nan and his father die, young Jack goes off to seek his fortune, and in the adventures that follow, we see the striking differences in ethics and empathy between one so bred and the generality of infected mankind. After many exploits in India and Tartary and an obligatory marooning on a

—what a sight presented itself. The young lady, then in her twelfth year, was seated on a chair, her poor victim kneeling before her, with a pin run through her Ear. Vide Page 9 Vol 2d

97. "The young lady and her victim kneeling." Argus, *The Juvenile Spectator,* Part II, 1812.

deserted isle, he returns to England, which in a sense he also conquers by going into business and making a fortune, his nobility still untainted.

In *Sandford and Merton,* a black boy befriended by Harry tells of his humble, even primitive, home but also, pointedly, of the noble and just rules governing the life of his tribe. The child embodies two complementary strains in the Rousseauist ideal, the noble savage and the noble African, the latter enslaved by socialized man's rottenness and greed. The English prototype of this motif is probably Aphra Behn's *Oroonoko; or, The History of the Royal Slave* (c. 1688), fashioned into a tragedy by Thomas Southerne and staged about 1695. But that too credible picture of adult, passionate love and psychological integrity in Oroonoko was less influential in children's books and adult "polite" literature than were Rousseau's philosophical abstractions and Day's asexual, highly moralized characters.

In *The Dying Negro* (1773), a poem for adults, Day attacked slavery, which for a time was a fashionable concern. Sympathetic books about such figures, and about other nonwhites made familiar to Englishmen from Cook's voyages, appeared well into the next century. *Prince Lee Boo* (1789), by George Keate; *The History of Tommy, the Black Boy from Jamaica* (c. 1795); Pilkington's *The Asiatic Princess* (1800); *The Ransomed Slave; or, The Fortunate Release* (1804, 1806); *The Island of Slaves* (c. 1809); *The Adventures of Congo in Search of His Master,* calculated echo of "Keeper's search" ([1823], 1825, 1828, 1832); *Radama; or, The Enlightened African* (1824); and *The Black Man's Lament* (1826) are a few examples. Passions over this issue were deflected, however, by hostilities within English society sharpened by the start of the French Revolution and the heating up of the Industrial Revolution. The indisputable cruelties of the latter created an unlikely climate for concern about the lot of distant groups already labeled racially inferior by men like David Hume, philosopher and English government officer (1766).[9]

THE ROUSSEAUISTS' MORAL TALES

The modifications the so-called Rousseauists made to his philosophy were in some cases drastic; most works share a group of definitive ideals, some of which set them apart from other tellers of moral tales: They favor simplicity in food and clothing, and a lack of affectation in temperament; sincere feelings and empathy with the weak and animals, freely expressed, but never compromising innate courage and chivalrous

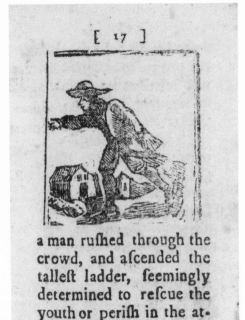

[17]

a man rushed through the crowd, and ascended the tallest ladder, seemingly determined to rescue the youth or perish in the attempt. A sudden gust of

98. "A man rushed through the crowd." [Thomas Day], *The Grateful Turk* [An American chapbook], 1796.

conduct; work with the hands appropriate to the character's sex and station, but humble chores like gardening for boys to keep them in touch with nature; love of only the right books, namely purveyors of information, moral lessons, and examples of fine feeling, but no fairy tales and nothing magic or supernatural; and, most important, strong ethics and love of the divine, but no religious teachings.

Although their moral commitment and rejection of fairy lore parallel books by reformists led by the fervent Anglican Sarah Trimmer, their deliberate exclusion of Church doctrine and implicit abjuration of revealed truth in Christianity separates and distinguishes the Rousseauists. Their sense of the presence of the divine in all recalls the universalist ideal of the knowledge of God accessible to all through reason in Alexander Pope's *Essay On Man;* but feeling and intuition, not reason, guide the African or the Turk in tales in *Sandford and Merton* to values and sensibilities identical to those of Harry Sandford and the eventually reformed Tommy Merton. Nevertheless, Trimmer's reformers and the Rousseauists did not seriously clash; they coexisted, for in practical matters their main goals coincided.

Part I of *Sandford and Merton* (1783) was one of the earliest books of this school to appear, and its popularity led Day to add Parts II and III (1786, 1789), bound as well as in cheap papercovers to reach poor children. The saga opens when Mr. Merton meets Harry, after he has saved the terrified Tommy from a snake, and invites him to dinner. When Harry refuses the wine and eats only simple foods, he earns Mrs. Merton's scorn but her wiser husband's respect. After comparing the robust, friendly, and courteous Harry to his own peevish, weak, spoiled son, Merton forms a scheme to have Tommy live with Harry and a tutor, Mr. Barlow.

From there on this homely episodic novel leads us through days of sunshine and rain, laughter and humiliation, progress and backsliding, as Tommy struggles to shed his doting mother's influence. Day's accounts of Tommy's reformation are frequently punctuated by Barlow's digressions that often take the form of tales, old and new, like "Androcles and the Lion," "The Grateful Turk," and "The Swedish Explorers," a miniature Robinsonnade about a small group of Crusoes lost in the icy northern wastes. There are many such, and they are welcome relief from Barlow's preachings. They and some very human boyish pranks are enduringly vital.

Sandford and Merton is an early example of the good boy–bad boy contrast that was quickly adapted to many spheres of life, including the animal kingdom. Stories of good and bad sisters or brothers, friends, apprentices, schoolboys, and even canine siblings flourished, some quite appealing in the simple way of the small child's world, all patterned to point a moral. William Hogarth's *Industry and Idleness* series for young adults and children was an important early stimulus for this moralizing comparison motif. It was in fact coopted as the title or subtitle for many children's books.

The contrast was also encouraged by several French Rousseauists' efforts, like Mme. d'Épinay's *Conversations with Emily* (1774; trans., 1787) and Arnaud Berquin's *L'Ami des Enfans,* in twenty-four monthly installments from January 1782 to December 1783. *The Children's Friend* was translated and issued twice monthly, 1783–86. Translated anew by the Reverend Mark A. Meilan, it was published by Stockdale in 1786 and reissued through John Bew and P. Geary later in 1786. T. Hookham put out a twelve-volume *Friend of Youth* in 1787–88—part translation and part original tales by Meilan.[10] *L'Ami des Enfans* was translated yet again by the Reverend W. D. Cooper [Richard Johnson] and published by E. Newbery in 1787 as *The Looking-Glass for the Mind; or, Intellectual Mirror:* "Being an Elegant Collection of the most delightful Little Stories and Interesting Tales: Chiefly translated from that much admired work L'AMI DES ENFANS. With Seventy-four Cuts . . . by I. [John] Bewick." The seventeenth edition (1827; 18th ed., 1830) was "Printed for John Harris, G. Whittaker, Harvey and Co., Longman and Co., J. and C. Rivington, T. Cadell," and ten other firms, thus ensuring wide distribution. Cadell & Elmsley had published independently the first, far less successful translation (1783–86).

This is a charming little work in which very human little children's follies, kindnesses, and cruelties are corrected by the experience of joy or pain and unhappiness based on their choices: Nancy, who dearly loves but loses her pet canary because she forgets her mother's warning to feed it; Joseph and the bad boys, who gleefully taunt Crazy Samuel; Tommy, who very humanly pines for summer in winter and for fall in spring and who "learns" the absurdity of this; Anabella, who gazes in wonder at the market wares and loses her mother; a governess who helps four squabbling sisters to learn that cooperating leads to fun at play whereas willfulness leads to lonely boredom; and Miss Caroline, whose childlike simplicity, unadorned beauty, and comfort are ruined when she gets what she demands—a silk gown and powdered-pomaded-burnt (with hot tongs) hair. On an outing Miss Caroline's friends laugh at her folly as she stumbles about, ruins her dress and complex coiffure, and arrives home filthy, soaked, and miserable. Her wise mother kindly offers to replace her spoiled finery: "Oh no, mamma . . . I am perfectly convinced, from experience, that fine clothes cannot add . . . [to] happiness." She begs for her old dress and consigns powder, silks, and the rest to her future, in ten years. But moral lessons cannot dampen the pleasure of tales that begin like this: "A pert little hussey, whose name was Cleopatra, was continually teasing and commanding her poor brother. . . ." The "tyrant" is reformed and the reader, amused.

Perhaps this very popular little trade book influenced Maria Edgeworth. Her tales cover many similar incidents, but her antidotes to error are typically more austere than Johnson's. Richard Edgeworth hatched a plot to write little tales, preceded by a preface much like a modern "instructor's manual" explaining to parents how to educate their young and providing the means in his exempla. He soon had Maria acting

LOUISA'S TENDERNESS TO THE LITTLE BIRDS IN WINTER.

HOWEVER long the winter may appear the spring will naturally succeed it. A gentle breeze began to warm the air, the snow gradually vanished, the fields put on their enamelled livery, the flowers shot their buds, and the birds began to send forth their harmony from every bough.

Little Louisa and her father left the city, to partake of the pleasures of the country.— Scarcely had the blackbird and the thrush begun

CLEOPATRA; OR THE REFORMED LITTLE TYRANT.

A PERT little hussey, whose name was Cleopatra, was continually teasing and commanding her poor brother. " So, you will not do what I bid you, Mr. Obstinacy ?" she would often say to him : " Come, come, Sir, obey, or it shall be worse for you."

If Cleopatra's word might be taken for it, her brother did every thing wrong; but, on the contrary, whatever she thought of doing was the masterpiece of reason and sound sense. If he proposed any kind of diversion, she was sure to consider it as dull and insipid : but it often happened, that she would herself the next day

99. "Louisa's Tenderness." [Richard Johnson], *The Looking-Glass for the Mind*, 1827.

100. "Cleopatra; or the Reformed Little Tyrant." [Johnson], *Looking-Glass for the Mind*, 1827.

more as author than amanuensis, and indeed she finished most of the tales and wrote the sequels he desired: *Parent's Assistant* (1795), *Practical Education* (1798), *Early Lessons* and *Moral Tales* (1801), and *Popular Tales* (1804).

Edgeworth never openly refuted Rousseau's system, but he did not let Day dissuade him from educating Maria well, and he never forgot the bitter lesson of his eldest son's miseducation. None of the zaniness of the system remains, but neither do the warmth, spontaneity, optimism about the human heart, or trust in pleasure as a preceptor. His coldly rationalist "Rousseauism" retains only what it can bend to an essentially secular puritan spirit: far from being banished, judiciously chosen books might actually replace human society; contrary to both Locke and Rousseau, discipline should associate pain with undesirable habits

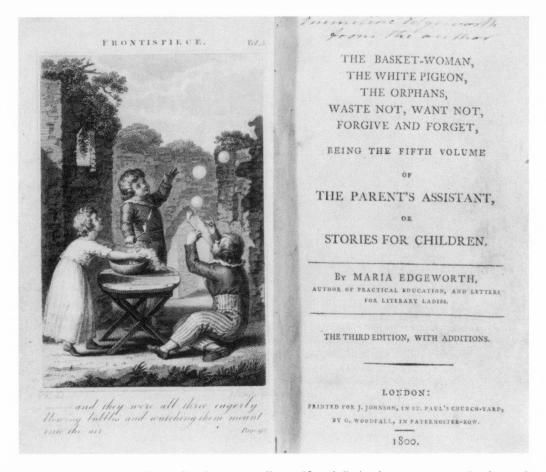

FRONTISPIECE.

THE BASKET-WOMAN,
THE WHITE PIGEON,
THE ORPHANS,
WASTE NOT, WANT NOT,
FORGIVE AND FORGET,

BEING THE FIFTH VOLUME

OF

THE PARENT'S ASSISTANT,

OR

STORIES FOR CHILDREN.

BY MARIA EDGEWORTH,
AUTHOR OF PRACTICAL EDUCATION, AND LETTERS
FOR LITERARY LADIES.

THE THIRD EDITION, WITH ADDITIONS.

LONDON:
PRINTED FOR J. JOHNSON, IN ST. PAUL'S CHURCH-YARD,
BY G. WOODFALL, IN PATERNOSTER-ROW.

1800.

... and they were all three eagerly
blowing bubbles and watching them mount
into the air.

101. Frontispiece and autographed title page. Maria Edgeworth, *The Parent's Assistant*, vol. 5, 1800.

"immediately, repeatedly, uniformly." Again contrary to Locke and Rousseau, toys and games to entice learning are scorned in favor of educational and scientific "toys" or practical tools, wheelbarrows over spinning tops. But little girls need dolls to prepare them for their roles as wives and mothers. These ideals are explained in the prefaces of *Assistant* and *Education;* but they did not, amazingly, doom Maria's work. Her genius for telling a story overcomes even the most suspect moral expediencies.

Like the tales in *Looking-Glass for the Mind,* Maria Edgeworth's often hinge on choices that are contrived by adults. Among the most objectionable yet fascinating to moderns are her Rosamond stories, especially "The Purple Jar," as F. J. Harvey Darton eloquently argues.[11] This and "The Birthday Gift" first appeared in *Parent's Assistant* (2d ed., 1796), and "The Purple Jar" was moved to *Early Lessons* in 1801. In both, as in so much of the early literature, our discomfort stems from our radically different point of view. To Edgeworth and her readers, it was not merely fair but essential to test whether a child's lessons "had taken," like a smallpox vaccine. Thus, the fact that Rosamond's mother does not tell her the jar contains nothing but colored water is irrelevant: Rosamond may admire beauty, but she must not be allowed to remain so foolish that she would trade any of life's necessities for *any* thing of mere beauty—stark, to us, but realistic and prudent in Edgeworth's world.

Once we accept the terms of the story, however, we find ourselves liking the mother—or, in "Gift," the father—no better. What saves these stories is the little girl who, unlike her meek, dutiful, dull sister, Laura, is innocently incorrigible. She *intends* to do right, means to recall the rules, but all too humanly forgets. In "The Purple Jar" the choice is between that glass-and-colored-water "Aladdin's lamp" and a stout pair of shoes. The dreamer in Rosamond wins out over the carefully drilled daughter; she takes the jar and goes without the needed shoes. Said Edgeworth, pain "immediately, repeatedly, and uniformly" drove home the point! In "The Birthday Gift" the sisters decide to make gifts for their cousin, to be presented at a wonderful party. Their papa reminds them of the virtues of practical, simple gifts and seems to hint that the cousins are ill-bred, a bit wild, and not fit to receive delicate or fancy ornaments. Laura at once takes his point; but Rosamond dreams of beauty and elegance, of something lovely beyond the ordinary. She decides on a filigree basket, fragile, difficult and costly to make, but exquisite to behold. She is an artist at heart, and she labors long hours to achieve beautiful results. But at the party, the gifts are put in a separate room to await their unveiling; the cousin sneaks in, spies Rosamond's masterpiece, and carelessly pulls it apart. Father knew best?

Maria Edgeworth respected children enough to wish not to lie to them or distort the truth "for their own good" (as Sarah Trimmer insisted was both necessary and right) in cases where the upper orders committed wrongs. Among Edgeworth's tales for the very young are several that expose the greed, cruelty, or thoughtlessness of the respectable and affluent. One of the most touching is "Simple Susan," a tale Newbery would have loved. Like Goody Two-Shoes, Susan and her family are threatened by the landlord's powerful agent, who wants their farm and does all he can to drive them out. He allows his haughty, ill-bred daughter to torment Susan without check. She invades the cottage and, begged not to, eats an entire honeycomb meant to last the child's

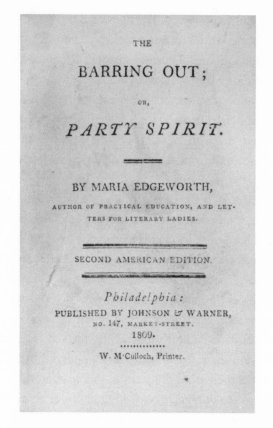

THE

BARRING OUT;

OR,

PARTY SPIRIT.

BY MARIA EDGEWORTH,

AUTHOR OF PRACTICAL EDUCATION, AND LET-
TERS FOR LITERARY LADIES.

SECOND AMERICAN EDITION.

Philadelphia:
PUBLISHED BY JOHNSON & WARNER,
NO. 147, MARKET-STREET.
1809.
....
W. M'Culloch, Printer.

ill mother several days. She demands and gets Susan's prize chicken. Her father orders Susan to surrender her pet lamb to the butcher so that he can feast the landlord superbly on his coming visit. The butcher contrives to hide the lamb, and everyone nervously awaits the master's arrival. As it happens he is a good, shrewd man—unlike others of the gentry in her tales—and speedily ends his agent's tyranny and aids Susan's family.

Similarly, in her *Moral Tales* for somewhat older children, and *Popular Tales* for them and late adolescents (and many an adult), Edgeworth anatomizes the world around her impartially, meticulously, and morally, to be sure, but always with unerringly true psychological and social reality, and often with a neat dose of very welcome wit.

A number of these seem almost to be covert anti-Rousseau tales. They may be that and also a reaction to some of the excesses in children's books that imitators of the best works were prone to indulge in. The greatest surfeit was in feeling, touchstone of all good in Rousseau.

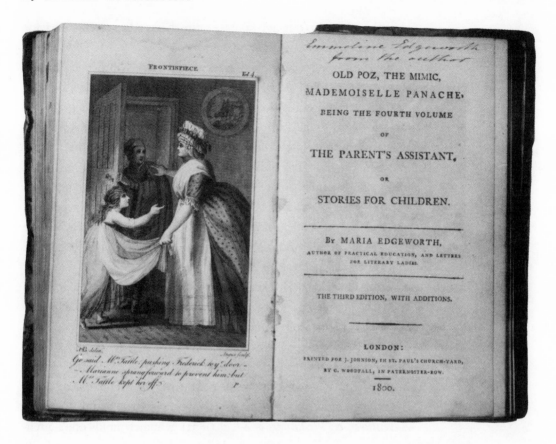

FRONTISPIECE

OLD POZ, THE MIMIC,

MADEMOISELLE PANACHE,

BEING THE FOURTH VOLUME

OF

THE PARENT'S ASSISTANT,

OR

STORIES FOR CHILDREN.

BY MARIA EDGEWORTH,
AUTHOR OF PRACTICAL EDUCATION, AND LETTERS
FOR LITERARY LADIES.

THE THIRD EDITION, WITH ADDITIONS.

LONDON:
PRINTED FOR J. JOHNSON, IN ST. PAUL'S CHURCH-YARD,
BY C. WOODFALL, IN PATERNOSTER-ROW.

1800.

Edgeworth has many stories that reveal better than could any treatise the danger and folly of untrammeled emotion in human life. One reads like a corrective to *Émile:* "Forrester," a tale of a noble youth who is impatient of all social forms and "authoritarian" rules because, he wrongly argues, they were merely cooked up to repress men's better selves. His saga is funny and sad, as he strikes all the worst poses for the sake of being natural; refuses to study and rashly leaves his guardian's home; tries to treat with mankind from his ideals, regardless of life's realities and others' desires; and fails disastrously and painfully enough to decide to transform himself by gargantuan effort. He is headstrong, idealistic, warm, silly, and petulant when crossed, loyal to the point of folly, intelligent enough to grow and change, and likable withal.

This moral tale—like "Angeline," a female Forrester filled to bursting with immoderate feeling and sensibility, or like "Mademoiselle Panache," a Sophia gone awry by misguided education, and like many others—teaches through vicarious experience in the realism of Edgeworth's art but also through salutary satire that renders certain behavior and beliefs untenable because ridiculous.

Edgeworth influenced many writers in the first half of the century, some pedestrian imitators, some fine. Mary Belson Elliott's little tales lack the incisive ironic thrust of Edgeworth's but are appealing, for she too knew how to tell a story, to draw one swiftly into a little world and the concerns in it. She wrote one novel, *The Orphan Boy* (1812), rather interesting until it falters toward the end, as though she had run out of ideas. The Fairchild children read it in Mary Sherwood's *History of the Fairchild Family,* and it was rather popular. But her little moral tales are her best work—"Idle Ann," "Beauty but Skin Deep," "The White Chicken," "Dumb Animals"—slight but lively little sagas with sure touches of still vital realism.

Like Elliott, Mary Hopkins Pilkington was influenced by Edgeworth and wrote moral, but not highly religious or evangelical, tales. Her version of Mme. de Genlis's *Contes Moraux, Tales of the Cottage* (1795), was well received, as were her *Biographies for Girls* and *for Boys* (1799), but they seem lackluster today. Most of her "account[s] of the birth, life and death of young" women lack appeal, charm, or wit. Her works designed to entertain more and preach a bit less were more successful. *Marvelous Adventures; or, Vicissitudes of a Cat* (1802) genuinely holds one's attention today, avoiding as it usually does excess sentiment and being lively and at times droll. But another work which she edited, *Pity's Gift* (1798), cannot have pleased Maria Edgeworth with its maudlin extravagances, and it certainly aroused Trimmer's reformers.

THE TOO VISIBLY GOOD HEART: SENSIBILITY AND SENSE

Concern over cruelty to animals, and by extension to the weak and helpless generally, was clearly an issue raised, and settled in favor of the victims, well before Rousseau's *Émile* was translated, as A. Charles Babenroth has long since demonstrated.[12] Certainly *Émile* and the books it influenced helped to make a fashion of displays of one's sensibility. In adult literature, many considered this deplorable. In children's books, such excess was unseemly to moderate parents, and even immoral and pernicious to conservative ones.

But for a large number of parents and writers, a child's inability to value properly the animal life about him implied that he did not understand God's plan for man, the earth, and its lesser creatures, as Samuel

12 PITY'S GIFT.

THE DUTCH DRAFT DOGS.

WE are told by a traveller who has lately performed the tour of Holland, that the very dogs of that country are conftrained to promote the trade of the Republic; infomuch, that there is not an *idle* Dog of any fize in the Seven Provinces. You encounter at all hours of the day an incredible number loaded with fifh *and* men, under

THE SPARROW'S NEST.

BILLY JESSAMY, having one day espied a sparrow's nest under the eves of the house, ran directly to inform his sisters of the important discovery, and they immediately fell into a consultation concerning the manner in which they should take it. It was at last agreed that they should wait till the young ones were fledged, that Billy should then get a ladder up against the wall, and that his sisters should hold it fast below, while he mounted after the prize.

As soon as they thought these poor little creatures were properly fledged, preparations were

104. "Not an *idle* Dog of any size in the Seven Provinces." [Mary Pilkington, ed.], *Pity's Gift*, 1798.

105. "The Sparrow's Nest." [Johnson], *Looking-Glass for the Mind*, 1827.

Pickering lucidly shows.[13] Extravagant love for or grief over animals was precisely what many books after 1790 depicted. *Pity's Gift*, a medley of poems and stories, repeatedly exploits the pathos of suffering beasts; lingers lugubriously over details of domestic animals led to slaughter; puts into the mouth of a dying horse the sensitivity and poetic expression of a Warton; lauds the dove that Noah sent to test the waters, as if it, not God, had arranged matters; weeps in its small beer over the death of a canary, sole support of its master; tells a grisly tale of a man who "Lived in times of old," father of grown children and young, who *justly* tortures, maims, and kills one or two to teach them better manners to God's feathered creatures; and ranges Europe—England was evidently short of atrocities to fill the 147 pages—for samples of such doings.

Not every volume on this theme was as extreme; most are less offensive than *Pity's Gift,* though similarly steeped in bathos. In *The Biography of a Spaniel* (1806), as master and loyal pet expire together, the dog is immensely gratified to hear his master breathe, "Bury us together." It seems likely the genre would have died a natural death, but some adults could not wait. One was the redoubtable Sarah Trimmer, who launched an attack in the pages of the influential *Guardian of Education* against "the RIGHTS OF ANIMALS" as a denial of God's ordering of creation.[14]

Elizabeth Newbery was before her in a calmer, more convincing indictment of such excess with Elizabeth Pinchard's *Blind Child; or, Anecdotes of the Wyndham Family* (1791), which discourages hardheartedness but urges moderation and balance in teaching children about animals. The same point had also been made in Carnan and Newbery's *Letters Between Master Tommy and Miss Nancy Goodwill* (1770) and before that in John Newbery's *Valentine's Gift* (1765). However, by the late 1790s, the reformers had gotten well beyond merely writing books to correct or neutralize their enemies. They had begun to seize control of and set standards for early education, as well as to decree appropriate choices in leisure reading for all classes. In contrast to the stance of their earliest works, they now strove to dictate rather than to persuade. The improvement campaign had become a bitter war for full power.

8. The Propaganda War in Lilliput

The war in the Lilliputian world of children's books was only part of the larger economic and class conflict that engulfed England. Since the 1760s, there had been a growing conviction of the rights of the individual among the lower-middle classes and artisans.[1] In the 1770s many of these Englishmen supported the American colonists' demands for social justice and greater economic independence and condemned the tyranny of their government. With the outbreak of the American Revolution, discord between classes and political factions intensified. Consequently, many greeted the French Revolution (1789) as a continuance of the struggle of ordinary men for freedom and as a harbinger of just change.[2]

Initially, the supporters of the revolution were an oddly mixed lot: Among the lower classes, many poor English laborers and artisans sympathized with the impoverished French who sought to change a social structure that allowed them no share in its privileges. Some intellectuals, artists, and literati, including most of the Romantic poets, dreamed of a secular apocalypse in which man and society would be cleansed of the accumulated abuses and rot of centuries and then spiritually and socially renovated. Even certain of the "wilder-living" aristocracy flirted with the idea of demolishing age-old restrictive laws and inhibitory customs, for they did not at first see that this threatened the scaffolding supporting privilege, and them.[3]

As the unprecedented anarchic fury of the mobs disrupted social and religious order in France and then was turned on the nobility, England's upper orders came to share fears expressed by the conservative middle class from the start. A flood of emigres, stripped of everything and with tales of horror to impart, swiftly completed the disaffection of the upper

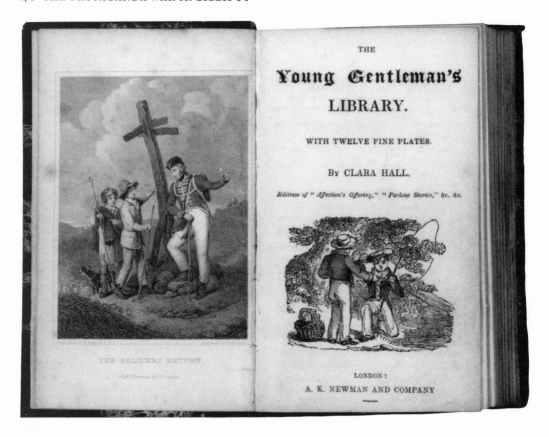

THE

Young Gentleman's

LIBRARY.

WITH TWELVE FINE PLATES.

BY CLARA HALL.

Editress of " Affection's Offering," " Parlour Stories," &c. &c.

LONDON :
A. K. NEWMAN AND COMPANY

106. "The Soldier's Return." Clara Hall, *The Young Gentleman's Library*, [*c.* 1820s].

classes. Artistic and literary figures suffered a similar revulsion at accounts of The Terror. Their informal political alliance cut across class lines and helped to set the stage for the brutal conditions that are often associated with the Industrial Revolution alone but that also grew out of this period of deep alarm at the potential treachery and destructiveness of mechanics, artisans, and the working poor. Fearful self-interest corroded the goodwill toward the poor that had fueled many philanthropic efforts in the eighteenth century, and it steeled the sensibilities of the comfortable, respectable classes against the ordeals of the poor.

Among the lower classes, those ruled by strong religious principles, especially the Methodists, or those who hoped for advancement within the system often sided with the establishment against Jacobin or revolutionary notions.[4] But many, notably skilled laborers or artisans, found in the Jacobins' writings that which spoke to the harsh inequities of life for the English poor. The political and religious establishment grew uneasy at what it correctly perceived to be a widespread sympathy with Jacobin ideals among the lowly. Thomas Paine's *Rights of Man* (1791) advocated universal suffrage and the sovereignty of the people in a democracy and demanded a state education system for all. Enormously popular, the tract was published with Paine's permission to be sold at cost (or given away) for widest dissemination. Of course, the government ordered them and Paine taken into custody. One hundred thousand tracts were sold in one week. Paine fled.[5]

In the humbler spheres of child life and children's books, many attitudes and ideals that had flourished in trade books during the free-wheeling transitional years were now suspect as potential seeds of revolution. The books of Newbery and his colleagues from 1740 to 1765, and socioeconomic developments between 1750 and 1785, had encouraged children to believe that the handicaps of birth might be overcome by action—industry, virtue, learning, even luck. Environment might be so arranged as to outweigh "blood." This had no doubt whetted their thirst for books and learning. Ambitious upstarts, like Giles Gingerbread or Primrose Prettyface, who gobbled up their lessons and schemed and dreamed of rising to wealth and high estate, were replaced by the likes of inoffensive Jack in *The Adventures of Jack the Broom Boy* (London: T. & R. Hughes, 1807). This boy too is smart and hardworking, but his dreams soar no higher than making better brooms and getting a horsecart to haul them in. A paradigm of becomingly modest aspiration, cheerful and contented Jack is shown walking beside the splendid cart, "And great is our hero's renown."

Clearly, by the 1790s dissatisfaction with the lowly or even destitute condition one was born to seemed dangerous to an oligarchy cradled in the reassuring assumption that its God-given superiority was the just and necessary foundation for its material and social preeminence. Egalitarian notions were abhorrent and, in these revolutionary days, extremely threatening because they inevitably undercut hallowed privilege. This explains the vitriolic criticism of books like *Primrose Prettyface, Goody Goosecap,* and even *Goody Two-Shoes* and also accounts for the mounting religious propaganda directed at children and the poor by Trimmer, More, and many other writers between 1780 and 1815. Censuring dangerous books and reinforcing religious restraints were complementary lines of attack pursued to restore fealty to the infallible and essential established order.

It may be difficult at first for moderns to see that certain writers of class-differentiated propaganda tales and lessons were motivated in

He was sickly, and had lost his left arm. It was some minutes before Mrs Howard could speak.

Vide Page 152. Vol. 2.nd

58

tho' homely, and if you were to meet him going to the Ludlow Market, you would say without hesitation, that he had the air of an industrious and thrifty man—and this was the fact, for after having cleared off his score at the public house, paid for the medicines as I have mentioned, put his cottage into decent and comfortable repair, bought warm clothing for his family, and sent his little ones to school, he found means to lay by a small sum out of his weekly wages, (very small at first it must be owned,) and it was to ask my advice upon the best and safest mode of disposing of this money, that he called on me, exactly three years after he had come to this wise resolution of giving up his visits to the Horse-Shoe, and of applying all his earnings to the support of his family. A little before that time, Savings Banks had been introduced among us, and every one was anxiously enquiring into the advantages which they were said to possess: when Isaac, therefore, asked my advice, as I had reflected a good deal upon the subject, I was enabled to explain their nature, and to recommend them to him very strenuously. The following is the substance of what I then told him, and I send it to you, because you may very probably know some person who,

IMPROVEMENT IN ISAAC'S FAMILY.

107. The soldier "was sickly, and had lost his left arm." Argus, *The Juvenile Spectator*, Part II, 1812.

108. "Improvement in Isaac's Family." [Thomas Beddoes?], *The History of Isaac Jenkins*, 1831.

some measure by an incontestable concern for the plight of the indigent. But some indeed were. To the hardships created in the lives of the working poor by agrarian and industrial disruptions had now been added "laws and penalties of great savagery directed" at them. Their desperation deepened as, between 1790 and 1840, many grew poorer in a nation growing richer and more powerful.[6] Some writers wished to ameliorate, however, the inhumanity of a system in which there were "220 offenses for which the death penalty could be imposed," a system worsened by renewed assaults on a source of comfort and hope the trading and laboring classes had come to rely on: books and learning. In 1788 George Hadley resurrected Bernard Mandeville's meanspirited arguments that the poor did not need education, that it made them proud and unfit for service, and that with education they would do inferior work but demand higher wages. Revealingly, Hadley added that charitable efforts to educate the poor were misguided and dangerous because the wealth of the nation rested squarely on the subordination of the poor, and their subjugation depended on their continued ignorance.[7]

The Blagdon Controversy of 1800–1803 was in fact an attack on Hannah More's numerous Sunday Schools and was part of a general effort to end such ventures. Accused of encouraging Methodism, which conservatives violently opposed, failing to see that it was a strong anti-Jacobin force,[8] More and her schools were targets of a virulent, two-year publicity campaign that nearly drove her from her project. The controversy faded. Though scarred, she and the schools survived. But the establishment mood was such that Davis Giddy's 1807 speech in the House of Commons, assailing education for the poor because it corrupted their morals and made them bad servants, made no stir: His argument was, for many, a given.[9]

The eighteenth century is justly famed for its great philanthropy, but like all ages and cultures it was often at the mercy of unconsciously conflicting faiths. Many of those who sincerely advocated and worked for improved conditions for all Britons and education for the poor were at the same time wholeheartedly committed to the inviolability of the divinely sanctioned social hierarchy. Many, like the conservative More and Trimmer, were viewed with suspicion by their more reactionary compeers. But these two women were among the best of their group and never abandoned the cause of the lower classes. Their efforts to aid the poor were reshaped, however, to accommodate contradictory allegiances. Moral books written during this period for the poor and for children of all classes clearly reveal this split.

"THE TWO NATIONS" IN CHILDREN'S LITERATURE

"I scribbled a little pamphlet called *Village Politics* by 'Will Chip'. . . . It is as vulgar [i.e., common] as heart can wish; but it is only designed for the most vulgar class of readers. . . . [This] sort of writing is repugnant to my nature, though it is a question of peace rather than politics" (Hannah More). *The Family Magazine* [is designed] "for Inferior Classes of people . . . To counteract the pernicious Tendency of Immoral Books . . . [and to make] good apprentices, and conscientious, faithful servants" (Sarah Trimmer). *Primrose Prettyface* "very wrong[ly teaches] . . . girls of the lower order to aspire to marriages . . . [to] persons in stations so far superior to their own, or put[s] into the heads of young gentlemen, at an early age, an ideal, that when they grow up they may, without impropriety, marry servant maids" (Sarah Trimmer). "The people [in novels] . . . are at home one minute, and beyond the sea the next. Beggars to-day, and Lords tomorrow. Waiting-maids in the morning, and Duchesses at night. . . . These books give false views of human life . . . teach contempt for humble . . . duties, for industry, [and for] frugality. . . . This corrupt reading is now got down even among some of the lowest class. And it is an evil which is spreading every day" (Hannah More).[10]

Trimmer and More were only two of the many persons who expended their energies and private funds to educate the poor in the Sunday School movement. From the 1780s the schools turned out "tens of thousands of adolescents" able to read—lured by the chapbooks and broadsides the reformers judged immoral (some of it was indelicate) or by the "political poison" of the "school of Paine."[11] More and Trimmer are important because their writings reached numerous children and adults at all levels of society and wielded great influence.

Their books were part of a campaign to reanimate love of Church and State. A vital first step was to revive and reinstate to its former puissance the Christian idea that poverty was not necessarily an evil, wealth not necessarily a boon. Another was to emphasize the notion that the poor had much to lose if French views prevailed in England. It was also crucial to persuade the young that, high or low, birth was ordained by God and fit His scheme of cosmic justice, an idea necessary to establish to ensure that they upheld that order. The glue to hold all this together was benevolence and mutual responsibility: Books and tracts for poor children and adults stressed the religious duty implicit in service, however lowly. Their betters' equivalents emphasized greater adult obligation to the deserving poor and increasingly depicted young ladies and gentlemen in scenes of selfless charity. Unexceptionable forms of the "Lady Bountiful" motif (*Goody Goosecap*), such propaganda forestalled guilt in the comfortable and comforted the lowly, but left them where God had put them.

Hannah More's system of Sunday Schools in the Mendip region educated thousands of children and even adults.[12] As she viewed the array of cheap materials sold to them she grew alarmed that the very tool designed to save could be twisted to their destruction. To counteract subversive sentiments excited by Paine's *Rights of Man,* she had reluctantly written *Village Politics* (1792), a dialogue between Jack Anvil, the village

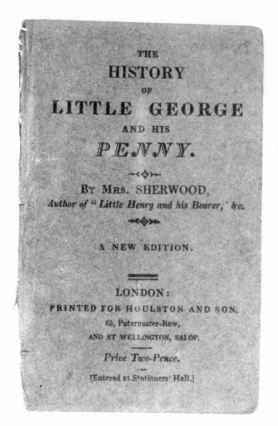

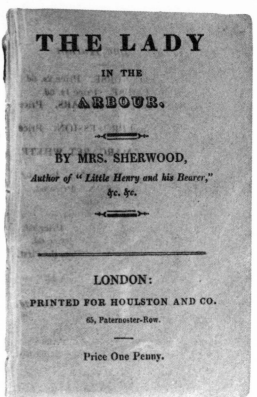

109. Four colored chapbook covers. [Mary Martha] Sherwood, *Little George, The Lady, The Rosebuds,* and *Poor Burruff,* n.d.

blacksmith, and Tom Hood, the mason who has read Paine and is anxious to convert Jack with his arguments against English society and the ruling classes. Of course, Tom has only a hash or parody of Paine's sophisticated language and logic in his noodle. The doughty Jack's commonsense rebuttals of Hood's jumbled notions is speedy, complete, *and* entertaining. He assails French democracy as murderous, the tyranny of thousands, and labels its rationalizations for its barbarities as satanic. He ends his oration by declaring that he will pray, fight, or die for England! Addressed by Will Chip to "all mechanics, journeymen, and labourers in Great Britain," *Village Politics* was widely read by all classes. Just as Paine's *Rights* had turned out to be the most persuasive rebuttal of Edmund Burke's *Reflections on the Revolution in France,* so *Village Politics* was the most successful refutation of *Rights* among the lower classes.

But Paine was not finished, and neither was More. His *Age of Reason* (1794), a fiery impeachment of the Church and clergy, could no more be kept out of England than *Rights*. The bishop of London appealed to

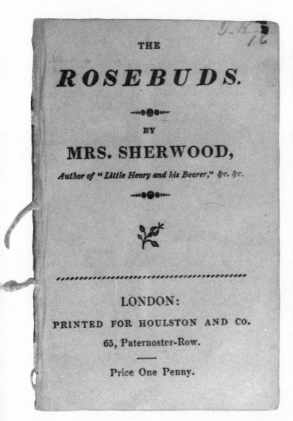

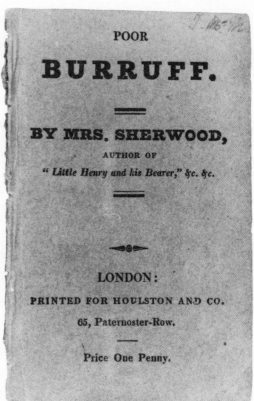

More to write a rebuttal to this, something like her *Village Politics*. At the time she was devising a great plan to provide massive readings for the poor, enough to replace the chapbooks and tracts she thought bawdy and subversive. *Cheap Repository Tracts* (1795–98) was the result.[13] More felt compelled to refuse the bishop's plea for help because she saw how the *Tracts* could be used to teach many lessons needed to save both England and the poor from Jacobin and other ungodly influences. There were three monthly tracts (tales, ballads, and Sunday readings), a total of 114—at least 50 of which More wrote herself, under the pseudonym of "Z," though she was ably assisted by the Clapham Sect. The tracts sold for ½ pence to 1½ pence, and their success was enormous: "By July 1795, 700,000 copies had been sold; by March 1796, over two million."[14]

One of the tracts most widely read by rich and poor was *The Shepherd of Salisbury Plain*, which shows how poverty is a blessing in disguise, for the Christian. It also introduces one nation, England's comfortable classes, to the details of life in a second nation, her poor. It is about a

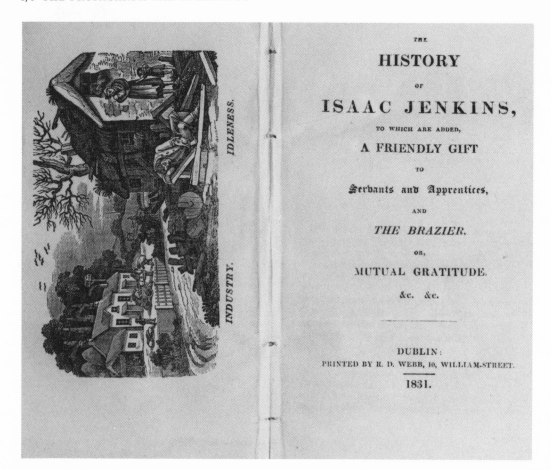

THE
HISTORY
OF
ISAAC JENKINS,
TO WHICH ARE ADDED,

A FRIENDLY GIFT
TO
Servants and Apprentices,
AND
THE BRAZIER.
OR,
MUTUAL GRATITUDE.
&c. &c.

DUBLIN:
PRINTED BY R. D. WEBB, 10, WILLIAM-STREET.
1831.

110. Frontispiece: "Industry and Idleness." [Beddoes?], *Isaac Jenkins*, 1831.

shepherd's struggles to feed his ailing wife and eight children on a shilling a day. Part I contains a dialogue between Mr. Johnson, a charitable gentleman, and the nameless Shepherd, whom he meets on the plain. With a curious but typical assumption of one-sided intimacy, Johnson questions Shepherd about his family, background, beliefs, habits, and current situation. Shepherd is anxious to reply and delights Johnson with the saga of his impoverished but happy family, enriched by love and the faith that God has chosen that they live as they do for some higher purpose. Johnson gives him a crown, tells him to buy them a good meal, and promises to visit him again. He does in Part II, arriving unannounced on a Sunday to find the family gathered in their spotless cottage, with biblical broadsides on the walls and a meal of bread and potatoes on the table. He rebukes Shepherd for not buying "a morsel of bacon." Mary, the wife, then bashfully explains that the money has gone to pay the doctor for her treatment, for they abhor debt and "some debts are sins."

So touched is the worthy Johnson that he decides to aid Shepherd, and when the village clerk dies, Johnson appoints Shepherd to that post, at a modest salary. Mary will open a dame school to supplement their income. When Mr. Johnson explains why the salary is small—"I am not going to make you rich but useful"—the noble Shepherd replies, "Indeed, my cup runs over with blessings, I hope God will give me humility." Overcome by their good fortune, man and wife burst into tears.

A common question among disaffected laborers and paupers in England in these years was, "What have we got to lose?" This More cunningly answered in the ballad "The Ploughman's Ditty," which pictures England overrun by barbarous Jacobins:

On Saturday night
'Tis still my delight,
    With my wages to run home the faster;
But if Frenchmen rule here,
I may look far and near,
    But I never shall find a pay master.
. . . .

My cot is my throne,
What I have is my own,
    And what is my own I will keep, Sir;
Should riot ensue,
I may plow, it is true,
    But I'm sure that I never shall reap, Sir.

Now, do but reflect
What I have to protect,
    Then doubt if to rise I shall choose, Sir;
King, Church, Babes, and Wife,
Laws, Liberty, Life;
    Now tell me I've nothing to lose, Sir.

The ditty depicts the ploughman's wife murdered, his babe's head on a pike, and the general devastation of *his* nation. This is the good old emotionally slanted stuff of effective propaganda. It worked. Many credited (or, like William Cobbett, blamed) More personally for turning the defection of "the vulgar" to patriotism (or to "bloody piety").[15]

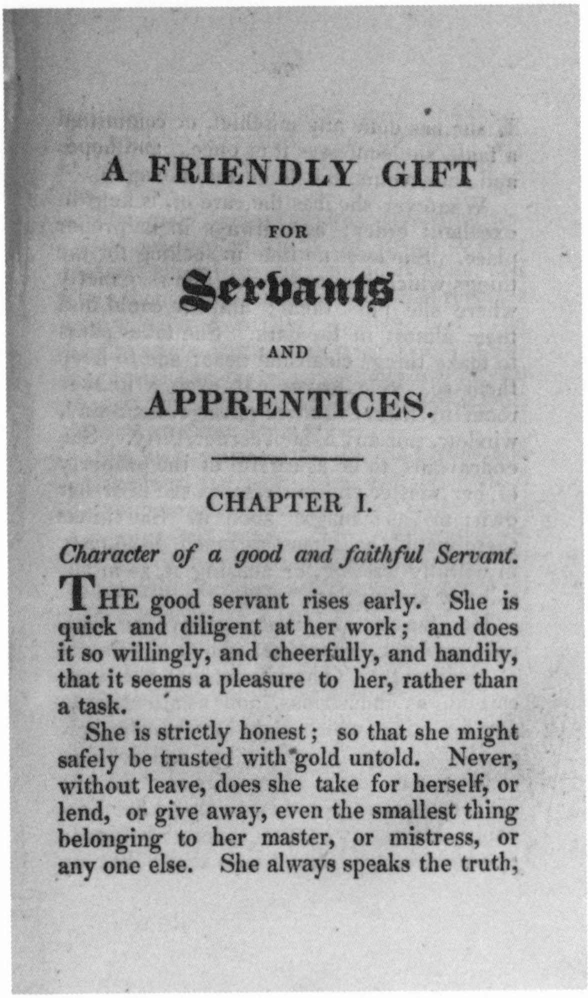

A FRIENDLY GIFT

FOR

Servants

AND

APPRENTICES.

CHAPTER I.

Character of a good and faithful Servant.

THE good servant rises early. She is quick and diligent at her work; and does it so willingly, and cheerfully, and handily, that it seems a pleasure to her, rather than a task.

She is strictly honest; so that she might safely be trusted with gold untold. Never, without leave, does she take for herself, or lend, or give away, even the smallest thing belonging to her master, or mistress, or any one else. She always speaks the truth;

III. *A Friendly Gift for Servants and Apprentices.* [Beddoes?], *Isaac Jenkins,* 1831.

In numerous tales and songs in the *Tracts,* More combatted superstition (*Tawney Rachel*), dishonest business dealings (*The Roguish Miller*), poaching (*Black Giles*), the dangers of evil company or books, and gin (*The Carpenter, The Two Wealthy Farmers,* and *The Gin Shop*), and she lauded thrift (*The Good Cook*), industry (*The Two Shoemakers*), patience and duty (*Patient Joe, the Newcastle Collier*), and religious faith and loyalty to one's land (*Dan and Jane* and *The Good Militiaman*). They are simple tales, simply told, and there is a vitality in most; More's huge, diverse audience loved them.

Sarah Trimmer began her campaign to guide the poor and servants early. The same year she put out *The History of the Robins* to instruct youngsters of the respectable classes on the proper use and place of animals in God's order, she also put out *The Two Farmers* (1786), with identical lessons on animals and mankind but also with pointed extensions of her hierarchical vision of the world into the relation between servant and master. Like older communal literature and More's *Tracts,* this was directed at lowly adults and children, especially those in "hall or Kitchen" who, "If they would be good [children or] servants and obey God," must gratefully accept the place He allotted them. She also wrote charity and Sunday School readers, data about which is scarce. *The Charity School Spelling Book* appeared *c.* 1790. Part I was 36 pages long in separate editions for boys and girls (I, 5th ed., 1799); Part II was 162 pages long and conveyed much information along with its moralizing (II, 4th ed., 1798).

Perceiving, as More would, the need for good books to oust the ribald or insubordinate, Trimmer started *The Family Magazine* (1788–89), intended to entertain and spiritually uplift servants, thereby making them more contented, and useful. Her venture failed financially, but another work, *The Servant's Friend* (1787), was a single volume, a novel of life below stairs, with much sermonizing by the Reverend Mr. Brown and his servant, Thomas Simkins. When the new cook brings into the household evil books—novels, chapbooks, and ballads—which threaten to lead Kitty, the impressionable maid, astray, the good master and Simkins (the maid's future husband) save her by prayer. Babenroth describes another tale for the lowly, "The Thrifty Widow of Hasketon," in which Trimmer demonstrates how thrift, industry, and faith can overcome desperate poverty, despite the disadvantage of age (fifty-five, with young children). As Babenroth observes, however, Trimmer glosses over the fact that the widow's succor rests on the improbably low rent her landlord exacts—and two cows she chances to own.[16]

Trimmer may have slipped on the matter of the cows, but her picture of the landlord was no mistake. She, More, and many writers of this school deliberately twisted reality to present the most generous image possible of those with position or wealth. This was the policy stated in her journal for the respectable classes, *Guardian of Education,* and the basis for her harshest attack on Newbery's *Goody Two-Shoes:* To show a Sir Timothy Gripe and a prosperous Farmer Graspall as villainous and greedy undercut Church and State.[17] Therefore, neither she nor More did so. The highborn were always generous and kindly; the rich were ever scrupulous and fair.

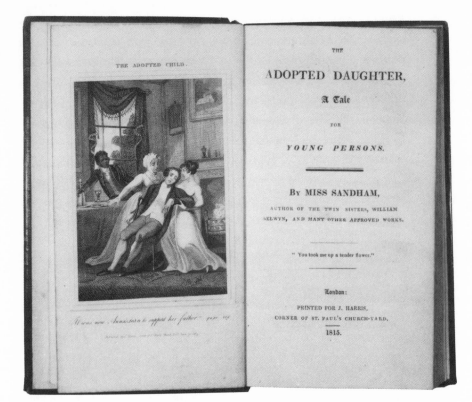

THE ADOPTED CHILD.

THE

ADOPTED DAUGHTER,

A Tale

FOR

YOUNG PERSONS.

By MISS SANDHAM,

AUTHOR OF THE TWIN SISTERS, WILLIAM
SELWYN, AND MANY OTHER APPROVED WORKS.

" You took me up a tender flower."

London:

PRINTED FOR J. HARRIS,
CORNER OF ST. PAUL'S CHURCH-YARD,

1815.

It was now Anna's turn to support her father page 119

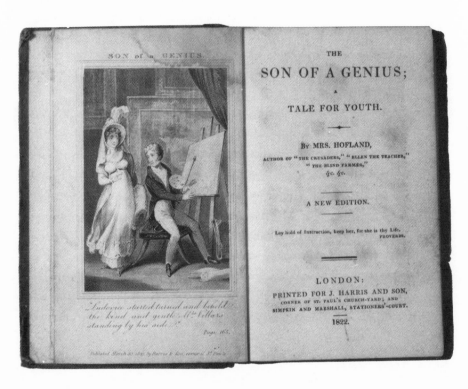

SON of a GENIUS.

THE

SON OF A GENIUS;

A

TALE FOR YOUTH.

By MRS. HOFLAND,

AUTHOR OF "THE CRUSADERS," "ELLEN THE TEACHER,"
"THE BLIND FARMER,"
&c. &c.

A NEW EDITION.

Lay hold of Instruction, keep her, for she is thy Life.
PROVERBS.

LONDON:

PRINTED FOR J. HARRIS AND SON,
CORNER OF ST. PAUL'S CHURCH-YARD; AND
SIMPKIN AND MARSHALL, STATIONERS'-COURT.

1822.

"Ludovico started turned and beheld
the kind and gentle Mrs Villars
standing by his side."
Page 163.

Between 1790 and 1815, the influence of More and Trimmer, whose *Guardian* was as much a manual for prospective writers as a guide for parents' selections, manifested itself in a flood of moral tales and poems

112. "It was now Anna's turn to support her father." [Elizabeth] Sandham, *The Adopted Daughter,* 1815.

that, unlike those of Edgeworth, emphasized religion and painted over the sins of the rich or great for reasons of national security. Of course, the lines were not always clear or easily distinguishable; many authors fell between the evangelical and the rational, sharing aspects of both.

113. Ludovic gazing in the mirror. [Barbara] Hofland, *The Son of a Genius,* 1822.

Among these are Mary Belson Elliott, Mary Pilkington, Elizabeth Pinchard, Mary Robson Hughes (*Aunt Mary's Tales,* for girls, 1811; boys, 1815), Alicia Catherine Mant (*Ellen; or, The Young Godmother,* 1812), Barbara Hofland (*The Son of a Genius,* 1812), and Maria Elizabeth Budden (*Always Happy . . . Anecdotes of Felix and . . . Serena,* 1814, and *Right and Wrong . . . the History of Rosa and Agnes,* 1815).

Lucy Aikin's *Poetry for Children* (1801, 1803), though chiefly a collection, contains a few original poems. "The Beggar Man" opens:

> Around the fire one wintry night
> The farmer's rosy children sat;
> The faggot lent its blazing light,
> And jokes went round and careless chat.

The scene is interrupted by an aged beggar, whom they welcome and comfort. The book also contains "The Happy Man," which revels in the golden gifts of poverty; "The Vanity of Greatness," which exposes the tinsel-joys of the opposite state; and numerous lyrics on religious and social duty.

Ann and Jane Taylor's *Original Poems* (Pt. I, 1804; Pt. II, 1805) is considered a successful early effort to write unaffectedly for children, without undue moral or religious freight. Like Aikin's and Mary Elliott's poetry (*Simple Truths, in Verse,* 1812?), it contains homely, realistic scenes from the child's world, but it is somewhat less didactic. Yet religious elements exist in the Taylors' poems as much as in Aikin's and Elliott's. "The Church-Yard" foreshadows the charnel scene repeated in Sherwood's famed *History of the Fairchild Family:*

> The moon rises bright in the east,
>   The stars with pure brilliancy shine;
> The songs of the woodlands have ceas'd,
>   And still is the low of the kine.
> . . . .

My child, let us wander alone,
    When half the wide world is in bed,
And read o'er the mouldering stone,
    That tells of the mouldering dead;
And let us remember it well,
    That we must as certainly die,
For us too may toll the sad bell.
    And in the cold earth we must lie.

You are not so healthy and gay,
    So young, and so active, and bright,
That death cannot snatch you away. . . .[18]

114. Frontispiece and title page. Mary Belson [Elliott], *Simple Truths, In Verse*, 1822.

115. Sherwood, *Little George and His Penny*, n.d.

This is not to deny the many lighter, comic, and occasionally truly poetic poems the Taylors wrote, but is meant to balance the picture. For they, Aikin, Elliott, and most poets and prose writers in these years participated to a greater or lesser extent in the vast work of reestablishing the religious, moral, social, and political verities necessary to bolster Church and State, as articulated by Hannah More and Sarah Trimmer. They succeeded in that great work. But the end of the Napoleonic Wars (1815) hardly marked the end of publications of this sort, nor of their consensus about the urgent need to keep a tight rein on the literature to which the lower classes were allowed access.

The evangelical mission implicit in many authors' writings continued with unabated fervor throughout much of the century—certainly past 1840. The Religious Tract Society, established in 1799 to take up the work started in the *Cheap Repository Tracts*, became a Christian international and ecumenical society. It published England's first lasting (because subsidized) monthly children's periodical, *The Child's Companion; or, Sunday Scholar's Reward*, from 1824 to 1846, when it became *The Child's Companion and Juvenile Instructor*, and appeared until 1930.[19] The Tract Society and the Society for Promoting Christian Knowledge, along with organized efforts among the increasingly powerful and monied Wesleyans, were the main institutional forces that continued the religious offensive. Many authors of the More-Trimmer school wrote for one of these, or for religious tract series put out by booksellers like Houlston and Hatchard.

Mary Martha Sherwood and her sister Lucy Butt, later Cameron, were among these. Cameron's talent was the lesser, and her best-known

SIMPLE TRUTHS

To meet him, all his children run,
And gather round him on the sod;
He shares the welcome meal of home,
Nor rests till he has thank'd his God.

Vide Simple Truths Hymn XVIII page 136.

SIMPLE TRUTHS,
In Verse;
FOR THE AMUSEMENT
AND
INSTRUCTION OF CHILDREN,
AT AN
EARLY AGE.

By MARY BELSON,
AUTHOR OF
"Innocent Poetry," "Grateful Tributes," "The Orphan
Boy," "Precept and Example," "Industry and
Idleness," &c. &c.

THIRD EDITION, REVISED.

LONDON:
W. DARTON, 58, HOLBORN-HILL,
OPPOSITE ELY-PLACE.

1822.
[*Price Eighteen Pence.*]

FRONTISPIECE.

See Page 27.

THE
HISTORY
OF
LITTLE GEORGE
AND HIS
PENNY.

By MRS. SHERWOOD,
Author of "Little Henry and his Bearer," &c.

NINETEENTH EDITION.

LONDON:
PRINTED FOR HOULSTON AND CO.
65, Paternoster-Row.

26   THE CARELESS BOY.

from his knees, and felt very much comforted; and just that minute he heard some-body calling, " Horace, Ho-race," and in a minute Wil-liam came running towards him. At first he was too much out of breath to speak : at last he said, " O, brother!

THE CARELESS BOY.   27

I am glad to find you here, for it has saved my running all the way to the house. I have got leave of mamma and grandpapa for you to come to us; and they are stop-ping to look at the school near the park-gate; and I have got leave to come and

116. Horace prays for forgiveness for his many sins. [Lucy Butt] Cameron, *The Careless Little Boy*, n.d.

works, like *The Two Lambs* (*c.* 1803), are rigidly allegorical, though some of her chapbooks, like *The Careless Little Boy* (n.d.), are more ap-pealing. More relentlessly Calvinist and just as didactic, Sherwood's work is superior, for it stems from an imagination fascinated by the ma-cabre and by the psychological realism of terror and guilt. She uses evo-cative detail and is well able to spin a yarn. By virtue of her experiences in India, she was one of the early writers of foreign missionary tales, a body of literature that bolstered England's imperialistic policies later in the century.[20]

Sherwood published over three hundred books, tracts, and chap-books. Many of her works still entrance, but so alien are her views that one must test this oneself. There is no doubt, however, of the fascina-tion of portions of her famed *History of the Fairchild Family* (Pt. I, 1818; Pts. II and III, 1847). This was a series of episodes from a family's life "calculated to shew the importance and effects of a religious education." It contains a compelling tale of psychological terror that arises realisti-cally from the conduct of the Fairchilds. Lucy, Emily, and Harry quarrel

12   THE LADY

never come again?" and Mary began
to cry.

"Yes," said the lady, "I will hope
to come to-morrow; so do not cry,
Mary. You will, I trust, see me again."

Mary was comforted with this, and
went to the wood the next day as early as Jane would give her leave; but
when she got into the little valley, by
the brook, no lady was in the arbour.
Mary thought the place looked very,
very sad; and she sat down on the
green step at the foot of the bower.
There Mary waited and waited till the
sun went down behind the wood, and
the wind began to blow very cold. The
little girl began to cry; and while she
was crying, she heard her own name,
which some one was repeating in a
loud voice. She looked up, and saw
Jane Price, who was come to look
after her. "What are you doing
here, child?" said Jane, very angrily.
"Why don't you come home?"

IN THE ARBOUR.   13

"I am waiting for the lady," replied Mary.

"And what is the use of waiting
for her?" said Jane; "what has she
ever given you but a few sticks? what
use are friends to poor folks, who
cannot find in their hearts to give
them a farthing? Go home, naughty
girl; and if ever I find you here again,
I will make you remember."

Jane then dragged the little girl
from her seat, and was pulling her
roughly away, when the lady was

117. "Go home, naughty
girl." Sherwood, *The Lady*,
n.d.

over a doll, and in the heat of the fray, Lucy bites Emily and gets
scratched. The gentle Mr. Fairchild reproves them and then calmly pro-
ceeds to whip their hands long and well. But this he deems insufficient
to make them sensible of what such acts lead to, so he prepares a lesson
for them. Each child is kissed and given dinner, the ugly fight apparently
forgotten, until Mr. Fairchild readies himself to take the children for a
walk, to "shew them something . . . which, I think, they will remember
as long as they live," he tells his wife. The children grow frightened as
he leads them through eerie Blackwood, for their mother has told them
they will see one "who hated his brother, . . . something very dreadful."
"Will he hurt us, Papa?" cries Henry. "He cannot hurt you now," mur-
murs Mr. Fairchild. Led through the thick dark wood with serene reas-
surances, the innocents stumble along in growing terror. Finally, they
arrive at a ruin of a house with a wildly overgrown garden near which
stands a gibbet, "on which the body of a man hung in irons: it had not
yet fallen to pieces, although it had hung there some years. The body
had on a blue coat, a silk handkerchief round the neck, with shoes and

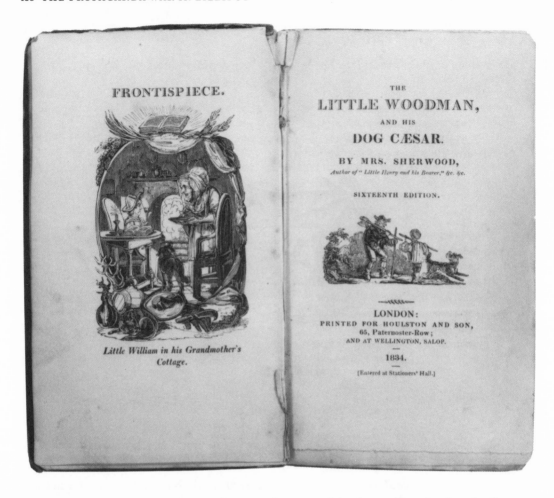

FRONTISPIECE.

Little William in his Grandmother's
Cottage.

THE
LITTLE WOODMAN,
AND HIS
DOG CÆSAR.

BY MRS. SHERWOOD,
Author of " Little Henry and his Bearer," &c. &c.

SIXTEENTH EDITION.

LONDON:
PRINTED FOR HOULSTON AND SON,
65, Paternoster-Row;
AND AT WELLINGTON, SALOP.

1834.

[Entered at Stationers' Hall.]

stockings, and every other part of the dress still entire: but the face was so shocking, that the children could not look at it."

There, in the dark, with the chill wind whistling through the dead trees, the corpse rocking to and fro to the accompaniment of the creaking iron of the gibbet, Mr. Fairchild unhurriedly tells them of the brothers' rivalry and the murder, and of the gibbet and the custom of allowing a murderer's body to hang until it falls to bits—warning to all. As he speaks, the winds rises, the body swings harder, and the iron creaks more loudly. "Oh! let us go, Papa!" sob the children. He takes them away—*after* he finishes his lesson.

As a child, Sherwood begged her father for a funeral invitation showing "representations of every horrible circumstance belonging to natural death—graves, and skeletons, and coffins, and shrouds, skulls and cross-bones." She mused, "I cannot comprehend where the temptation

118. Frontispiece and title page. [Mary Martha] Sherwood, *The Little Woodman, and His Dog Caesar*, 1834.

119. Frontispiece. [Mary Martha] Sherwood, *The History of Little Henry and his Bearer*, 1814.

lies of poring over such dismal matters . . . I sought them so diligently that I contrived to be taken to see the vault in Stanford Church, and when the funeral arrived, with all the paraphernalia of nodding plumes . . . coal-black steeds and mourning coaches . . . I stood . . . and gave myself up thoroughly to the contemplation of the scene."[21] Whatever the inner sources of her art and propaganda, she could write, and did until her death (1851).

Another prominent evangelical writer of children's books was Samuel Griswold Goodrich, an American Calvinist who decided to save England from ungodly forces and who wrote under the name "Peter Parley." His numerous *Tales of Peter Parley* (1824–32) were soon copied by no less than six bogus "Parleys," as Darton amusingly recounts.[22] Though mediocre and preachy, his 116 sternly moralistic books sold over seven million copies in about thirty years. The imitators seem to have done well also. Together, they added considerably to the moral and evangelical books flooding the children's market between 1790 and 1860. Their sales reveal the depth of that vein of "Puritan character" in the English. They also reveal, but partially only, the extent to which the reading and book-buying habits had grown from their shaky beginnings with the juvenile trade of the 1740s.

This picture of children's literature would be not only incomplete but distorted as well if we did not add that nearly as many books, chapbooks, and broadsides of an entirely different sort were also sold in these years. For the war in Lilliput waged by the reformers of morals and the preservers of society had not gone unchallenged. At first, it seemed impossible to take exception to their material or principles. But as its promulgators attempted to drive out all other literature and to lay waste to the treasures of the imagination and fancy, safer and stronger reasons for resisting their control emerged.

Imaginative, lighthearted, humorous, and adventurous books had by no means ceased to be, but they had, to an extent, gone underground. In 1801 or 1802, however, at the very peak of the power of the *Guardian of Education* and works of like spirit, Trimmer and More's campaign began to be quietly undercut by efforts that would shortly end their rule and secure coexistence for Mab, Oberon, Whittington, Bevis, and great flocks of "butterflies of fancy" in *papillonnades,* as I call them—imitations of William Roscoe's *Butterfly's Ball* (1806).

9. Oberon Leads the Counteroffensive

It did not take very long for reaction to set in against the rigors of the socioreligious reformers' ideas about fit reading for the young. By 1785 they had received from John Marshall his much publicized statement of conversion,[1] and in the following five years they consolidated their power to such an extent that most respectable booksellers were trimming to Trimmer's line to turn a profit. In 1800, Elizabeth Newbery published a list of her stock that is revealing in two ways: First, it shows a heavy representation of moral didactic books; yet second, it also contains several books of the fanciful and playful sort that could hardly have been approved by the More-Trimmer supporters but that she resolutely carried notwithstanding.[2] In short, the reformers did not completely control her selections. In 1802, Charles Lamb wrote his famed letter to S. T. Coleridge complaining (mistakenly) of "Anna Barbauld's" information-mongering influence on nursery fare and bemoaning the loss of lovable Newberys like *Goody Two-Shoes* and of imaginative, adventurous books.[3]

The counteroffensive, under way in earnest by 1803, came from the sources represented by Newbery and Lamb: It was a trade revolt against stultifying controls that had quashed publishers overlong; it was also a revulsion among those of enlightened artistic and literary predilections against an airless, inhumanly narrow view of the child's mind, capacities, and needs. In short, the recoil based itself in part on recent developments in English Romanticism, particularly the repatriation of the imagination as a vitally constructive part of human nature. Romanticism had not yet arrived in the world of children's books. But strangely enough, neoclassical and pre-Romantic devices had, the latter shortly before the former, both aided and abetted by that irrepressible urge of

120. "He desired of [the mother] one of them in marriage, leaving to her the choice which of the two she should bestow on him." *The Popular Story of Blue Beard*, [*c.* 1846].

121. "The Ghost of the Murdered Lord Lovel." Clara Reeve, *The Old English Baron*, 1813.

THE HISTORY OF

BLUE BEARD.

THERE was a man who had fine houses, both in town and country, a deal of silver and gold plate, embroidered furniture, and coaches gilded all over with gold. But this man had the misfortune to have a blue beard, which made him so frightfully ugly, that all the women and girls ran away from him.

One of his neighbours, a lady of quality, had two daughters, who were perfect beauties. He desired of her one of them in marriage, leaving to her the choice which of the two

confirmed tradesmen to produce abundant entertainment in the spirit of John Newbery. John Harris, successor to the Newberys, was one important bookseller who resisted the reformers and helped to breach their iron code.

Harris purchased the firm "at the corner of St. Paul's Church-Yard" and much of its stock in 1801. Like his predecessor, he carried old and newly commissioned improving books—moral, social, and instructive. However, in 1802 he published four works that are important in complementary ways: The first was the notorious *Renowned History of Primrose Prettyface*, which was promptly castigated in Trimmer's monthly the *Guardian of Education*.[4] Next was Clara Reeve's *Edwin, King of Northumberland, A Story of the Seventh Century*, influenced by Horace Walpole, whose *Castle of Otranto* (1764) was a harbinger of Romantic themes. Harris also revived Reeve's *Old English Baron: A Gothic Story* (1776–77)—first called *The Champion of Virtue, A Gothic Story*, retitled

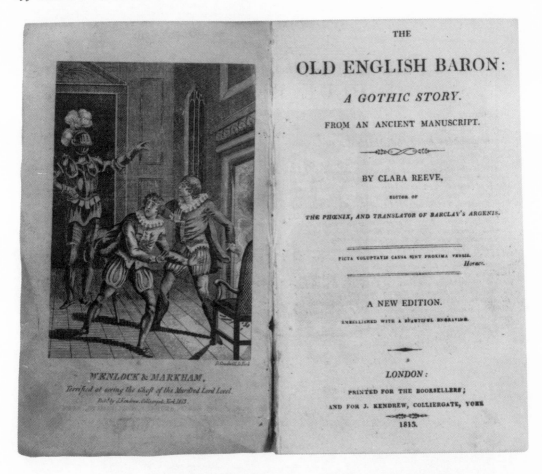

THE

OLD ENGLISH BARON:

A GOTHIC STORY.

FROM AN ANCIENT MANUSCRIPT.

BY CLARA REEVE,

EDITOR OF

THE PHŒNIX, AND TRANSLATOR OF BARCLAY'S ARGENIS.

FICTA VOLUPTATIS CAUSA SINT PROXIMA VERIIS.
Horace.

A NEW EDITION.

EMBELLISHED WITH A BEAUTIFUL ENGRAVING.

LONDON:

PRINTED FOR THE BOOKSELLERS;

AND FOR J. KENDREW, COLLIERGATE, YORK

1813.

WENLOCK & MARKHAM,
Terrified at seeing the ghost of the Murdered Lord Level.
Pub.d by J.Kendrew, Colliergate, York 1813.

in the second edition—and issued this with Walpole's *Otranto* (1808, 1811). Third, he published August von Kotzebue's *The Guardian Angel, A Story for Youth*, which Trimmer pounced on as "totally unfit," a "tale of wonders and false sentiment" likely only to attract "corrupt" youths.[5] And last, he reissued *Oriental Tales* (E. Newbery, 1795) with a provocative new dedication.

Moreover, Harris joined with Vernor & Hood, J. Walker, and other firms to publish these and similar books. Exasperation with tomes solely for piety, propriety, gradgrinding, and fact-jobbing was evidently widening. The 1802 books furthered the quiet counterrevolution: *Primrose Prettyface*, with thirty-one new cuts, amounted to a declaration of independence from, if not war on, the reformers' commandments, in particular those designed to stymie the lower orders' scramble up from their appointed niche. The publication of Reeve's gothic stories is a direct borrowing from the legitimate literature of the pre-Romantic move-

A new way to assist to carry a heavy load.

page 12.

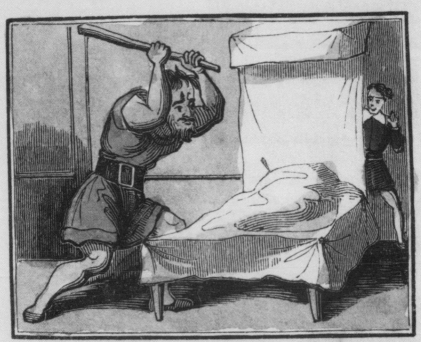

The Giants' way of showing a welcome to his visitors.

"Two of us in the church-yard lie,
 "My sister and my brother,
"And in the church-yard cottage, I
 "Dwell near them with my mother.

"You say that two at Conway dwell,
 "And two are gone to sea,
"Yet you are seven : I pray you tell,
 "Sweet maid, how this may be."

Then did the little maid reply,
 "Seven boys and girls are we;
"Two of us in the church-yard lie,
 "Beneath the church-yard tree."

"You run about my pretty maid,
 "Your limbs they are alive :
"If two are in the church-yard laid,
 "Then you are only five."

122. "The Gallant Little Tailor," *Popular Tales of the Olden Time,* [*c.* 1830].

123. "The Little Maid and the Gentleman," a chapbook version of William Wordsworth's "We are Seven," *Lyrical Ballads,* [*c.* 1820].

ment, with its interest in the exotic past, events of great passion and terror, and the sublime—hallmarks of the reemergent imagination in the late eighteenth century, now offered to the young.

Of related import is Kotzebue's tale. That grinder-out of highly emotional, farfetched plays enjoyed a vogue from about 1798, which, ironically, was frowned on by William Wordsworth as well as Sarah Trimmer.[6] Wordsworth objected to Kotzebue's debasement of feeling and of the esthetic sensibility that Wordsworth and other Romantic poets saw as a vital source of human moral awareness and as the foundation of noble pleasure in life. Trimmer saw sin, and dangerous freedom, of course. The significance of Kotzebue's advent in children's books is its indication of the strength of the backlash against the rigid limitations prevailing.

Finally, the dedication "to Isabella" of *Oriental Tales* (1 June 1802) is one of the earliest articulations of the strongest rebuttals to the fear-rooted censorship of everything fanciful. The dedication defends imag-

124. "She went to the Fruiterer's." [Sarah Catherine Martin], *The Comic Adventures of Old Mother Hubbard and her Dog*, [1806].

124a. "She went to the Barber's." [Martin], *Old Mother Hubbard*, [1806].

inative tales on the grounds that children should be induced to love reading no matter what the means and "that much good advice and information can be conveyed in a Fable and a Fairy Tale" which are, in their way, as amusing and "improving as an account of Sir Isaac Newton's Philosophy, or an Abridgement of Locke on the Human Understanding"—a case surely of throwing the cat amongst the pigeons![7] This is the Romantic vision of the human mind newly applied to children's minds, a vision we find in Wordsworth's "To H[artley]. C[oleridge]. Six Years Old" and in Blake's *Songs of Innocence & Experience*: It exalts the imagination as the touchstone of one's humanity, the wellspring of art, of ethics, and of all that is best and most vividly alive.

The increase of such books Sarah Trimmer deplored: "They have multiplied to an astonishing and alarming degree, and much mischief lies hid in . . . them"; she felt there was *no* "species of Books for Children and Youth . . . which has not been made in some way or other an engine of mischief."[8]

Although Harris always carried moral didactic books, for which there was much demand, he brought out Mme. d'Aulnoy's tales as *Mother Bunch's Fairy Tales* in 1802, and in 1803, her *Renowned History of*

Prince Chery and Princess Fair Star and *Renowned History of the White Cat, and Other . . . Stories*, and Charles Perrault's *Histories; or, Tales of Past Times*. In 1804 he revived E. Newbery's 1788 *Life and Adventures of Peter Wilkins*, best of the early adult Robinsonnades adopted by children, and issued his first romance, *Valentine and Orson*, which Trimmer promptly sniffed had "nothing to recommend it."[9] In 1805 he published S. C. Martin's *Comic Adventures of Old Mother Hubbard and her Dog* and *A Continuation*, and in 1806, *A Sequel*.

Nor was he alone in breaching the walls of decorous and arid propriety: Benjamin Tabart, Howard and Evans, Thomas Batchelor, Thomas Evans, Richard Phillips, John Roe, Ann Lemoine, John Jennings, and many other respectable booksellers began in 1803–4 to bring out fairy tales, the discredited *Gesta* romances, English folklore, and ballads. Their effusions were reinforced by provincial booksellers and chapbook sellers in London and the provinces: Kendrew, Burbage, and Angus. By 1820 their numbers had swollen amazingly: Lumsden, Rusher, Bloomer, Marsden, and so on. Even stalwarts of the reformers' school joined in, if but timidly: The pious Houlston of Wellington, Salop, and London put out, among others, Jeanne Marie le Prince de Beaumont's *Beauty and the Beast*, and *The History of Prince Fatal and Prince Fortunatus, with an Account of Astolpho's Journey to the Kingdom of the Moon* (c. 1817), and *Nurse Dandlem's Little Repository* (c. 1820), an original (preconversion) John Marshall confection kept alive in chapbooks. And the staid Dartons joined in 1806 with *The Death and Burial of Cock Robin* and *The Moving Adventures of Old Dame Trot and Her Comical Cat* in 1807. The dike was breached; fresh waters flowed.

NONSENSE AND FUNNY-SENSE: COMIC POETRY

The real breakthrough in imaginative and humorous or adventurous books came in poetry rather than prose perhaps because the latter had been so exclusively preempted in the service of Church and State; perhaps it was mere chance. One of the things that comes through poorly in written criticism such as this is the living voice of an age. Generally in earlier times people sang more, possibly a benefit of the absence of synthetic music and canned lyrics. From what one can gather, this was true everywhere. Certainly, ballads, broadsides of songs set to well-known tunes, and even songbooks were abundant sellers in eighteenth- and nineteenth-century Britain. Moreover, this lyrical impulse was cre-

8

THE COOK COOKED.

A hare, who long had hung for dead,
  But *really* brew'd sedition,
Once set a scheme on foot, and said,
She could not take it in her head,
  That *hares* should be nutrition :

A turkey next began to speak,
  But said her task was harder,
Because the cook had tucked her beak
Behind her wing, for half a week
  That she'd been in the larder.

THE COOK COOKED.

125. "A hare who . . . *really* brew'd sedition." [Taylor], *Signor Topsy-Turvy*, [1810].

atively wedded to homely enterprise in the street cries—of London, Glasgow, Edinburgh, or wherever a chapbook edition originated—to alert the public to the peculiar attractiveness or usefulness of small businesswomen's and -men's produce, wares, or skilled services, like rush chair mending. A considerable portion of the disreputable "Jemmy" Catnach's lucrative one-fourth-pence, one-half-pence, and one-pence business in Seven Dials (1813–39), apart from the lurid accounts of murder, mayhem, and grisly justice at Tyburn Tree, was in catches, glees, and broadside ballads, some a bit bawdy but most just comic or sentimental.

To be sure, the children chanted their street songs and game songs, many of which were printed in both shoddy and superior chapbooks and in anthologies and were thus passed along to this day. Partly out of this rich melange emerged collections of songs for the nursery.[10] As we have seen, the first such nursery collection was compiled by Mary Cooper in *Tommy Thumb's Pretty Song Book* (1744). Competing volumes were issued by Crowder and Collins, *The Top Book of All* (c. 1760), and by Newbery, *Mother Goose's Melody; or, Sonnets for the Cradle* (c. 1760). The next major work was perhaps that of the chapbook publishers Cluer Dicey and Richard Marshall, who issued the famous nursery rhyme *Simple Simon* in 1764. Imitators and reprinters of Cooper's and Newbery's songs—Isaiah Thomas in America and John Marshall and numerous other chapbook publishers in London and the provinces—busily filled the needs of patrons during the sixties, seventies, and eighties.

Inspired by Newbery's *Mother Goose's Melody*, the precise antiquarian Joseph Ritson issued a collection in 1784 that stimulated poetry in an era when prose was largely controlled by the moral utilitarians and devoted to repressing laughter and fancy. *Gammer Gurton's Garland; or, The Nursery Parnassus* contained the original (in print) of "Goosey, Goosey Gander" and "Little Bo-Peep." Many of its songs were evidently widely known and often sung in their day. *Garland* was enlarged and reissued about 1799 and was further enlarged by Francis Douce [?] in a new edition of 1810 which contained the first printed version of "Humpty Dumpty" and an imitation of *Old Mother Hubbard*, "The Surprising Old Woman." Many of our staples of Mother Goose's nursery rhymes were added to the cannon in these years. Some, like "Hot Cross Buns," originated in street cries (to sell the buns traditionally eaten on Good Friday) that had already appeared in print (this one as a "catch" by Luffman Atterbury in *A Seventh Collection of Catches, Canons & Glees*, 1768).[11]

In the aggregate, such works reveal a yearning for the surcease of duty and moral "busy-ness" and for the resurgence of imagination and of comic amusements. This desire was perfectly fulfilled in *Old Mother Hubbard*, which seemed to open the floodgates, letting pour through a great tide of engagingly droll and occasionally witty poetry. Most of it was meant for sheer enjoyment, but its spirit infected writers of instructive books as well, and some of these soared for the first time above the dull paths their ilk usually crept on. Typically, any truly popular new book was imitated as swiftly (and deftly) as the trade could manage, often quite surprisingly successfully in these years.

Mother Hubbard was not new but was rather a stock figure from folk or nursery tales. I know of one inexpensive version of *Mother Hubbard* (*c.* 1770–90), put out by John Evans, publisher of farthing chapbooks and songsheets in Long Lane, West Smithfield, London; doubtless there were others. But the poetry was evidently refurbished by Sarah Catherine Martin in 1804, as were the illustrations. It was loved and recited, and imitated and followed by sequels and continuations for decades:

126. [Ann Taylor], *My Mother*. Bound with four imitations, *My Brother, My Aunt, My Grandmother, My Grandfather*, [c. 1815–35].

127. *My Brother*, [c. 1815–35].

Old Mother Hubbard
Went to the cupboard
To fetch her poor dog a bone;
But when she came there
The cupboard was bare
And so the poor dog had none.

She went to the baker's
To buy him some bread;
But when she came back
The poor dog was dead.

Mother Hubbard appeared 1 June 1805, the 24th edition coming in 1807; *A Continuation* came out in 1805, its 12th edition in 1807; and *A Sequel*, published 1 March 1806, sold ten thousand copies in six months. "A Near Relation of Mother Hubbard" authored *Whimsical Incidents; or, The Power of Music, a Poetical Tale*, a merry bit of rhyming, on 25 October 1805. *Pug's Visit; or, The Disasters of Mr. Punch; A Poetical Tale* followed in 1806—all brought out by Harris. The "Hubbards" were all pirated in chapbooks and widely imitated.

Others joined in with their versions of the first amusing poetry for children since Mary Cooper's books in the 1740s, versions generally without moral or educational purpose. Thomas Hodgkins (i.e., William Godwin's firm) published *The King and Queen of Hearts*, Charles Lamb's anonymous but pleasant reworking of once current political jibes, in 1805; and Benjamin Tabart issued the important *Songs for the Nursery* (1805), which included "Little Miss Muffet" and "Little Bobby Shaftoe," and *Memoirs of The Little Man and the Little Maid* (1807), the first children's version of which appeared in Newbery's *Mother Goose's Melody*. Joining the trend, though in more original and ironic (and thus moral) verse, Ann Taylor wrote *Signor Topsy Turvy's Wonderful Magic Lantern* (1810), a series of comic-satiric poems that enlighteningly reverse the order of things in life, especially between men and beasts, with vivid illustrations.

In addition, Dean & Munday of Threadneedle Street, frequent co-publishers with A. K. Newman (The Minerva Press), put out batches of refreshingly silly entertainments: *Dame Wiggins of Lee and Her Seven Wonderful Cats. Written Principally by a Lady of Ninety* (1823); *Deborah Dent and her Donkey* (c. 1820s), daffy doings at Brighton; *Madam Fig's*

Who ran to help me when I fell,

And would some pretty story tell,

Or kiss the place to make it well?

My Mother.

Who lov'd to see me pleas'd and gay,

And taught me sweetly how to play,

And minded all I had to say?

My Mother

Who, as I on the couch did lie,

Took off his shoes ere he came nigh,

And through the room stole softly by?

MY BROTHER.

Who, watchful ever to impart

Sweet pleasure to his sister's heart,

Became her horse, and lent his cart?

MY BROTHER.

OLD WOMAN OF CROYDON

There was an Old Woman of Croydon
To look young she affected the Hoyden
And would jump and would skip,
Till she put out her hip ;
Alas ! poor Old Woman of Croydon.

OLD WOMAN OF GOSPORT

There was an Old Woman of Gosport,
And she was one of the cross sort,
When she dressed for the Ball
Her wig was too small,
Which enrag'd this Old Woman of Gosport.

7 times 12 are 84.
O happy little tawny Moor.

8 times 8 are 64.
A Baron bold in days of yore.

128. "Alas! poor Old Woman of Croydon." *The History of Sixteen Wonderful Old Women,* 1820.

128 a. "There was an Old Woman of Gosport." *Sixteen Wonderful Old Women,* 1820.

129. "7 times 12" and "8 times 8." *Marmaduke Multiply's Merry Method of Making Minor Mathematicians,* [*c.* 1840–50].

Gala (*c.* 1820s), the comic tussles between a greengrocer and his social-climbing wife; and *Aldiborontiphoskyphorniostikos; A Round game for Merry Parties* (*c.* 1822), by R. Stennet, grafting Eastern tales like *Ali Baba* to tongue twisters like "Peter Piper": "M, Muley Hassan Mufti of Moldavia put on his Barnacles to see little Tweedle gobble them up, when Kia Khan Kreuse transmogrified them into Pippins, . . . Snip's wife cried, Illikipilliky, lass a day, 'tis too bad to titter at a body. . . ." On goes the sheer nonsense. Imagine *that* being recited speedily at a children's party.

Tongue twisting and poetry games became the rage. Some were ancient, like *The Gaping, Wide-mouthed, Waddling Frog* (Dean & Munday, E. Marshall, *c.* 1815–20); but many imitations appeared. E. Marshall seemed to have specialized in these, which were beautifully printed for him by David Carvalho from designs by Robert Cruikshank: *The Frisking, Barking, Lady's Lap-Dog, A Game of Forfeits; The Hopping, Prating, Chattering Magpie; The Pretty, Playful, Tortoise-Shell Cat,* and *The Noble Prancing, Cantering Horse*—all published around 1820 and all nicely hand-colored.

Most such stuff has long since been forgotten, but the rollicking comic backlash spawned at least one lasting genre, the limerick. Harris's *History of Sixteen Wonderful Old Women* (1820) led the way:

> There was an Old Woman of Harrow
> Who visited in a wheel-barrow,
> > And her servant before
> > Knock'd loud at each door;
> To announce the Old Woman of Harrow.

E. Marshall, who was proving as resourceful as his kinsman John, immediately countered with two works. *Anecdotes and Adventures of Fifteen Gentlemen* (*c.* 1821) and *Anecdotes and Adventures of Fifteen Young Ladies* (*c.* 1822), printed by Carvalho with designs by R. Cruikshank. Darton demonstrates that both text and inspiration for an illustration in Edward Lear's *Book of Nonsense* (1846) were provided by *Gentlemen*:[12]

> There was a sick man of Tobago
> Liv'd long on rice-gruel and sago;
> > But at last, to his bliss,
> > The physician said this—
> To a roast leg of mutton you may go.

130. *A Good Child's Book of Stops*, [*c.* 1830s].

131. "Let's haste away!" [William Roscoe], *The Butterfly's Ball and the Grasshopper's Feast*, 1807.

Assuredly this prolonged rash of delicious humor was a healthy reaction to years of grim earnestness. But its benefits were not limited to the healing relief of jollity; they spilt over quite wonderfully into the field of instruction. For the first time in children's literature many little works successfully combined learning and laughter. One of the earliest is the charmingly illustrated and colored *Juvenile Numerator* (London: Stevens & Co., 1810). It is the old counting rhyme "1, 2, Buckle my shoe!" that goes to "19, 20, My Belly's Empty. / So pray Dame give me some pudding."

Harris's *Peter Piper's Practical Principles of Plain and Perfect Pronunciation* appeared in 1813 and sold well through many editions, though it was attacked in 1820 for slyly bawdy innuendoes.[13] One of its tongue twisters is widely known even today: "Peter Piper picked a peck of pickled peppers. . . ." But Harris's triumph was the 1816 *Marmaduke Multiply's Merry Method of Making Minor Mathematicians; or, The Multiplication*

Table, illustrated, which went through countless editions in England and America: "3 time 10 *are* 30 / My face is very dirty. . . . 5 times 12 *are* 60 / The House is like a Pig's sty! . . . 10 times 12 *are* 120 / I laugh and sing and live in plenty" and on to "12 times 12." Marmaduke had a learned family, some of whom rushed into print: *The Pence Table Playfully Paraphrased. By Peter Pennyless* (1818); *The Mint; or, Shillings transformed into Pounds. By Peregrine Proteus* (1819). And *Harris's Cabinet: Pence Tables* (1819?) is rhymed and illustrated, like John Wallis's *Paul Pennylove's Poetical Paraphrase of the Pence Table* (c. 1814). The impulse was clearly catching.

Publishers, naturally, were not slow to adapt these devices to language. Thomas Love Peacock's *Sir Hornbook; or, Childe Launcelot's Expedition. A Grammatico-Allegorical Ballad* (1814) was much touted in Peacock's own circle and that of the Godwins, who published it. But it is a turgid, pedantic exercise, ridiculously encumbered with footnotes

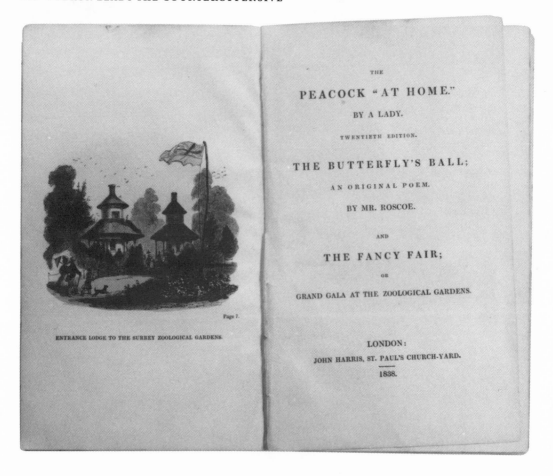

ENTRANCE LODGE TO THE SURREY ZOOLOGICAL GARDENS.

THE
PEACOCK "AT HOME."
BY A LADY.
TWENTIETH EDITION.

THE BUTTERFLY'S BALL;
AN ORIGINAL POEM.
BY MR. ROSCOE.

AND

THE FANCY FAIR;
OR
GRAND GALA AT THE ZOOLOGICAL GARDENS.

LONDON:
JOHN HARRIS, ST. PAUL'S CHURCH-YARD.
1838.

to explicate nearly every line. Far more simple and pleasing is Harris's *Paths of Learning Strewed with Flowers; or, English Grammar Illustrated* (1820), which may have been influenced by Elizabeth S. Graham's *Voyage to Locuta* (Hatchard, 1818). Both are amusing and visually delightful.

Quite different in tone is Harris's *Infant's Grammar; or, A Pic-Nic Party of the Parts of Speech* (1822), a more vigorously comic mock epic influenced by the many imitations of William Roscoe's *Butterfly's Ball* (1806). It opens:

> One day, I am told, and, as it was cold,
> I suppose it occur'd in cold weather.
> The NINE PARTS OF SPEECH, having no one to teach,
> resolv'd on a PIC-NIC together.
>
> The ARTICLE mov'd, and the PRONOUN approv'd
> That the NOUN should preside at the feast;

132. Frontispiece: Surrey
Zoological Gardens.
[Catherine Ann Dorset],
The Peacock "At Home,"
1838.

132 a. *The Lobster's Voyage
to the Brazils,* 1808.

132 b. [??] "The Eagle
Rock—Surrey Gardens."
*The Fancy Fair; or, Grand
Gala at the Zoological
Garden,* 1838.

Till a *Magpie*, at length, the banquet announcing,
Gave the signal, long wish'd for, of clamoring and pouncing :
At the well-furnish'd board all were eager to perch,
But the little Miss *Creepers* were left in the lurch.

Description must fail, and the pen is unable
To recount all the luxuries that cover'd the table.
Each delicate viand that taste could denote,
Wasps *à la sauce piquante*, and Flies *en compôte ;*

Worms and Frogs *en friture,* for the web-footed Fowl,
And a barbecued Mouse was prepared for the Owl ;
Nuts, grains, fruit, and fish, to regale every palate,
And groundsel and chickweed served up in a salad.
The *Razor-bill* * carved for the famishing group,
And the *Spoon-bill* † obligingly ladled the soup ;

* *Razor-bill.* A migratory sea-bird which visits the northern shores in spring, and leaves them in winter : they lay a single egg on the ledges of the rocks without any nest, and on which it is said to be fixed with a cement.

† *Spoon-bill.* So called from the construction of the bill, which is flat

But the ADJECTIVE said, though the Noun might be head,
    The VERB should be none of the least.

And on it goes to the arrangements, the dressing up, the banqueting, and the dancing that are cleverly worked into an exposition of the rules of grammar.

Works like this competed with the duller improving and information books that descendants of the first reformers continued to publish with dreary regularity. But the old order had been restrained; and the new had made a lasting place for itself.

FLIGHTS OF BUTTERFLIES—THE PAPILLONNADES

It is odd that pre-Romantic elements should have found their way into nursery and youthful libraries before neoclassical ones; but humanity often confutes mere chronology. The spiritual descendants of Alexander Pope burst into the world of children's books in late 1806 led by William

133. "The banquet is announced." [Dorset], *The Peacock "At Home,"* 1838.

134. "The card party." [Dorset], *The Peacock "At Home,"* 1807.

Roscoe's *Butterfly's Ball and the Grasshopper's Feast*, published in book form the next year by John Harris. Before the year was out, Harris had another writer producing imitation "butterflies"—or papillonnades, as I have dubbed them after the French "Robinsonnades." Within the next year, four others had joined her in the profitable and extremely delightful enterprise of loosing more papillonnades on England's young. So polished were some that a reviewer complained they were too good for children.[14] He was wrong, to be sure, but they were—many of them—very good indeed. In fact, an unusual phenomenon occurred in them: Whereas the first of a type is often finest and its imitations wanting, in these the imitations, especially Catherine Ann Dorset's, outshone the original.

Roscoe's cheery little poem with designs by William Mulready opens with the frontispiece showing a boy inviting a group of children to go out the open door:

Come take up your Hats, and away let us haste.
To the Butterfly's Ball, and the Grasshopper's feast.
The Trumpeter Gad-Fly has summon'd the crew,
And the Revels are now only waiting for you.
On the smooth-shaven Grass by the side of a Wood,
Beneath a broad oak which for ages has stood,

135. "First came the Lion."
W. B., *The Elephant's Ball
and the Grand Fete
Champetre*, 1807.

136. "The Musical Band."
W. B., *The Elephant's Ball*,
1807.

> See the children of earth, and the tenants of Air,
> To an evening's amusement together repair.[15]

These are assuredly not Pope's heroic couplets, yet the happy lilt of the
tetrameter dactyls does contain a regularity that brings order to this diverting account of little creatures' and little folks' versions of adult galas.
Indeed, it is in this adapting of the mock epic in its gentlest form that
Roscoe brought lighter neoclassical strains to nursery fare.

Catherine Dorset excelled in so precisely gauging this note in the
poem and in recreating the delicate aura of the mock epic at its gentlest
and airiest. Several of her nursery miniatures rival *The Rape of the Lock*
in their delicious yoking of the high and the low, the regal and the ridiculous, the sublime and the showy—all held together with the merest
whiff of lighthearted mockery at the very human foibles her characters
display. *The Peacock "At Home"* (1807) flew from her pen:

> The Butterfly's Ball, and the Grasshopper's Feasts,
> Excited the spleen of the Birds and the Beasts:
> For their mirth and good cheer—of the Bee was the theme,
> And the Gnat blew his horn, as he danc'd in the beam. . . .
> The Quadrupeds listen'd with sullen displeasure.

But the Tenants of Air were enrag'd beyond measure.
The PEACOCK display'd his bright plumes to the Sun,
And, addressing his Mates, thus indignant begun:
"Shall we, like domestic, inelegant Fowls,
"As unpolish'd as Geese, and as stupid as Owls,
"Sit tamely at home, hum drum, with our Spouses,
"While Crickets, and Butterflies, open their houses? . . .
"If I suffer such insolent airs to prevail,
"May Juno pluck out all the eyes in my tail;
"So a Fete I will give, and my taste I'll display,
"And send out my cards for Saint Valentine's Day."

Dorset's shrewd but tolerant eye for social pretensions and absurdities supplied the richly detailed vignettes of dinners, dances, card games, and the ever delectable joys of neighbor watching and fashion gauging that animate the pages of this and her other similarly successful papillonnades. In 1807 *The Lion's Masquerade: A Sequel to The Peacock "At Home"* followed. Like the creatures left out of the butterfly's grand fete, the lion takes umbrage and "vainly sought rest, / For something like envy had poison'd his breast." Naturally, the solution is to give his own ton masquerade, to which the learned Pig, a Cat in pattens, a great Hog in armor and a large wig (borrowed from Carnan's *The Lilliputian Mas-*

At the banquet the guests in amazement were lost,
And the *King of Siam* took the right of his host.
Beside him, a vase fill'd with water was plac'd,
Of chrystal, and gold, very skilfully chac'd:
With flowers of the orange the handles were bound,
And Otto of Roses was sprinkled around—
Before him were cocoa nuts, figs, wheat and rice,
The wood of acacia, banana and spice:
With arrack, and every delicate wine,
That each nation can press from the clustering vine.

137. "The guests in amazement were lost." Catherine Ann Dorset, *The Lion's Masquerade: A Sequel to the Peacock "At Home,"* 1807.

138. [Catherine Ann Dorset], *Think Before You Speak; or, The Three Wishes,* 1810.

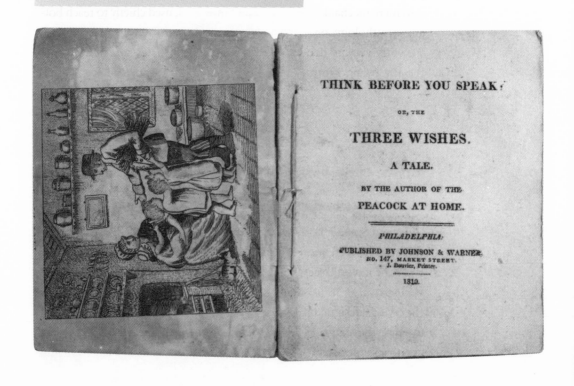

querade . . . [for] Lilliputians and Tommythumbians, 1783), the King of Siam, and many other worthies repair.

To discuss even the Harris papillonnades that appeared between 1807 and 1810 would consume more pages than can be spared. Suffice it to note that he had five known writers hot at it: Dorset was quickly joined by "W. B." with *The Elephant's Ball and Grand Fete Champetre* (1807); then A.D.M., *The Butterfly's Birthday, St. Valentine's Day, and the Whale's Ball*; Mrs. Mary Cockle, *The Fishes Grand Gala*; Dorset(?), *The Lioness's Rout*; Theresa Tyro, *The Feast of the Fishes; or, The Whale's Invitation to His Brethren of the Deep*; *The Lioness's Ball*; *Flora's Gala*, with copper plates after Maria Flaxman's designs; *The Lobster's Voyage to the Brazils*; *The Horse's Levee; or, The Court of Pegasus*; and two sharper satires, *Grand-Mamma; or, The Christning [sic] 'Not At Home'* and *The Rose's Breakfast*—all in 1808; in 1809, Roscoe, *The Butterfly's Birthday. By the Author of the Butterfly's Ball* and, *The Mermaid "At Home!"*; Dorset, *The Peacock and Parrot on Their Search for the Author of the Peacock at Home* (1816) and *The Fancy Fair; or, Grand Gala at the Zoological Gardens* (1838).

There were certainly flocks of papillonnades uncocooned by other publishers loath to miss out on the craze. Predictably, some dwindled into mere mechanical applications of the form, used chiefly to teach botany, ornithology, or the like. But surprisingly, many were imbued with the witty vivacity that stamped the earliest. The dates are uncertain and the list by no means complete, but some that appeared from other presses are *The Water-King's Levee; or, The Gala of the Lake* (W. Lindsell, 1807?); *The Eagle's Masque. By "Tom Tit"* (J. Mawman, *c.* 1807; 2d ed., 1808); *The Jack Daw "At Home"* (A. K. Newman, *c.* 1810); *The Peahen at Home; or, The Swan's Bridal Day* (J. L. Marks, *c.* 1840); the exceedingly beautiful *Chrysallina; or, The Butterfly's Gala, addressed to two little girls,* by R. C. Barton (T. Boys, 1820); and, late and sadly degenerated into prose, if with good illustrations, *The Dog's Dinner Party* (George Routledge and Sons, *c.* 1870) and *The Cat's Tea Party* (Routledge, *c.* 1871). Of course there were more, for they were deservedly loved, though not by everyone it would seem: In 1808 J.L.B. wrote for John Wallis *The Butterfly's Funeral, a sequel to the Butterfly's Ball & Grasshopper's Feast,* with engravings designed by Maria Flaxman. But these poetic exequies failed to stem the flight: Reports of the death of the brave papillon were greatly exaggerated.

"WHEN THE GREEN WOODS LAUGH WITH THE VOICE OF JOY"

Truly fine poetry was late coming to the nursery and even to the library of older children. For a long time, it seemed as though Anna Barbauld had been correct in her judgment that poetry could not stoop to infancy, without ceasing to be. Of course much comic poetry was written, as we have seen, some very fine indeed. And also there was a spate of moral and cautionary rhymes and jingles put out by poetasters of the More-Trimmer school. Though these were not utterly without appeal, their obsessive moralizing and grim devotion to regular meter and rhyme did snuff out imagination, as in Mary Belson Elliott's *Simple Truths, in Verse* (1812) and Elizabeth Turner's *Daisy; or, Cautionary Stories in Verse* (1807), *Cowslip; or, More . . . in Verse* (1809), and *The Crocus* (1816). Such books were cranked out through the 1840s and after.

Charles and Mary Lamb's *Poetry for Children* (1809) has bits in some poems—though rare, even in this book—that soar above the drivel around them, like "Cleanliness":

> Come my little Robert near—
> Fie! what filthy hands are here—
> Who, that e'er could understand
> The rare structure of a hand,
> With its branching fingers fine,
> Work itself of hands divine,
> Strong, yet delicately knit,
> For Ten thousand uses fit. . . . [16]

An early serious attempt by an established poet to bend to the child's world was Christopher Smart's *Hymns, for the Amusement of Children* (1771); it was promptly pirated in two issues of a Dublin edition in 1772 (London: Carnan, 2d ed., 1773; 3rd, 1775; 4th, 1786; Philadelphia: W. Spottswood, 1791).[17] The book was very popular. It is a religious work, but the poems depict a gentle and intimate world, like Anna Barbauld's, and they have touches of beauty and a fragile gaiety, as in "Mirth" (Hymn XXV):

> If you are merry, sing away,
>   And touch the organs sweet. . . .
>
> Ye little prattlers, that repair
>   For cowslips in the mead,
> Of those exulting colts beware.

46   HYMNS FOR CHILDREN.

XXXIII. — For SATURDAY.

NOW's the time for mirth and play,
    Saturday's an holiday ?
Praise to heav'n unceasing yield,
I've found a lark's nest in the field.

A lark's nest, then your play-mate begs
You'd spare herself and speckled eggs ;
Soon she shall ascend and sing
Your praises to the Eternal King.

HYMNS FOR CHILDREN.   47

XXXIV. — For SUNDAY.

ARISE—arise—the Lord arose
    On this triumphant day :
Your souls to piety dispose,
    Arise to bless and pray.

Ev'n rustics do adorn them now,
    Themselves in roses dress ;
And to the clergyman they bow,
    When he begins to bless.

Their best apparel now arrays
    The little girls and boys ;
And better than the preacher prays
    For heaven's eternal joys.

139. Hymns for Saturday
and Sunday. [Christopher
Smart], *Hymns, for the
Amusement of Children*, [c.
1772].

But blythe security is there
    Where skipping lambkins feed.

With white and crimson laughs the sky,
    With birds the hedge-rows ring;
To give the praise to God most High,
    And all the sulky fiends defy,
        Is a most joyful thing.[18]

The second important poet to write poetry accessible to, if not precisely for, children was William Blake. It is not certain how much of his work was known, or when. Assuredly, it was not widely read; his first book, *Poetical Sketches* (1783), is extant only in printer's proofs, so far as is known. Moreover, his even more important *Songs of Innocence* (1789) and *Songs of Innocence & Experience* (1794) were engraved and colored by Blake and later by his wife, Catherine, like most of his work.

THE

COURT OF OBERON

OR

TEMPLE OF THE FAIRIES

Published Aug 20 1823 by Harris & Son,
Corner of St Pauls.

140. Title page. *The Court of Oberon; or, Temple of the Fairies,* 1823.

141. Autograph manuscript version. [Marie Le Prince de Beaumont], *Beauty and the Beast,* translated by Adelaide Doyle and illustrated by Richard Doyle, 1842.

Yet he was not altogether unknown. In 1806 Benjamin Heath Malkin issued *A Father's Memoirs of his Child* in which are printed several important poems that the *boy* knew from unspecified sources: "How Sweet I Roamed," and "I Love the Jocund Dance," from *Poetical Sketches*; and "The Tiger" [*sic*], "The Divine Image," "Holy Thursday," and the incomparable "Laughing Song" from *Innocence & Experience*:

When the green woods laugh with the voice of joy
And the dimpling stream runs laughing by,
When air does laugh with our merry wit,
And the green hill laughs with the noise of it,

When the meadows laugh with the lively green,
And the grasshopper laughs in this merry scene,
When Mary and Susan and Emily,
With their sweet round mouths, sing Ha, ha, he![19]

Malkin had seen Blake's prophetic books, of which he said "his personifications are bold, his thoughts original, and his style of writing altogether epic in its structure." More acumen had Malkin than many who merely called Blake mad.[20] Coleridge got hold of a copy of *Songs of Innocence & Experience* late—1818—but also thought him a "man of genius."[21]

One can only speculate whether Ann and Jane Taylor, from a family of engravers, Blake's craft, saw some of his poems before writing *Original Poems, for Infant Minds* (1804), Pt. II (1805). They were among the earliest children's authors to offer Blake to the young. In the revised 1818 edition of *City Scenes; or, A Peep into London for Children* (1801), Ann and Jane include "Holy Thursday" in their chapter on "Charity Children." Influenced by Blake or not, they were talented and their poetry mixed the homely, the humorous, even the grimly religious, but occasionally as well true poetry, as in "Autumn":

The sun is far risen above the old trees
    His beams on the silver dew play;
The gossamer tenderly waves in the breeze.
    And the mists are fast rolling away.[22]

Even a hasty scan of their little books, including *Rhymes for the Nursery* (1806), yields several such fragile gems.

With the best of the Taylors' art, Oberon, King of Fancy, may be said

142. "Some say this Monster was a witch." Victor Hugo, *Hans of Iceland,* illustrated by George Cruikshank, 1825.

to have achieved his final triumph: To the joys of fanciful and magical tales, comic poems, funny lessons, and delicious, sheer nonsense were now added the first fruits of golden poesy.

THE COURT OF OBERON

In 1823 John Harris published *The Court of Oberon; or, Temple of the Fairies*, with tales of Mother Goose (Perrault), Mother Bunch (d'Aulnoy), and assorted popular tales, nicely if conventionally illustrated. The same year C. Baldwin brought out *German Popular Stories. Translated from the Kinder und Haus Marchen. Collected by M. M. Grimm*, 2 vols. (1823–26), illustrated with an appropriately eccentic verve and eerieness by George Cruikshank. His illustrations of 1825 for the first English edition of Victor Hugo's *Hans of Iceland* (Paris, 1823; London: J. Robins) evince the same spirit. These years mark a watershed in children's books, chiefly because of the translations from the

The Giant and the Harp.

page 34.

The Giant's endeavours to regain his Harp.

page 34.

Jack exchanging the Cow for the curious Beans.

page 5.

143. "Jack and the Bean-
Stalk," *Popular Tales of the
Olden Time,* [c. 1830].

144. "Jack and the Bean-
Stalk," *Popular Tales of the
Olden Time,* [c. 1830].

scholarly collections of the Grimms. Thereafter, most parents and adults interested in children's literature accepted without qualms the once dubious fairy tales. Only the exceedingly conservative and religious extremists still rejected them.

The way to this coup had to an extent been prepared by two separate groups. The first was the numerous children's chapbook sellers who had given sanctuary not only to fairy tales but also to popular folk tales and the old English romances. It would be impossible to even list a tenth of the chapbook publications in this area in England, Ireland, and Scotland. A complete list would require many sizable volumes. It is worth noting, however, that though keeping abreast of most new developments in every sort of children's book, chapbooks regularly offered adventures, fairy tales, romances, and Eastern tales and continued to do so after respectable publishers had joined in competitively.

The second group to help prepare the way for new developments included many respectable publishers who, as we have seen, put out single volumes and collections of two or three tales. Significantly, Benjamin Tabart, with help from William and Mary Jane Godwin, also attempted

Jack begg'd to come in with so winning an air,
That she promis'd to hide him & pointed out where;
He'd no sooner crept in than the Door open'd wide,
And in stalk'd the Giant with a very long stride.

145. The Servant-Maid
hides Jack. B.A.T., *The
History of Mother Twaddle,
and the Marvelous Atchievements of Her Son Jack,*
1807.

a far more ambitious scheme. Until recently, however, Tabart's role in
this had not been appreciated. Brian Alderson has added vital details to
the picture: In 1804 Tabart began to issue his *Collection of Popular Stories
for the Nursery; Newly Translated and Revised from the French, Italian and
Old English Writers.* The stories were issued separately in "Lilliputian
Folios," with three colored engravings, sixpence each. He also offered
the set in three parts, to be sold as one or separately. There were about
thirty-five booklets in all. The project continued to 1809 when the
fourth volume appeared, Eastern stories and "Jack and the Beanstalk."
In 1818 Tabart issued his *Popular Fairy Tales,* which contained twenty-six
tales he had collected and edited.[23]

By an amusing coincidence, John Harris published *The History of
Mother Twaddle, and the Marvellous Atchievements [sic] of her Son Jack, by*

B.A.T. [Isabella Jane Towers], a verse form of "Jack and the Beanstalk," in 1807, just before Tabart's collection. In *Mother Twaddle* Jack comes by the remarkable bean after his mother finds sixpence and sends him to the market to buy a goose. Of course, he meets the peddler and returns home with his bean, whereupon he is roundly denounced for his idiocy. But he plants the bean, climbs the stalk, and discovers the giant's castle and untold wealth. With the aid of a servant-maid enslaved by the giant, he decapitates this monster, weds the maid, sends for his mother, and lives happily ever after in luxury. Interestingly, Tabart's version, not Harris's, has prevailed. This has the cow, the hen that lays golden eggs, the fairy harp, the man-eating giant (Fe, Fi, Fo, Fum!), and the breathtaking flight down the stalk, ending with the timely dispatching of the giant with Jack's trusty axe.

Thus was the way prepared for the termination of overt hostilities between the two main factions in children's books—moral utilitarians and those tolerant of fancy. The contest never fully ceased in the century—indeed it continues to this day—but a truce was tacitly declared. A measure of the success of Oberon's counteroffensive was that it was no longer acceptable to sneer at him or the minions of his court.

10. The Right to Laugh, the Right to Dream

When in 1843 Henry Cole, later Sir Henry Cole, set about producing the volumes that were to become "Felix Summerly's Home Treasury of Books, Pictures, Toys, etc., purposed to cultivate the Affections, Fancy, Imagination, and Taste of Children" (1843–47), he outlined his intent against a background of unacceptable literature that he dubbed Peter Parleyism. This, he proclaimed in his prospectus, had stamped the character of "Children's Books published during the last quarter of a century." And, he asserted, it was to counter such narrow, impoverishing effusions that he would retrieve from England's neglected past the best of her imaginative, adventurous, and rightly affecting literature and would present it, for the first time, to her young.[1]

Darton relates, with gestures of fairness to the patently dense Parley and with a restrained and gentlemanly amusement, the saga of the misguided American who thrust himself into the scene, determined to save the Mother Country's young from contamination, with his insipid and rubbishing substitutes for English culture, apparently completely unaware that he was not a member of the exclusive club represented by "the Prince Consort's right-hand man [Cole]"—and was not welcome.[2] It makes a good tale, but it is hardly the whole story: The output of respectable booksellers, elegant chapbook publishers like Belch and Park, and even the scruffier sort like Catnach and Pitts, provided Britain's children with much "English culture" that the cultured had, until this time, chosen to ignore.

If we take Cole or "Felix Summerly" at his word, we would have to conclude that the More-Trimmerites, the Sherwoods, and the Parleys had prevailed unequivocally. Yet we have seen that this was not the case.

146. "The mighty Cornish Giant." "Jack, the Giant-Killer," *Popular Tales of the Olden Time,* [*c.* 1830].

147. Jack kills the Giant and rescues his victims. "Jack, the Giant-Killer," *Popular Tales of the Olden Time,* [*c.* 1830].

FRONTISPIECE.

The mighty Cornish Giant, the first one whom Jack slew.

page 7.

Imaginative books had secured a place with English parents and children of all classes and of most religious and political persuasions: The fairy tales, ballads, medieval romances, transcribed oral and folk tales, long available in despised chapbooks, were now regularly published by respectable booksellers. Indeed, the same reasoning Cole implicitly offers to rout Parleyism was anticipated more wittily and succinctly in the 1802 dedication to Harris's *Oriental Tales,* which helped pave the way for the vital changes described in the last chapter. States Cole, "The many tales sung or said from time immemorial, which appealed to the other and certainly not less important elements of a child's mind, its fancy, imagination, sympathies, affections are almost all gone out of memory, and are scarcely to be obtained."[3] The dedication to *Oriental Tales* undercut both fanatical moralists *and* arid information mongers.

What had happened? Had the crusaders for Church and State via juvenile books really won complete control? They had not, but they had

The Death of the Cornish Giant.

page 8.

Jack releasing the Giants' prisoners.

page 13.

also not been idle. Nor, we may be assured, was Cole being disingenuous. He plainly tells us that he had no fewer than five chapbook versions of "Red Riding-Hood" before him as he began to rewrite the tale.[4] We must thus assume we are confronting the long-standing class prejudice that blinded so many to any value in chapbooks and that allowed only bare tolerance for most of the tribe of tradesmen-publishers.

Cole performed a great service for English children's literature, but it was not the rescue of the heritage of "Merry Old England." His *Home Treasury* (1843–47) contained nursery rhymes, imported fairy tales, medieval romances and ballads, English folk tales, and Bible events—in other words, almost nothing new or unfamiliar to generations of youngsters. However, by openly turning his critical sensibilities on the literature, Cole gave it a new dignity in important circles, and he secured the talents of England's finest artists for the venture and used works of great masters from the past. His double goal, to elevate the language as well as the illustrations, marked a turning point in the field.[5]

Yet Cole's sense that Parleyism had grown in the 1830s was not entirely unfounded. The appearance in the late 1820s and 1830s of works like *Coming of the Messiah* (1827), as well as a rash of reputed miracles, convinced many that the Second Coming and the Millenium Kingdom under Christ's rule were at hand. Formerly a fringe sect of the ignorant and the lower orders, millenarianism infected the middle and even upper classes in the thirties and forties. The religious hysteria touched the learned Thomas Arnold, moving him to declare his conviction that the "day of the Lord," the "termination of one of the great . . . [ages] of the human race," was imminent. This was a phenomenon that in time played itself out, for the obvious reason, though it did leave a residual passion for ghosts, mediums, spiritualism, astrology, and the like, which lingered for many decades.[6] But it was not, as Cole feared, proof of a "Yankee" invasion.

Indeed a tribe of Parleys who were largely native wrote Goodlies and Godlys for a large audience. The 116 books of the real Peter Parley (Samuel Goodrich) sold, over a thirty-year period, an amazing seven million copies, treasured by British readers. As astonishingly, six British pseudo-Parleys issued at least equally as massive an output under his name for profit: Samuel Clark, Edward Lacey, William Martin, George Mogridge, Thomas Tegg, and Charles Tilt.[7]

Tegg and Mogridge were the most prolific and influential, and were

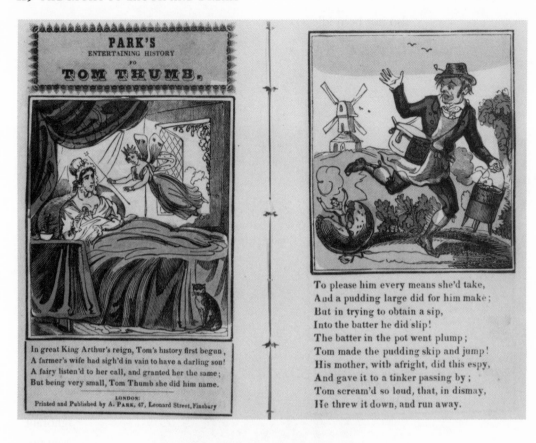

148. "In great King Arthur's reign, Tom's history first begun." *Park's Entertaining History of Tom Thumb,* [*c.* 1830s].

very different. Mogridge wrote under the names of Parley, Old Humphrey, and Ephraim Holding, cranking out sternly pious, spare-the-rod-spoil-the-child tales "for amusement." He wrote for both the Religious Tract Society and Houlston's *Juvenile Tract Series.* Goodrich doubtless deplored the theft of his name, but he would have had no quarrel with what Mogridge used it to purvey. In contrast, Tegg actually obtained Goodrich's permission to publish certain books and agreed to a modest reimbursement on them—which he never made. His Parleys were moral but more secular; and he apparently wrote them himself. A deceptively simple man, Tegg betrays a fanatical concern for the letter of the scripture and for devout display in his autobiography. Yet he cheated Goodrich, off whom he made a fortune, and ran afoul of Thomas Carlyle, whose garbled legal petition for redress failed. And when Goodrich died, he claimed with overweening effrontery, in his twelfth edition of Parley's *Tales about Animals,* that he, Tegg the publisher, had written the entire series and was the original and only Parley.[8]

149. *The New History of Tom Thumb . . . by Margery Meanwell,* 1838.

150. Top: Mrs. Crabtree's discipline. Bottom: A Servant brings an acceptance to the tea party. Catherine Sinclair, *Holiday House,* 1851.

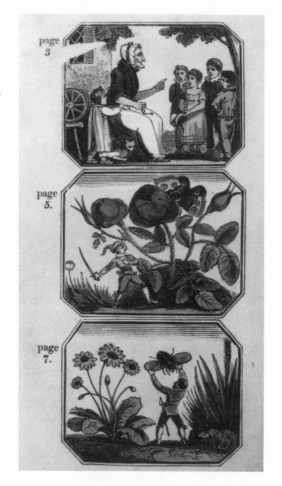

During the 1830s and 1840s and beyond, the efforts of the Parleys and their ilk were reinforced by the constant reissuing of works by Mary Sherwood, Lucy Cameron, and many others, most of whom wrote for some religious tract series and whose works came out in penny and halfpenny chapbooks. The enormous sales, if sometimes exaggerated by the practice of giving away tracts, still reveal the continuance of an audience for pious books, one perhaps for about two decades enlarged by millenarian fears or hopes. However, the "Puritan character" or strain in the English psyche coexisted with other quite different tastes, which probably accounts for such a mixed book market. Cole's fear that the Godlys signaled a turning away from a cosmopolitan spirit back to the narrow Puritanism or evangelicalism of the 1700s was mistaken. The religious element of British taste did not eradicate an appreciation of quite different fare.

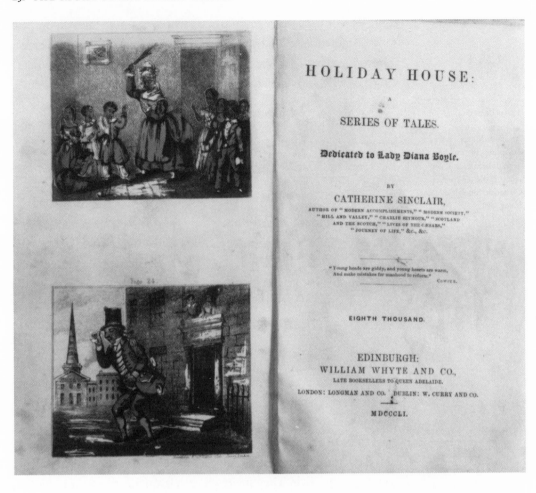

Yet another factor may indeed have made England's social and cultural prospects seem darker to Cole than they were. In the mid-1820s, the nation suffered a severe economic slump and, from the 1820s through the 1840s, violent labor problems, part of her adjustment to the Industrial Revolution. The prevailing climate was troubled, and booksellers were not immune: It was as if the trade went into a period of relative decline—not in terms of output, which remained huge if a bit stale, but in the creative urge that had yielded such amazing variety and excellence between 1803 and 1825, which now seemed to falter. Whatever caused this dearth of quality seems to have begun to abate by the late 1830s.

THE MICROCOSM OF THE "NEW" CHILD'S WORLD

Catherine Sinclair's *Holiday House* (1839) was important for several reasons. First, it was a very amusing book whose coming indicated the possible reanimation of vital creative impulses in children's books. Second, it introduced a sprightliness in its young characters, most notably Laura Graham, who with her brother, Harry, tumbles regularly into mischief. They are heedless and frolicsome "despite" the often brutal and always harsh and strident tactics of their nurse-governess, a daughter of Mrs. Mason-Teachwell-Bell devoted to the pain principle. The very rough-and-ready (with her hands) Mrs. Crabtree does not, however, have things all her own way. And therein lies the third significance of the book.

On the death of their mother, Sir Edward, the children's father, is ordered to Europe for a rest cure, leaving them in the care of their delightful grandmother, Lady Harriet, and their uncle, Major David Graham. This microcosm sets forth most clearly the new feelings about the child's world and puts into perspective for us the relationship among rigid rules and piety embodied in Crabtree, gentle tolerance as seen in Lady Harriet, and whimsy and occasional anarchy represented by her son David.

Harry and Laura get dirty, break vases, set the bed curtains on fire and then perilously hide in a closet in terror and shame; taunt and are nearly trampled by a bull; and accidentally decoy a mean and overbearing host, Lord Rockville, into the same uncomfortable position. Harry runs from the violence-bent Crabtree and locks himself safely in a room; Laura cuts her hair. They invite all their acquaintance to tea, without permission, only to have Crabtree humiliate them by refusing to serve the crowd a morsel more than the children's usual two biscuits and tea. They *are* a trial to their nurse. But as Sinclair makes clear, much of their naughtiness and most of their stubbornness are reactions to Mrs. Crab's hard hand and shrewish tongue. Sinclair contrasts her methods to those of Lady Harriet and Mrs. Darwin, whose introduction into the household cinches the case against the school of cruel knocks. Both women are gentle, calm, and sensible, and their warmth tempers necessary firmness. And both know that lessons gained from experience carry more weight than all the preaching and scolding in Christendom.

Our rejection of Crabtreeism is further ensured, moreover, by the presence of the children's Uncle David, a great wag who loves a laugh and is serenely untroubled by minor naughtinesses—an ideal uncle. He irreverently jokes about Lord Rockville's ruthless disregard for his

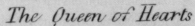

151. The Queen and Her
Pages. [Charles Lamb],
*The King and Queen of
Hearts*, 1806.

152. Gerda in the Palace.
Hans Christian Andersen,
"The Snow Queen," *The
Shoes of Fortune and Other
Tales,* translated by C.
Boner, drawings by Otto
Speckter, 1847.

153. Andersen,
"The Leap-Frog," *The Shoes
of Fortune,* 1847.

guests' comfort, and he advises them to refuse to visit. He delights them
with nonsensical tales about giants, fairies, and the successes of not especially reverent heroes. And he teaches Harry wondrously unedifying
lyrics:

> I wish I were a brewer's horse,
> Five quarters of a year.
> I'd place my head where was my tail,
> And drink up all the beer!

And when he condescends to give solemn advice, it is quite good of its
sort but hardly in the expected vein: "Never crack nuts with your teeth!"
Of all the balancing elements used by Sinclair to give us the proper perspective on the Crabtree school of child rearing, Uncle David is the
most forward looking, for his love of fun and nonsense, his delight in
illogic, and his inability to be dismayed by minor peccadilloes soon
came into their own with Carroll's Alice and Lear's owl and pussycat.

NEW FAIRY TALES

Although there were few entirely new creations in the period up to
about 1845, one form that showed continued growth was fairy tales.
Clearly, they remained a vital oral tradition that flourished in the privacy
of many families of all classes. Robert Southey is credited with writing
"The Three Bears," though he said he had been told the story by an
uncle. It first appeared in print in 1837 in his journal *The Doctor* (vol. 4,
chapter 129, 1834–37). But a handmade book with colored pictures, created in 1831 by Eleanor Mure for the children in her family tells the same
story in verse—a delightful testimony to the abiding and intimate appeal of such lore.[9]

Those devoted to the genre were greatly cheered by translations of
new Danish fairy tales by Hans Christian Andersen. The first of these
was done by Mary Howitt, who with her husband, William, produced
many gently moral books for the young.[10] Her *Wonderful Stories for
Children* (Chapman and Hall, 1846) was quickly followed by Charles
Boner's *Danish Story Book* (J. Cundall, 1846). Boner also translated *The
Shoes of Fortune, and Other Tales,* which includes "The Fir Tree," "The
Leap-Frog," "The Snow Queen," in seven parts, and "The Red Shoes,"
(Chapman and Hall, 1847); and his *Little Tuk and Other Tales by Hans
Christian Andersen* contains among others "The Darning Needle," "The

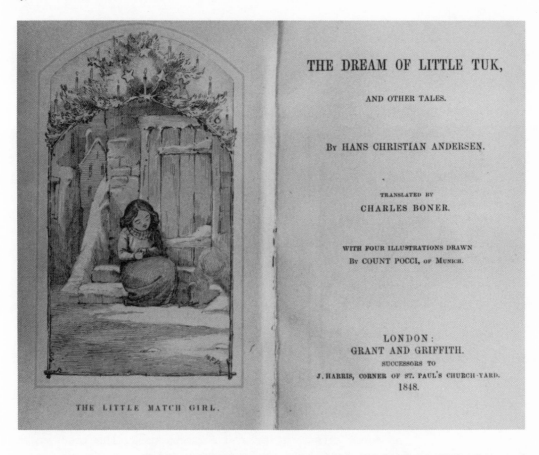

THE LITTLE MATCH GIRL.

THE DREAM OF LITTLE TUK,

AND OTHER TALES.

By HANS CHRISTIAN ANDERSEN.

TRANSLATED BY
CHARLES BONER.

WITH FOUR ILLUSTRATIONS DRAWN
By COUNT POCCI, OF MUNICH.

LONDON:
GRANT AND GRIFFITH.
SUCCESSORS TO
J. HARRIS, CORNER OF ST. PAUL'S CHURCH-YARD.
1848.

154. "The Little Match Girl." Hans Christian Andersen, *The Dream of Little Tuk, and Other Tales*, 1st English ed., 1848.

Shadow," "The Street-Lamp," and "The Little Match Girl" (Grant and Griffith, successors to John Harris, 1848). Thwaite also mentions another early translator, Caroline Peachey, whose *Danish Fairy Tales and Legends* (Pickering, 1846) contained "The Ugly Duckling" and "The Little Mermaid."[11] At long last the vestiges of doubt and suspicion at the effect of faery on the child's imagination were put to rout.

DEVELOPMENTS IN STORIES FOR OLDER BOYS AND FOR GIRLS

As we have seen, the distinction between books fit solely for girls or for boys, and the differentiation between ages or phases of development in childhood, took root with the labors of the reform writers, who were participating in a larger movement to redefine femininity and its roles and uses for society (see chapter 6), as well as to redefine the degree and nature of learning deemed proper for the various classes. A double standard was erected that allowed boys relative freedom but that made it a socioreligious crime for respectable females, ladies, to behave in ways

155. China: 25, The Great Wall. 26, Street Scene. 27, Gathering Tea Plants. The Rev. Isaac Taylor, *Scenes in Asia,* 1821.

156. Hindoostan: 49, The Four Casts. 50, The Tiger's Visit. 51, The Faquirs. 52, "Pagan" Worship of "Jaggernaut." 53, A Widow Burning Herself. 54, A Christian Missionary Preaching. Taylor, *Scenes in Asia,* 1821.

previously deemed natural and unexceptionable. This code was so deeply implanted that some of its prohibitions and subtle judgments about the nature of females linger to this day. Further age distinctions in reading material also crystallized at about this time. With the revolt against the conservative reformers came new material for "juvenile" books, works assuredly not for the nursery set yet not quite for mature adults either. They can perhaps be called books for young people, for "the teens," as a John Marshall 1828 end list states.

Many were adaptations of adult works by authors like Sir Walter Scott, August Kotzebue, Clara Reeve; and perhaps here too belong several by Charles Lamb: *Tales from Shakespear* [sic]. *Designed for the Use of Young Persons,* 2 vols. (1807), *Adventures of Ulysses* (1808)—the issue of "Heathen mythology" for the young was by no means settled[12]—and probably even *Prince Dorus; or, Flattery Put Out of Countenance* (1811), whose grandiloquent rhymelets could hardly have been meant for younger children. Also, many entirely new works of fiction began to appear which offered the young unusual combinations of the romantic

and adventurous with striking realism about human affairs and personal relations.

Before 1835 this new sort of book, though often written mainly for older boys *or* girls, was probably read by both sexes. Over the next half century, intentional gender differences became more firmly established. The more energetic developments in youths' books occurred predictably in books for males, as a number of tributaries poured into their new adventure worlds. But young ladies' books explored new psychological horizons, sedately but nonetheless with courage and great insight.

The vigor of medieval romances, *Crusoe,* the Robinsonnades, and Cook's travels enhanced books for boys. But new elements were also important. Books of information like those written for Harris by the Reverend Isaac Taylor and his son Jefferys (father and brother to the poets Ann and Jane), like *Scenes in Europe* (1818), *Asia* (1819), *Africa* (1820), *America* (1821), and *England* (1822)—just one of many such series—whetted youthful appetites for travel. The more obviously technical books also stimulated excitement, as did *The Ocean . . . Wonders*

and Important Products of the Sea (Harris, 1833), with its surprising engraving of two men in a diving bell and a lone diver walking on the
bottom of the sea.

Such ingredients come together in the books of Frederick Marryat,
captain in the Royal Navy, who took up writing adventures rooted in
his personal experiences. His output was voluminous, and the early
books were for adults: *Frank Mildmay* (1829), *Peter Simple* (1833), and
Jacob Faithful (1834). But the stories often involved harshly realistic rites
of passage from boyhood to young manhood or from the humiliating
burden of being thought a fool or nonentity to the development of a
strong, rich individuality. They were enjoyed by the young. His first
children's work was *Mr. Midshipman Easy* (1836). Like all his books, it is
highly moral but contains little moralizing, and it has touches of brutal
realism. Action demonstrates the right; decent behavior wins in the face
of temptation. Among others he wrote for boys were *The Pacha of Many
Tales* (1836), *The Phantom Ship* (1839), *Poor Jack* (1840), *Masterman Ready*
(1841), and *The Settlers in Canada* (1844).

Of necessity, books for girls were less exotic and adventurous, but
they were not without action or excitement. The romantic interest of
early favorites like *Primrose Prettyface* was recast for historical tales and
adaptations by Scott, Reeve, and others. The interest in the past was

157. Diving Bell. *The Ocean,* 1833.

158. "The Wreck of the Pacific." Frederick Marryat, *Masterman Ready,* 1841–42.

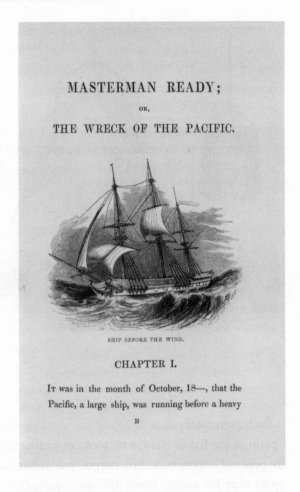

intensified by many competent and interestingly written historical information books printed from the 1820s on. A pioneer in fiction was Barbara Hofland, who wrote books for boys as well as girls. Her *Son of a Genius* (1812) was followed by *Daughter of a Genius* (c. 1810s); she also wrote *The History of an Officer's Widow and her Young Family* (1809), *Barbadoes Girl* (c. 1810), and *Theodore; or, The Crusaders* (c. 1821).

A most influential writer of stories for girls, Charlotte Yonge, began publishing shortly after our period ends. But so important are her contributions that they require brief mention. She also wrote books for young children, like *Countess Kate* (1862) and *The Prince and the Page* (1865), effective stories which, like Sinclair's, create realistic child characters. But her greatest work was in the gray area between young persons' and adult books. *The Heir of Redclyffe* (1853) is the romance that brought her fame. Today it might be called a woman's novel, but her contemporaries saw it as no such thing: Men and women enjoyed it; soldiers at the front in the Crimean are said to have wept over it. Like most of her work it stands on its own, even if it is often recalled today because Jo March cries over it while consuming apples (Louisa May Alcott, *Little Women,* 1868). Yonge followed *Heir* with a long series of competently written romantic adventures. But some scholars think her masterpiece is one about a family's life, *The Daisy Chain* (1856), story of Dr. May—whose wife dies in the opening pages—and his eleven children. The novel probes its many characters subtly and realistically, yielding illuminating insights into the dynamics of rich and complex relationships.[13]

THE RECLAMATION OF DRAMA IN BOOKS AND FOR PERFORMANCE

The subject of plays for children was a prickly one during the eighteenth century. The closing of London theaters under Cromwell had been followed by their reopening in 1660 with the introduction of plays influenced, many felt, by French drama's witty ribaldry. Censure by England's many varieties of Puritans quickly followed: It was axiomatic that plays imperiled youth, and must be avoided. Throughout the century, this note was repeatedly sounded. But many ignored it, including, predictably, certain aristocrats and gentry, but also many pious middle-class persons, who if they did not condone participation in dramas, did not forbid seeing or reading them. In fact, though there was heavy pressure on all decent souls to eschew plays, the actual role of plays in children's lives varied.

In evangelical circles, though plays and acting were generally frowned on, many made an exception for Hannah More's *Sacred Dramas, chiefly intended for Young Persons on Subjects taken from the Bible, including Moses in the Bull-rushes* (1782). These plays had often been acted, long before their publication, by the students at the school in Park Street, Bristol, operated by More and her four sisters. The religious and conservative extolled their "quality and her bold experiment." Satirists like the noted "Peter Pindar" (Dr. John Wolcot) waxed cynical:

> The Holy Dramas of Miss Hannah More
> Where all the Nine and little Moses snore.[14]

Static and mainly declamatory though they were, *Sacred Dramas,* like More's earlier pastoral drama, *The Search after Happiness* (1773; 9th ed.,

1787), lent a mantle of respectability to dramatic performance. This the Mores reinforced by their practice of marching their charges off to see "proper" plays at Bristol's Theatre Royal. Jonas Hanway recommended *Sacred Dramas* to be read, but *not* performed. Erasmus Darwin—joining in the campaign of the late eighteenth and early nineteenth centuries to turn ladies into angelically feminine "walking ghosts"—opined that the danger in acting was it destroyed "that retiring modesty and blushing embarrassment to which young ladies owe their most powerful external charms." But where More led, many followed. If little Sally Horne, daughter of Dr. George Horne, dean of Canterbury, later bishop of Norwich, could safely attend More's school and without contamination participate in her plays, then who could not?[15]

As liberal forces among the book writers and publishers began to throw off conservative esthetic and social fetters, successful sales signaled decidedly altered public attitudes and led to the general acceptance of these secular innovations. Elizabeth Pinchard published *Dramas for Children: containing The Little Country Visitor . . . The Village Wedding, The Distrest Family and Charles the First* [In prose], "by the Author of *The Blind Child*" (London, 1807). Barbara Hofland wrote *Little Dramas for Young People by Mrs. Hoole* (London: Longman, 1810), and Longman also put out *Juvenile Dramas*, 3 vols. (1808). *New Sacred Dramas*, in imitation of More, appeared in 1820; and *Hodgson's Juvenile Dramas, Abridged and Adapted from the Original Editions*, 6 vols. (Hodgson & Co.) in 1822. A single-volume version with seventeen plays "to be acted in private by young persons," *Hodgson's Juvenile Drama [sic], A Collection of Plays*, followed (c. 1825). *Dramas from the Novels . . . of the Author of Waverly* (vol. 1) was published by Black in 1823. And a mysterious volume is listed in *The English Catalogue of Books, 1801–1836* (London, 1914): *Plays for Children* (London: Baldwin, 1827), by Maria Edgeworth, which I have been unable to trace but which is evidently not her *Comic Dramas* (London: R. Hunter, 1817, 1827) under a different title.[16]

Apart from the sheer numbers of plays to read and act, the subjects are extremely revealing—adaptations of novels, adult plays, and poems, in other words, themes that before "Oberon's Counteroffensive" would have been utterly unacceptable to most families. Hodgson's books are most telling in this regard. Apparently edited and abridged by the printer Orlando Hodgson himself, the books consist of two- or three-act plays, with set and stage directions that include such exotic fare as

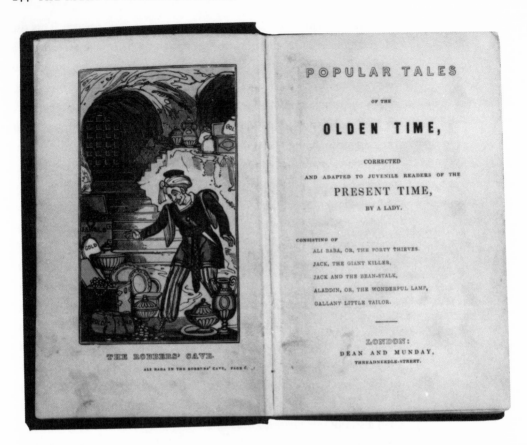

Thalaba, based on Southey's poem about a Muslim tyrant; *Rob Roy
MacGregor; Robinson Crusoe; or, The Bold Buccaniers* [*sic*]; *The Vampire;
or, The Bride of the Isles; Zoroaster; Ali Baba; Blue Beard; or, Female Curiosity* and *Cherry and Fair Star; or, The Children of Cypress,* chapbook
favorites; *Magna Charta; or, The eventful Reign of King John; Ladaiska;
or, The Captive Princess,* and *The Vision of the Sun; or, The Orphan of Peru.*

This reclamation of amateur dramatics for respectable youngsters,
even though in private, indicates a profound shift toward a more liberal,
less grimly and fearfully moral view of the child's life and leisure pursuits. Such books were intended for the older child, but their impact
was very likely to have been heightened by the popularization of toy
theaters, paper cutout books from which a stage, sets, and characters
were constructed for the nursery set. Of course, youngsters had to speak
the simple parts in any playlets they enacted. These toy theaters were
available in a range of prices and must have instilled in young children
rather generally a taste for drama and theatricals.[17]

LOOKING BACK, LOOKING FORWARD

Not surprisingly, plays and dramatic performance in children's books evolved in a manner that is similar to that of older categories in this class of literature—fairy tales and romances and the novel. In other words, drama went through a period of rejection, on moral and social grounds; was then provisionally accepted because limited to biblical or moral subjects; and thereafter gradually gained a degree of freedom both in content and as performance, albeit in the private sphere. This is a fundamental pattern for the field which seems to unfold roughly according to a dynamic stemming from conflicts between various groups seeking to impose their pet utilitarian purposes, be they religious, social, or political, on books produced for the young, and periodically from conflicts between the utilitarians in uneasy alliance against all essentially nonutilitarian writers who tap the sources of imagination, spontaneity, and creativity for sheer human delight. These are paradigmatic operations that are frequently expressed overtly in children's books partly because of the nature of the literature, that is, as a tool or engine constructed to direct and control the development of the child.

Especially in its early stages, English children's literature was rooted in complex social, religious, and political conflict. It was yoked to the service of this or that party, faction, class, dogma, or philosophy and was constantly buffeted in controversies over who should control the child's world and mind. Very little of the early literature was belletristic, in the tradition of adult literature. Consequently, it may at times seem to be dull or childish. Closer examination often reveals a wealth of insight into the child and adult life of the age. To appreciate this important body of mixed literature requires the judicious examination of its contexts, its embeddedness in the rich and enormously intricate tapestry of the nation's social and economic history. This study has attempted to apply this basic rule at each stage.

Chapter 1 describes the social, philosophical, political, and economic conditions that made possible the birth not of English children's literature as such—an event that should be dated at least a century earlier and credited to Puritans—but rather of the trade in children's books. Men like Newbery, Baldwin, Crowder, Collins, and others, in London and a few major provincial centers, scented opportunities that had not existed before. They took advantage of changing conditions created by a new optimism about the improvability of human nature and society and by increasingly radical notions about what we today call upward mobility for even the lowliest, and they launched a new publishing venture. Their success was facilitated by economic factors: For a short period before the disorienting onslaught of the Industrial Revolution, small but sufficient economic gains were made among Britain's lower-middle classes, artisans, and even some working poor, making it possible for some of them to buy one-, two-, or even sixpenny books. Although early entrepreneurs sought and secured to some extent the trade of the more respectable and affluent classes, the sheer bulk of business needed to sustain them, let alone create growth, depended on numbers, and thus on the humbler classes as well as their betters.

One of the essential achievements of the Newberys, Baldwins, Marshalls, and Dartons was to use advertising to create and sustain the volume of sales needed for the expansion of their businesses. They skillfully manipulated rudimentary marketing devices to stimulate their customers' desire for new books on a regular basis. The affluent enjoyed their wares and were schooled to regulate pleasure and purchasing. The humble were taught to see books and learning as necessities, as means to vital ends, to economic and even social betterment. The instrument that instilled and influenced such habits was advertising: Through periodicals and their own juvenile and adult book end lists, through their company "libraries," or bookstores, and through toys and games that accompanied new books (for a small consideration), pioneering children's booksellers publicized their wares and excited in patrons a sense of need for books. Thus, they transformed patrons into consumers and created one of England's early and important consumer groups—children (and parents) with reading and buying habits and with a taste for their kind of books. Without that foundation, no trade in publishing children's books could have thrived, and the field as we know it would not exist today.

Once book publishers had created this new market, they had to feed, as it were, the appetites they had whetted. Although early publishers like Boreman, Cooper, and Newbery produced new books or new versions of old formats, they also found it necessary to publish cheap, illustrated works from the relatively large pool of books that had been available for at least a century. These forerunners of early children's books fall roughly into two groups: those of religious origin and a mixed bag of the essentially nonreligious. The former includes that reservoir of Puritan children's books and Puritan and Anglican primers. The latter comprised chiefly teaching tools, like the school Aesops, some early courtesy books, and a large body of previously communal literature enjoyed by adults and the young of virtually all classes. This included romances and ballads, adventures, fairy tales, and chapbooks, which were both the vehicles for temporarily discredited literature and the source of other types of books (riddles, puzzles, etc.).

Chapter 2 describes major religious sources, especially early Puritan books for children, and uses the socioreligious context to recreate a sense of the world as book writers, parents, and children would have experienced it. This is necessary with a literature so morbid and fixated on death and damnation that it is alien to us. For if we cannot imagine the external conditions and internal imperatives that shaped what early Puritans saw, felt, feared, and hoped for, then we can have no inkling of the sensibilities and motives that created books or of the way these books were experienced by their audience. It is important to understand that this literature was intended for childrens' leisure but in general *not* for pure pleasure. The very notion would have reeked of brimstone to most of the austere souls who sought to occupy their young with readings to assure they knew and practiced precepts likely to stave off damnation and an eternity of suffering. Even if pleasure of a sort might have been gleaned from macabre tales about the deaths and salvation or damnation of tots—often accompanied after the 1720s by lurid pictures—frivolous matters like pleasure and enjoyment were seldom part of writers' or parents' purpose.

Gradually Puritans succumbed to intellectual and material changes in the world. Their books began to reveal an altered spirit, as exemplified in the relatively less somber *Songs* of Dr. Watts and *Visions in Verse* by Nathaniel Cotton, in which death itself is relieved of its sting when a benign Providence, represented by a kindly angel, decrees that faith and rational conduct will assure salvation. Decreased emphasis on death and, even more important, the repudiation of otherworldly disdain (or horror) as the proper attitude to the business of this life eventually made Puritan or evangelical children's books acceptable to numerous Englishmen, whose temper was pious and austere. Shorn of the more extremist spiritual and dogmatic elements, such books gained widespread acceptance. The continued popularity of evangelical children's books in the mainstream of English life late into the nineteenth century depended on a devout and severe Puritan set of mind, common to the English character in the age, especially among the middling and lower orders, but increasingly too among their betters.

The greatest general benefit of Puritan and other religious children's literature to society stemmed from the Protestant idea of individual responsibility for the soul. Human beings might not be able to assure their salvation, said early Puritans, but they were required to try. To do this, they had to be able to read for themselves the documents of salvation: the Bible—and, added Anglicans, the Prayer Book. This, as well as a desire to succor the poor and render them useful, was the rationale behind the charity school movement, and later, behind Sunday Schools and even the schools of industry. To many, like Bernard Mandeville in the early eighteenth century and the politicians who echoed his cruel arguments at its end, this was a worse than foolish luxury: Literacy for the poor and lowly spelled doom for the stability of society and for the cherished privilege of those on top.

The struggles of charity schools to survive the exaggerated political charges and scare tactics their political opponents used in labeling them hotbeds of Jacobite agitation (i.e., favoring Catholicism, the divine right of kings, and the return of the ousted Stuarts to the throne) parallel with sad irony the political smear of Hannah More's too successful Sunday Schools. These taught thousands of poor adults and children and were accused of harboring Methodist propagandists, subverting the established church, and thus the state, in the vicious Blagdon Controversy (1800–1803). The arguments of the powerful to oppose literacy for the lowly were much the same at the start and at the end of the century.

Chapter 3 explores secular literature adapted to or developed for the children's book market. The popular Aesops, emblemaria, and courtesy books were not controversial like fairy tales, romances, and histories from the *Gesta Romanorum,* all of which originally entertained adult or communal audiences. These were relegated to children and servants, semiliterate adults, and were purveyed chiefly in the ill-favored chapbook until its reform starting around 1760.

Three points need emphasis: First, chapbook sales reinforced early efforts in children's trade books to stimulate and fulfill consumers' desire for reading matter and thus build markets. Second, much lore, the bits and pieces of a vast culture, was preserved in romances and histories that additionally fed their audience's thirst for adventure. Finally, this stimulation of imagination fed into the new, real adventures possible in the age, represented in dreams that individual effort, learning, and the acquisition of polite conduct could make modern Whittingtons (like Sir John Barnard, mayor of the city of London) and modern Cinderellas or Primrose Prettyfaces, (servant maids and other nobodies who became duchesses in the twinkling of an eye).[18]

Chapter 4 describes pioneers' efforts to create new types of juvenile books and explains both the success and larger implications of John Newbery's business. His brand of nationalism dovetailed with the message of individual social improvement, implicit in most books, especially the miscellanies. Such ideals were to fall into disrepute by 1790 because identified with Jacobin notions. They had been in conflict with the establishment and conservative social doctrine since at least as early as 1750, though the respectable and privileged had not then learned to fear them.

Chapter 5 continues the history of the trade years of children's books, before they were appropriated to the service of conservative bourgeois ideals by Trimmer's minions. These were years of feverish output, of steady increase in sales, and of corresponding influence of juvenile trade books. Few publishers maintained John Newbery's lofty if humbly expressed hopes for the individual child and the nation or society generally. That lapse had two important but contradictory consequences. First, it may have delayed somewhat the inevitable open conflict between tradesmen and respectable writers and parents seeking to reform the industry, which erupted around 1785–86. But at the same time, transitional trade books contained sentiments that made the conflict inescapable, in particular romantic hopes for social elevation from the lower orders by marriage. This is doubtless the reason for the otherwise puzzling inclusion by John Marshall of books about "*Love, Gallantry, etc.*" among works of "prejudicial Nonsense (to young Minds)" with the more predictable "*goblins, Witches,* [and] *Fairies.*" The reappearance of the somewhat coarser chapbook figures of 1750 to 1765 or so, like Tom Thumb, who showed up in works in the early 1770s, may have exasperated respectable adults; but books depicting servant girls raised to the estate of duchesses, on the strength of their virtue, learning, and beauty and in spite of their low birth, triggered large social and intimate personal fears.

Chapter 6 describes the early efforts of reformers of English children's books and strives to show Barbauld, the Kilners, and also the more doctrinaire and less prepossessing Ellenor Fenn and Sarah Trimmer as they would have been viewed by contemporaries who agreed with them. Thus the chapter maintains a double critical perspective: The first explains the frame of mind of these writers and their self-selected audience and is given greater emphasis; the second takes into account the implications of their propaganda, particularly as it was felt and understood by those against whose social aspirations it operated. Thus the beauties of Barbauld's work, the strength and cleverness of Trimmer's, the nearly pure delight of some of the Kilners', and the charm and sound sense of procedure of Fenn's are analyzed. But the seeds their writings contained for the second phase of the reformers' campaign are identified for future discussion. Although these include serious efforts to *re*-form the female ideal, imposing crippling and unnatural, or "denatured," distortions on the definition of femininity, the most serious—because it was the most far-reaching—of their propaganda efforts at this time was their success at taming lower-class aspirations, at immuring servants and others in their traditionally inferior position, the elites' solution to Britain's class conflicts.

The so-called Rousseauists' efforts at social improvement through juvenile books, and their likenesses to and differences from the religious reformers, are detailed and explained in chapter 7. The two groups cooperated because their social goals were so similar, though the Rousseauists abjured proselytizing directly for any church or even for Christianity. They stressed the rational nature of human beings, deriving all virtue from it, including the all-important ones of moderation and balance in nature. But they too believed society was naturally hierarchical and endorsed that view in their books. Yet some of them, like some fervent Anglicans, simultaneously supported humanitarian measures for less fortunate groups, the virtuous poor or pious black slaves, for example. Their literary achievements include many individual works, like *Sandford and Merton* and a number of Robinsonnades, and at least one author of significant artistic stature, Maria Edgeworth.

Taking up the thread of the story of the battle for control of the children's book trade by Trimmer, Hannah More, and the reformers, chapter 8 places this Lilliputian war in the context of the larger social conflicts. It shows what the ruling elite and middle-class reformers needed to do to subdue and repatriate the lower orders, and how they did it. The dealings of many of these figures were extremely complicated, however. Often their motives were ambiguous, as were those of More and Trimmer. Ironically, More—the cleverest propagandist the conservative establishment could boast—opposed the heartless repressions and extreme deprivations of the poor urged by fanatics in her own camp. They openly castigated her and her work to aid the lower classes and teach them to read. The task of rebuilding the Church and State's eroded facade in the face of Jacobin assaults and the just discontent of English laborers was aided by writers like Mary Martha Sherwood, Lucy Cameron, Mary Belson Elliott, and even the ostensibly apolitical Ann and Jane Taylor of Ongar. In their sociopolitical goals they succeeded, even creating a spirit of jingoism, ironically, as William Cobbett observed, among the very poor and oppressed—England's "second nation." Temporarily, they dominated much of the children's book trade. But the literary or esthetic part of their victory was short-lived.

Chapter 9 traces the counterassault by exasperated trade publishers and those enlightened persons who gagged at the stultifying products of a largely smug, mirthless, and unimaginative crew. The revolt had been very quietly building, even as the reformers consolidated their victories. The true innovations came in poetry, first with more collections of nursery songs than had been seen since Mary Cooper's years, and then with nonsense poetry, which flowered into truly witty and elegant verse and spilt over delightfully into the nation's first intrinsically entertaining instruction books. The papillonnades, imitations of Roscoe's *Butterfly's Ball,* were the crowning achievement of a troop of poets in the heretofore despised category of children's writers. Added to the canon of children's fare were gothic tales, new fairy tales from Germany and later Denmark and other Scandanavian countries, and plays of all sorts to be read and performed.

Chapter 10 explores the apparently precarious but long-lasting balance between the moral utilitarians and the apostles of fancy. The pattern that emerges continued to hold throughout the century. Each type had its fanatical adherents; each tried to dominate the field from time to time. But in fact they both held their own, for the moralists and the artists ministered to divergent, possibly inimical, but apparently ineradicable human needs.

THE SHADOW.

160. "The Shadow."
Andersen, *The Dream of
Little Tuk*, 1848.

ON THE HORIZON

The greatest innovations in the remainder of the century lay in technical improvements and illustrations: Kate Greenway, Randolph Caldecott, Beatrix Potter, Arthur Rackham—these would be names to conjure with. The basic patterns in the genres, ancient and modern, further refinements of the age distinction for children and adolescents and of gender-differentiated literature—all these continued to evolve throughout the century. The mass of literature for children until 1910 or so continued to reflect the social, political, and even religious conflicts in the adult world, though the issues differed chiefly because of the new element of imperialist wars of colonization.

Yet what makes the ongoing saga of this field so absorbing, apart from the inherent social drama, is the utter unpredictability of those flashes of genius that seem to have come with dazzling frequency in the Victorian and Edwardian years. Unlike much of the everyday meat and potatoes of children's books, neither the instant of the appearance of these special books nor the form they will take can be foreseen. Yet when they magically burst forth into view, we recognize them at once and with a thrill of delight—*Alice in Wonderland, Goblin Market, The Water-Babies, At the Back of the North Wind, Mopsa the Fairy, Through the Looking-Glass, The Owl and the Pussycat, Treasure Island, King Solomon's Mines, The Golden Age, Peter Rabbit* and *Squirrel Nutkin, Peter Pan, The Wind in the Willows, The Secret Garden,* and so on, it is to be hoped, without ceasing.

Notes

CHAPTER I

1. Sidney Roscoe, *John Newbery and his Successors, 1740–1814: A Bibliography* (Wormsley: Five Owls Press, 1973), introduction; this corrects many errors in Charles Welsh's *A Bookseller of the Last Century* (London, 1885). See also F. J. Harvey Darton, *Children's Books in England,* 3d ed., rev. Brian Alderson (Cambridge: Cambridge University Press, 1982), appendix 2, table 1, on the Newbery firms. I am indebted to Barbara Dunlap for the form this chapter has taken.

2. Robert Mahoney and Betty Rizzo, eds., *Christopher Smart: An Annotated Bibliography, 1743–1983* (New York and London: Garland Publishing, 1984), 159, item 368. This suggests Smart as the probable author; see also chap. 4 n. 15.

3. M. Dorothy George, *England in Transition: Life and Work in the Eighteenth Century* (New York: Penguin, 1953); Arthur Stanley Tuberville, ed., *Johnson's England: An Account of the Life and Manners of his Age,* 2 vols. (Oxford: Clarendon Press, 1933), 1:106–23, 129–32, 150–53, 278–88. See also T. S. Ashton, *Economic History of England: The Eighteenth Century* (New York: Barnes and Noble, 1955) and, for a general survey, J. H. Plumb, *England in the Eighteenth Century,* rev. ed., (New York: Penguin Books, 1963). J. Jean Hecht, *The Domestic Servant Class in Eighteenth-Century England* (London: Routledge and Kegan Paul, 1956).

4. John Locke, *An Essay Concerning Human Understanding,* ed. John W. Yolton (London: J. M. Dent; New York: Dutton, 1961). Book 2, chapters 1, 4, 10, 18, 19. Also *Some Thoughts Concerning Education,* ed. Rev. R. H. Quick (Cambridge: Cambridge University Press, 1902).

5. William Sherlock, *A Discourse Concerning the Happiness of Good Men, And . . . Wicked In The Next World* (1704); as quoted in Samuel F. Pickering, Jr., *John Locke and Children's Books in Eighteenth-Century England* (Knoxville: University of Tennessee Press, 1981), 213.

6. Tuberville, *Johnson's England,* 1:255, 2:265–82; Plumb, England, 77–90. See also T. S. Ashton, *The Industrial Revolution, 1760–1830,* rev. ed. (New York: Oxford University Press, 1964); G. M. Trevelyan, *Illustrated English Social History,* vol. 2 (London: Longmans, Green, 1949–52); Ivy Pinchbeck, *Women Workers and the Industrial Revolution, 1750–1850* (London: G. Routledge and Sons; New York: F. S. Crofts and Co., 1930); Dorothy Marshall, *Industrial England, 1776–1831* (London: Routledge and Kegan Paul, 1973); George, *England in Transition,* 100–116.

7. M. Gladys Jones, *The Charity School Movement: A Study of Eighteenth-Century Puritanism in Action* (Cambridge: Cambridge University Press, 1938), 17–19, 21–26, 41–60. See also Victor Neuburg, *Popular Education in Eighteenth-Century England* (London: Woburn Press, 1971).

8. Jones, *Charity School,* 17, 24, 26.

9. Neuburg, *Popular Education,* 25–55; Rosamond Bayne-Powell, *The English Child in the Eighteenth Century* (London: John Murray, 1939), 56–61.

10. Jones, *Charity School,* 49–52, 204–

6; Plumb, *England,* 84–90; Neuburg, *Popular Education,* 13–14.

11. Neuburg, *Popular Education,* 39–55, 61–63; Paul Sangster, *Pity My Simplicity* (London: Epworth Press, n.d.), 48–49.

12. Sangster, *Pity My Simplicity,* 50–51; Janeway insisted the *Tokens* were true.

13. Darton, *Children's Books,* preface to the first edition and page 1, excludes instructional and devotional works from his definition of bona fide literature, despite the fact that a variety of pleasurably instructive books evolved from some of the early forms.

CHAPTER 2

1. The quotation is from Newbery's *A Little Pretty Pocket-Book* (London: J. Newbery, 1744) which is addressed to Master Tommy and Miss Polly.

2. Maurice Sendak, *Pierre, A Cautionary Tale* (New York: Harper and Row, 1962); Richard Scarry, *Please and Thank You Book* (New York: Random House, 1973).

3. By then called evangelicals, Puritans dominated the field for nearly twenty years, see chapters 6 and 8.

4. David E. Stannard, *The Puritan Way of Death* (New York: Oxford University Press, 1977), 40, 126.

5. Legal sanctions against all who rejected the Church of England, and periodic assaults on groups like the Catholics, as in the Gordon Riots of 1780, demonstrate this.

6. Jones, *Charity School,* 8–9, 10–12.

7. G. E. Harrison, *Son to Susanna* (New York: Penguin, 1944), 47. See also Rebecca L. Harmon, *Susanna: Mother to the Wesleys (1669–1742)* (London: Hodder and Stoughton, 1968).

8. Jones, *Charity School,* 10–11.

9. A. Charles Babenroth, *English Childhood: Wordsworth's Treatment of Childhood in the Light of English Poetry from Prior to Crabbe* (New York: Columbia University Press, 1922), 2–6; Ivy Pinchbeck [and Margaret Hewitt], *Children in English Society: From the Eighteenth Century to the Children's Act of 1948,* 2 vols. (London: Rout-

ledge and Kegan Paul, 1969–73), 1:250–60.

10. Jones, *Charity School,* 14, 41, 46. On nurseries see R. W. Chapman, ed., *Boswell's Life of Johnson* (London: Oxford University Press, 1953), 827, and Tuberville, *Johnson's England,* 1:27, 50.

11. Jones, *Charity School,* 6; Louise F. Field, *The Child and His Book* (London: Wells Gardner, [1892]), 202.

12. J. G. Millingen, M.D., *Curiosities of Medical Experience* (London: R. Bentley, 1839), 172–76, 178–79. See also Daniel Defoe, *A Journal of the Plague Year* (London: E. Nutt, 1722). Written some years after the event (he was only six at the time), Defoe's account is a bit sensationalized and borrows from described scenes of later plagues like that in Marseilles. Compare his account to Samuel Pepys's contemporary entries for 1665–66 in *Memoirs of Samuel Pepys, comprising his Diary from 1659 to 1669, deciphered by the Rev. J. Smith . . . and a Selection of his Private Correspondence, edited by Lord Braybrooke,* 2 vols. (London: Colburn, 1825).

13. Millingen, *Curiosities,* 179. W. K. Ferguson and G. Bruun, *A Survey of European Civilization* (Boston: Houghton Mifflin, 1958), 514–15.

14. Darton, *Children's Books,* 56–59.

15. Gerald Gottlieb, *Early Children's Books and Their Illustration* (New York: Pierpont Morgan Library, 1975), 75–76. Mary F. Thwaite, *From Primer to Pleasure in Reading,* rev. ed. (Boston: Horn Book, 1972), 23.

16. *The Childrens Bible* (London: A. Law, 1759, 1763, 1769), preface.

17. Field details the history of these in *The Child,* chapter 6; Gottlieb, *Early Children's Books,* 63–65.

18. Quoted from Darton, *Children's Books,* 46.

19. Margorie Moon, "Practical Principles and Profitable Amusement" (A Lecture Given to the Friends of the Osborne and Lillian H. Smith Collections at Boys and Girls House, 30 September 1982), 6. Moon's paper brought this work to my attention.

20. Field, *The Child,* 112–16, 119–20.

21. H. B. Wright and M. K. Spears, eds., *The Literary Works of Matthew Prior*, 2 vols. (Oxford: Clarendon Press, 1977), 1:497.

22. Gottlieb, *Early Children's Books*, 22–24.

23. Darton, *Children's Books*, rev. Brian Alderson, 27–28.

24. Quoted from Thwaite, *From Primer to Pleasure*, 24.

25. The deductions in this section, which differ from those of Brian Alderson (see my chap. 3 nn.1, 2), are based on the close examination of these editions and the Latin text on which they were based, *Oculum animumque . . . emblematum* (Amsterdam, 1718), and of numerous eighteenth- and nineteenth-century children's emblem books.

26. A comparison of texts instantly reveals these debts and the possibly unintentional reversals that are commonplace in such borrowings in the periods.

CHAPTER 3

1. The emblemaria, strange composites of science and religion, sparked changes in the other types. Please see above chap. 2 n. 25. I am indebted to Edward Hodnett's analysis of early Aesops in *Aesop in England: The Transmission of the Motifs in Seventeenth-Century Illustrations of Aesop's Fables* (Charlottesville: Published for the Bibliographical Society of the University of Virginia by the University Press of Virginia, 1979). See also Ruth K. MacDonald's fine discussion of Aesops in the early 1700s, *Literature for Children in England and America from 1646 to 1774* (Troy, NY: Whitston Publishing Co., 1982), 81–102.

2. Darton, *Children's Books*, 17–18. Alderson claims more for the influence of the book than seems justified: It was apparently little known and its cuts may be based on continental emblemaria, see n. 1.

3. *Aesop's Fables With His Life: In English, French & Latin. The English by . . . Aphra Behn; . . . Illustrated . . . by Francis Barlow* (London: Printed by William Godbid for Francis Barlow, 1687), Fable LXIX,

"The Nurse and Wolf," 139. Sir Roger L'Estrange, *Fables of Aesop and other Eminent Mythologists: With Morals and Reflexions*. 2d ed. (London: R. Sare, B. Took, . . ., and G. Sawbridge, 1694), Fable CCXIX, "A Nurse and a Wolfe," 199–200.

4. Alderson convincingly argues great influence for this book, Darton, *Children's Books*, 13–16; Thwaite seems less certain, *From Primer to Pleasure*, 8–10.

5. Hodnett, *Aesop in England*, 9–21; on Kirkall's introducing the white-line technique, 13; Darton, *Children's Books*, 21. Reynolds Grignion (d. 1787) also engraved a work of Addison's for Baskerville. Wale (1721?–1786?) was a well-known book illustrator.

6. Field, *The Child*, 100–106; Darton, *Children's Books*, 42–43; Thwaite, *From Primer to Pleasure*, 3, 7.

7. Field, *The Child*, 93–94, 104.

8. Savile's *Gift* is replete with prudent, witty advice; Henry Fielding, *Joseph Andrews and Shamela*, ed. M. C. Battestin (Boston: Houghton Mifflin Company, 1961), 322.

9. *A Token for Children . . . The Schoole of Good Manners* in Alison Lurie and Justin G. Schiller, eds., *Classics of Children's Literature, 1621–1932* (New York: Garland, 1977), vol. II.

10. It is Newbery's stated purpose in *The Lilliputian Magazine*, pref., ii; A Dialogue, 1–7 (London: T. Carnan and F. Newbery, 1772).

11. Gordon Rattray Taylor, *The Angel Makers* (New York: E. P. Dutton, 1974), 4–5 and n. 8, 44, 73–76. On stricter class lines after 1780, see my chapters 4, 6, and 8. The Gordon Riots and other signs of disaffection fueled the respectable and upper classes' fears of the poor. George Rudé, *Wilkes and Liberty* (London: Oxford University Press, 1962); see 3, 4, 10, 14, 162–63, 192–97 on public disorders from the 1760s to June, 1780. M. Dorothy George, *London Life in the XVIIIth Century* (NewYork: Knopf, 1925), 118–20. David Thomson, *England in the Nineteenth Century (1815–1914)* (Baltimore: Penguin Books, 1963), 11–33, 39–43; Plumb, *England*, 153–62.

12. Dorothy Marshall, *Industrial England,* 89–110; George, *London Life in the XVIIIth Century,* 56–213; and Plumb, *England,* 91–97.

13. Jane Austen praised Edgeworth's *Belinda* (1801) in *Northanger Abbey* (1803, pub. 1818) and satirized humorless romances.

14. Quoted from Darton, *Children's Books,* 44.

15. David Daiches, *A Critical History of English Literature,* 2 vols. (New York: Ronald Press, 1960), 1:35–37, 39–40.

16. Daiches, *A Critical History,* 1:71–85.

17. R. S. Crane, "The Vogue of Guy of Warwick," *PMLA,* XXX, 2 (1915), 125 ff.; Daiches, *A Critical History,* 1:199–200; B. A. Brockman, "Robin Hood and the Invention of Children's Literature," *Children's Literature* 10 (1982): 1–17.

18. Sir Thomas Malory, *Morte Darthur* (New York: Appleton-Century-Crofts, 1940), ix–xii; Daiches, *A Critical History,* 1:51–66.

19. A second wave of Eastern influences came with the five later crusades, 1202–70, as Chaucer's allusions to this vast culture in *The Canterbury Tales* (*c.* 1387) suggest.

20. E. R. Curtius, *European Literature and the Latin Middle Ages,* trans. W. R. Trask (New York: Pantheon Books, 1953), 154–55.

21. Gottlieb, *Early Children's Books,* 110–12.

22. Justin G. Schiller, *Realms of Childhood* (New York: Justin G. Schiller, 1983), 35, 38, 39: The confusion of Mme. d'Aulnoy's *Contes des fées* (Amsterdam: Estienne Roger, 1708) with Jean de Mailly's "tales of the fairies" was due to the identical noms de plume, "Par Madame D***."

23. Darton, *Children's Books,* 89. Alderson compares Beaumont's version to an earlier one for adults by Gabrielle Susanne de Villeneuve.

24. Victor E. Neuburg, *Chapbooks: A guide to reference material on English, Scottish and American chapbook literature of the eighteenth and nineteenth centuries,* 2d ed. (London: Woburn Press, 1972), 6–7, 76–81.

25. Neuburg, *Popular Education,* 21–42; M. Gladys Jones, *Hannah More* (New York: Greenwood Press, 1968), 125–51.

26. See Neuburg, *Chapbooks: A guide, Popular Education,* and *Milestones in Children's Literature: The Penny Histories* (New York: Harcourt, Brace and World, 1968).

27. See chapters 4 and 9.

CHAPTER 4

1. This happens fairly frequently and, with other uncertainties about issues from 1740 to *c.* 1788, makes dating chancy. It is not impossible to come upon printings of editions, and even editions, unknown to bibliographers.

2. Roscoe, *Newbery and his Succesors;* Darton, *Children's Books,* app. 2, table 3; Marjorie Moon, *John Harris's Books for Youth, 1801–1843* (Cambridge: Five Owls Press, 1976) and *A Supplement to John Harris's Books for Youth* (Richmond: Five Owls Press, 1983); Sidney Roscoe and R.A. Brimmell, eds., *James Lunsden & Son of Glasgow: Their Juvenile Books and Chapbooks* (Pinner: Private Libraries Association, 1981).

3. Brian Alderson dates important works earlier, like Newbery's *The Valentine's Gift,* 1764 (not 1767) and M. Kilner's *The Adventures of a Pincushion, c.* 1780, (not 1783–84) and *The Memoirs of a Peg-Top, c.* 1780 (not 1784–85). See Darton, *Children's Books,* 127, 163, and chap. 5, n. 14.

4. See Pickering, *Locke and Children's Books,* 216; Percival H. Muir, *English Children's Books from 1600 to 1900* (London: Batsford, 1954), 60–61, 80.

5. Darton, *Children's Books,* 123, 355 n. 3. The comic fictional characters that appear in some subscribers' lists are so named as to make identification instantaneous, and their presence does not compromise the authenticity of the remainder of such lists, which contain information that is often of great value to scholars.

6. W. S. and C. Baring-Gould, *The Annotated Mother Goose* (New York: Meridian, 1962), chap. 2, reproduces the rhymes and many illustrations from *Tommy Thumb.* See also Iona and Peter Opie, eds.,

The Oxford Dictionary of Nursery Rhymes
(Oxford: Oxford University Press, 1951),
an indispensable guide, and Darton, *Children's Books,* 101–3; 353–54 n. 7. Baring-
Gould states that librarians at the Bodleian
and the British Library conjecture that
"the first collected editions of the 'Mother
Goose' rhymes were published as early as
1620, and followed by reprints in 1648,"
and that the "*original* publication of many
of the rhymes may have been in the form
of handbills . . . as early as 1600" from
presses in London, Bath, Bristol, and
Edinburgh (24 n. 1); see also my chap. 9
n. 11.

7. For the illustration, see Pickering,
Locke and Children's Books, 219.

8. Baring-Gould, *Mother Goose,* 34–35 n.
44: "Piss a Bed," with its gross references
to bodily functions, and "Taunymoor,"
with racial and crude sexual slurs, are the
two usually deleted.

9. See *Queen Mab* [d'Aulnoy] (London: J. Dodsley, 1770, 1782); afterwards
d'Aulnoy's tales were attributed to
"Mother Bunch."

10. Beverly E. Schneller, "Mary
Cooper: Eighteenth-Century London
Bookseller" (Ph.D. diss., Catholic University of America, 1987).

11. Darton, *Children's Books,* 135.

12. Thwaite, *From Primer to Pleasure,*
44–45; Darton, *Children's Books,* 56–59.

13. *I saw a Peacock with a fiery Tail;*
 *I saw a Blazing Star, that dropt
down Hail;*

. . . .

 *I saw a Well, full of Men's Tears that
weep;*
 *I saw Men's Eyes, all on a Flame of
Fire;*

. . . .

 I saw the Sun Red, even at midnight;
 I saw the Man, that Saw this dreadful sight.

14. I am indebted to Betty W. Rizzo in
part for data that led me to draw these
conclusions about the development of the
Lilliputian stories from the shorter tales of
the miscellanies, and of novellas from
these longer tales.

15. Mahoney and Rizzo, *Christopher
Smart,* 159. In my estimation, Rizzo proves
Smart's authorship in "The Lilliputian
Magazine," an unpublished paper [*c.* 1976],
with new external evidence from letters
and reviews.

16. Darton, *Children's Books,* 4–5.

17. The interpolated "Letters of Cousin
Sam to Cousin Sue" sternly anatomize the
moral failings of Sam's employers and
their class; the poems (compiled) attack
political folly, dubious mores like the cruel
and hypocritical treatment of unwed
mothers, and the dangers of luxurious indolence that breed emotional unbalance
and even somatic ailments, which are
graphically detailed. This tone differs from
the one of extreme deference of servants to
their always admirable masters and mistresses in the literature after 1785–90; see
chap. 8. On the dangers of vigorous disapproval of the establishment, see the following note and chap. 5, n. 8, and chap. 8.
William Blake, charged with sedition,
luckily proved his innocence, but many
minor printers, publishers, and booksellers
were jailed after 1789 for what to us seems
slender cause. Newbery's nationalistic
views are clothed in homely English, to be
sure; yet they are no less valid than the eloquently expressed ideals of George Eliot in
1879: "Not only the nobleness of a nation
depends upon the presence of this national
consciousness, but also the nobleness of
each individual citizen. Our dignity and
rectitude are proportioned to our sense of
relationship to something great, admirable, pregnant with high possibilities,
worthy of sacrifice, a continual inspiration
to self-repression and discipline." (Gerald
Newman, *The Rise of English Nationalism:
A Cultural History, 1740–1830* [New York:
St. Martin's Press, 1987], 53.) For an entirely different evaluation of Newbery's activities, products, and place in social history (and those of other trade publishers),
please see Geoffrey Summerfield's *Fantasy
and Reason* (Athens: University of Georgia
Press, 1984).

18. George, *England in Transition,* 74–

76, 134–45; Taylor, *The Angel Makers,* 301–2, n. 56; Plumb, *England,* 78–81; and Thompson, *England,* 12–17.

19. A ball and pincushion were sold with *Pocket-Book;* Locke recommended dice (counting) and dabs or dibstones (for girls, to increase dexterity) and polygons, which Newbery sold.

20. "The Virtues of Laughter," *Midwife* 3, no. 3 (4 August 1752): 79–81.

21. Newbery would likely have known of Sir John's book.

22. John Newbery, *The History of Little Goody Two-Shoes* (London: J. Newbery, 1765), 118.

23. Pickering, *Locke and Children's Books,* 75. For a similar response, see Ruth K. MacDonald, *Literature for Children in England and America from 1646 to 1774,* 19. On child rearing, see also Jane Bingham and Grayce Scholt, *Fifteen Centuries of Children's Literature: An Annotated Chronology* (Westport, CT, and London: Greenwood Press, 1980), 92–96.

24. Roscoe, *Newbery and his Successors,* 73–82. I am indebted to Betty Rizzo for the insight on the two directions of Newbery's plans.

25. Ibid., 73–74.

26. Quoted from Pickering, *Locke and Children's Books,* 223.

27. Mahoney and Rizzo, *Christopher Smart,* 159.

28. See Darton for the illustration, *Children's Books,* 131.

CHAPTER 5

1. Roscoe, *Newbery and his Successors,* introduction; Darton, *Children's Books,* 332–33.

2. Darton, *Children's Books,* 122–23, 332.

3. In *A Collection of Pretty Poems for Children Three Feet High,* Carnan and Newbery denied ties to "*F. Newbery, at the Corner of St. Paul's Church-Yard and Ludgate-street*" and castigated his "paltry Compilations," i.

4. Moon, *Harris's Books,* 1.

5. These three are a few of the many Newbery copublishers, identified from her title pages.

6. On Johnson and "The Rev. Mr. Cooper," see Moon, *Harris's Books,* 162, 163, 413; and M.J.P. Weedon, "Richard Johnson and the Successors to J N," *Library,* 5th ser., 5, no. 1 (June 1949): 23–65.

7. See discussion of John Marshall later in this chapter and comments on E. Newbery in chapter 9.

8. The Habeas Corpus Act was suspended in October 1790, and stringent treason and Sedition Acts passed in 1795 and 1799. Blake was charged with sedition on 12 August 1803 and acquitted on 10 January 1804. But his employer, Joseph Johnson, was jailed for nine months for printing a mildly radical book. See David V. Erdman, *Prophet Against Empire* (Garden City, N.Y.: Doubleday, 1969), 301–3, 403–8. See also *The Speeches of the Honourable T. Erskine . . . at the . . . King's Bench* (London: J. S. Jordan, [1797]), which tells of a T. Williams, bookseller, given a three-year term for selling Paine's *Age of Reason* on 24 June 1797. On the plea of the successful prosecutor who thought him more unlucky than disloyal, his sentence was magnanimously reduced to one year in prison, which he served.

9. Neuburg, *Chapbooks: A guide,* 76–87.

10. Justin G. Schiller, *18th Century Children's Books* (New York: J. G. Schiller, n.d.), Catalogue 43, item 159. This rare book dealer's occasional catalogues for early juvenilia are valuable, as are those of many others, like those of Howard Mott Inc. and Daniel Hirch Fine and Rare Books.

11. Please see chap. 3, n. 5.

12. Gottlieb, *Early Children's Books,* 76.

13. *The Microcosm, a periodical work,* by Gregory Griffin of the College of Eton (Windsor: C. Knight, 1787) was written by young Etonians chiefly and ran for forty issues—6 November 1786 to 30 July 1787—but was a special, nonreligious case. See also Thwaite, *From Primer to Pleasure,* 213–17.

14. See Pickering's discussion of Marshall, *Locke and Children's Books,* 176–80; also MacDonald, *Literature for Children*

...*from 1646 to 1774*, 147; her dating of Marshall's *Goody Goosecap* and *Primrose Prettyface* (1770) is earlier than is traditional, but probably correct.

15. *Tom Thumb's Folio; or, A New Penny Play-Thing for Little Giants* (London: T. Carnan, 1786), 13–14, 16, 18.

16. However, numerous trade books on the geography of the expanding world and on its diverse nations and cultures did appear from the 1750s on.

17. *Children's Books Published before 1830, Exhibited at the Malvern Public Library in 1911*, ed. F. C. Morgan (Hereford: F. C. Morgan, 1976). Plate 6, the frontispiece, title page, and cut for chap. 4 of this scarce edition are reproduced.

18. Muir, *English Children's Books*, 83.

19. Neuburg, *Penny Histories*, 31, 42; *Chapbooks: A guide*, 48–49, 54, 58–62.

20. Darton, *Children's Books*, 137–38.

21. Neuburg, *Chapbooks: A guide*, 58 ff.

22. Henry Thornton chose Marshall, known in 1795 for his bona fide firm and with Cluer, Dicey, and Marshall, chapbook dealers: See Jones, *Hannah More*, 141–44; Pickering, *Locke and Children's Books*, 177–78. Also Simpkins and Marshall are listed with Hatchard as printers for the Philanthropic Society (1815) for a line of devotional books.

23. Pickering, *Locke and Children's Books*, 79–80, 176.

24. Quoted from ibid., 176.

25. Jones, *Hannah More*, 143–44.

26. The grievances of masters against their servants are to be found in such journals as these throughout the century, for this was not a new area of conflict. But the tenor of complaints generally seems more harshly censurious toward the end of the century, a result I suspect of the widening gap in sympathy or understanding between classes in the wake of the revolutionary era. For a detailed discussion of the problem, please see Hecht, *The Domestic Servant Class*, chapter 3, and for more on proposed legal and informal measures to control movement between jobs as well as the conduct of servants, including societies for "Good Servants," see pp. 91–96.

CHAPTER 6

1. Sangster, *Pity My Simplicity*, especially chapter 2.

2. Edward V. Lucas, ed., *The Works of Charles and Mary Lamb*, 7 vols. (London: Methuen and Co., 1903–5), 6:474 (Lamb's letter to Coleridge); see also chap. 9 n. 3.

3. Thwaite, *From Primer to Pleasure*, 58–59.

4. See "Aikin and Barbauld" in George Watson, ed., *The New Cambridge Bibliography of English Literature* (Cambridge: Cambridge University Press, 1971), for her works, independent and with her brother, John.

5. Anna Laetitia Barbauld, *Hymns in Prose for Children*, in Lurie and Schiller, eds., *Classics of Children's Literature, 1621–1932*, X, iv; William Wordsworth, *The Complete Works*, ed. A. J. George (New York: Houghton Mifflin, 1932), "Preface to the Lyrical Ballads," 791.

6. Barbauld, *Hymns in Prose*, in Lurie and Schiller, eds., *Classics of Children's Literature*, X, 63–74.

7. Moon, *Harris's Books*, 918–24. See G. E. Bentley, Jr., *Blake Records* (Oxford: Clarendon Press, 1969), 617, on the link between Harris and Blake. It shows that Blake did work for Harris on another project. There is no further proof that I know of than this circumstantial indicator, and that deduced from the designs themselves, that he might have been commissioned for the task, however.

8. Fenn is traditionally credited with devising this system. She did systematize its use for progressive text levels, but the device was not new. I have seen trade use of it, the earliest being a children's chapbook excerpt from Fielding's *The Governess: The Story of The cruel Giant Barbarico, The good Giant Benefico, and the pretty Dwarf Mignon* (Boston: Mein and Fleeming, and London: John Mein, 1768). See the several alphabets appended to the fairy tale.

9. *Female Instructor; or, Young Woman's Companion* (Liverpool: Nuttall, Fisher, and Dixon, 1811, 1812), 216. Many such works appeared. [John Muir], *Female Tui-*

tion: An Address to Mothers (London: J. Murray, 1784, 1786), 61, and *Sacred Meditations and Devotional Hymns* (London: Murry, 1813), 242, attribute society's virtues *and* vices to female conduct, as source or cause and remedy. *Females of the Present Day, Considered as to their Influence on Society, By a Country Lady* (London: Hatchard, 1831) says a lady's job is "insensibly" to soften and uplift brutish male nature. The curious double bind of a requisite powerlessness and ultimate responsibility for the private conduct of others and for the state of public morality generally characterizes most of these works.

10. See Kilner, *Pincushion* (London, *c.* 1780), preface; *Peg-Top* (*c.* 1781), preface; Darton, *Children's Books*, 163, for dates. Mary Ann Kilner's pseudonym, "S. S.," was for Spital Square, where she briefly lived after marrying Dorothy's brother; Dorothy used "M. P.," for her residence at Maryland Point.

11. See Pickering's fine discussion of animal biographies, *Locke and Children's Books*, 19–39, 92–97, and of Locke and evangelical ideals, 3–19.

12. Edward Augustus Kendall's bird books were *The Sparrow* (1798), *The Canary Bird* and *The Crested Wren* (1799), and *The Swallow* (1800), E. Newbery, later J. Harris, publishers.

CHAPTER 7

1. Chapman, *Boswell's Life of Johnson*, 359–60.

2. Jean-Jacques Rousseau, *Émile, ou de l'éducation*, 2 vols. (Paris: Nelson, 1913), 25, my translation. Rousseau's feminine ideal concurred with the conservative trend; please see chapter 6 n. 8. The quotation is from *Female Instructor*, 216.

3. Taylor, *Angel Makers*, 117–25.

4. Walter Harris, *Treatise of the Acute Diseases of Infants* (London: T. Astley, 1742); William Cadogan, *An Essay upon Nursing, by a Physician* (London: J. Roberts, 1748; 13th ed., 1805). Both doctors campaigned fruitlessly to alter nursing and infant feeding practices, which were sometimes barbaric and included forced or

speed feeding. But by the 1790s the fashionable world touted the "new" methods as the "English" method, as a matter of nationalistic pride. See also Pinchbeck and Hewitt, *Children in English Society,* 1:300–302.

5. Laments the narrator (*Felissa; or, . . . a Kitten of Sentiment* [1811], 34–35), "My poor little lady . . . had never learnt to read; for her mama had been advised by . . . one Mr. Rousseau, to suffer her children to remain foolish till . . . eight. This her mamma found so easy and delightful . . . she adopted the plan."

6. Chapman, *Boswell's Life of Johnson,* 359, 405, 1288.

7. Bayne-Powell, *The English Child,* 55–56.

8. Field, *The Child,* 269–70.

9. R. H. Popkin, "The Philosophical Basis of Modern Racism," in *Philosophy and the Civilizing Arts,* ed. C. Walton and J. P. Anton (Athens: Ohio University Press, 1974), 125–65.

10. Darton, *Children's Books,* 148.

11. Ibid., 141–42.

12. Babenroth, *English Childhood,* 98–107, 108–18.

13. Pickering, *Locke and Children's Books,* 35–37.

14. Ibid., 39.

CHAPTER 8

1. Rudé, *Wilkes and Liberty,* 19–36; George, *Industrial England,* 143–62; Plumb, *England in the Eighteenth Century,* 119–22, 123, 133–36. See also Neil Mckendrick, ed., *Historical Perspectives . . . in English Thought and Society* (London: Europa, 1974).

2. Erdman, *Prophet against Empire,* 148–50; Plumb, *England in the Eighteenth Century,* 155–60.

3. Erdman, *Prophet against Empire,* 151–52; Plumb, *England in the Eighteenth Century,* 161.

4. Wesleyanism, for instance, was a strong anti-Jacobin force. See Jones, *Hannah More;* J. H. Whiteley, *Wesley's England: A Survey of Eighteenth-Century Social and Cultural Conditions* (London: Epworth

Press, 1945); and Sangster, *Pity My Simplic-*
ity.

5. Jones, *Hannah More,* 132–33; Neuburg, *Chapbooks: A Guide,* 87.

6. Taylor, *The Angel Makers,* 301–2;
Thomson, *England in the Nineteenth Cen-*
tury, 12–19.

7. Quotation from Neuburg, *Popular*
Education, 71, discussion, 70–73.

8. Jones, *Hannah More,* 172–83.

9. Neuburg, *Popular Education,* 71–72.

10. More, letter to Mrs. Boscowen,
1793, quoted from Jones, *Hannah More,*
143; Trimmer, *The Family Magazine,*
quoted from Pickering, *Locke and Chil-*
dren's Books, 119; Trimmer, *The Guardian of*
Education 1 (1802): 436; More, *Two Wealthy*
Farmers 1 (*c.* 1795): 19–23.

11. More was concerned about radical
political influences and bawdy ones because she was thus able partially to counter
the alleged link between reading and im-
morality in the poor. The Bell and Lancaster education controversy was less concerned with new methods of rote learning
and peer-assisted teaching (monitors) than
with the teaching of conventional, establishmentarian views, i.e., Bell's acceptance of the Church of England and the
existing social hierarchy versus the teaching of nonsectarian ideals of the Quaker
Lancaster, who separated learning from
religious dogma. Many were suspicious of
such a separation, especially for the poor.
England's first "nonpublic" university
without religious affiliation, London University, was founded in 1836, as an examin-
ing body, and in 1898 as a teaching body.

12. Jones, *Hannah More,* 156–58, 161ff.

13. Ibid., 137; Jones describes fully how
More made this venture work.

14. Ibid., 142.

15. Babenroth quotes a stanza of "The
Ploughman's Ditty," *English Childhood,*
157–58. It was in print through the 1850s
and was sung to the tune of a popular ballad. See also Jones, *Hannah More,* 145,
147–49, 201–3.

16. See Pickering, *Locke and Children's*
Books, 199–200; Babenroth, *English Child-*
hood, 118–60.

17. "A veil [should be] thrown over
their faults" (*Guardian of Education* 1
[1802]: 430).

18. Mary Martha Sherwood, *The His-*
tory of the Fairchild Family (London: John
Hatchard, 1818), 1:21–23.

19. Thwaite, *From Primer to Pleasure,*
213–22.

20. M. Nancy Cutt, *Mrs. Sherwood and*
her Books for Children (London: Oxford
University Press, 1974), 6–22. Famous in
this group were *The History of Little Henry*
and his Bearer and *The Ayuh and the Lady.*

21. F.J.H. Darton, *The Life and Times of*
Mrs. Sherwood, 1775–1851 (London: Wells
Gardner, 1910), 47.

22. Darton, *Children's Books,* 221–28;
see also chap. 10, my discussion of Parleyism.

CHAPTER 9

1. See my discussion of his reliability, in
chap. 6.

2. [E.] *Newbery's Catalogue Of Instruc-*
tive And Amusing Publications For Young
Minds (1800) listed fairy and Eastern tales.

3. Lucas, *Charles and Mary Lamb,*
6:474.

4. Sarah Kirby Trimmer, *Guardian of*
Education 1 (1802): 430ff; see also chap. 8
n. 10.

5. Ibid., 1(1802):317.

6. *The Complete Poetical Works of Words-*
worth (Boston: Houghton Mifflin Company, 1932), 792. He attacks "sickly and
stupid German tragedies," of which Kotzebue's were very prominent.

7. *Oriental Tales* (London: John Harris, 1802); the Dedication to Isabella is
quoted from Moon, *Harris's Books,* 155.

8. Sarah Kirby Trimmer, *Essay on Chris-*
tian Education (1812), quoted from Darton,
Children's Books, 160.

9. Trimmer, *Guardian of Education* 4
(1805): 75.

10. Charles Hindley, *Curiosities of Street*
Literture: "Cocks" . . . Broadsides . . . A Va-
riety of "Ballads" . . . Dying Speeches . . .
and Verses. [To which is affixed] An Histori-
cal Introduction on the Catnach Press (London: Reeves and Turner, 1871) and *The Lit-*

erature of the Streets, [*to which is affixed*] *The Full, True, & Particular Account of the Life: Trial, Character, Confession, and Behaviour . . . of Old Jemmy Catnach* (London: Reeves and Turner, 1871?). The latter describes Catnach's enormously popular and profitable "Songs three yards a penny" and half pence broadsides with two ballads (p. 9). The vogue of songs and singing was, as these volumes show with abundant examples of every sort, much a part of the life of the lowly in London.

11. This collection is one of thirty-two put out by Edmund Thomas Warren and known collectively as "the Warren Collection" (reprinted in 7 vols., Wilmington, Del.: Mellifont Press, 1970). I am indebted to Betty Rizzo for this reference. But also rhymes of "Mother Goose" and many such songs added to printed collections during the nineteenth century had probably first appeared in cheap printed handbills from 1600, few of which are extant; see my chap. 4 n. 6.

12. Darton, *Children's Books,* 203–5.

13. Moon, *Harris's Books,* 156–61, reprints the *London Magazine* review.

14. Moon, *Harris's Books,* 217.

15. Roscoe revised the poem several times; this is from the first edition.

16. Lucas, *Charles and Mary Lamb,* 4:363.

17. Mahoney and Rizzo, *Christopher Smart,* 162, 166, 167, 168, 170, 175, 177.

18. *The Collected Poems of Christopher Smart,* ed. Norman Callan, 2 vols. (London: Routledge and Kegan Paul, 1949), 2:999.

19. G. Keynes, ed., *Songs of Innocence & Experience* (1967).

20. J. A. Wittreich, Jr., *Nineteenth-Century Accounts of William Blake* (Gainesville, Fla.: Scholars' Facsimile, 1970), 42.

21. Judith O'Neill, *Critics on Blake* (London: Unwin & Allen; Coral Gables, Fla.: University of Miami Press, 1970), 13–14.

22. Ann and Jane Taylor, *Original Poems* (New York: Garland, 1976), 14.

23. Darton, *Children's Books,* 214–15.

CHAPTER 10

1. Quoted from Darton, *Children's Books,* 233–34.

2. Ibid., 234.

3. Ibid., 233.

4. *The Home Treasury: The Traditional Faëry Tales of Little Red Riding Hood*[,] *Beauty and the Beast & Jack and the Bean Stalk,* "Edited by Felix Summerly [Sir Henry Cole] (London: Joseph Cundall, 1845)" in *Classics of Children's Literature* (New York: Garland, 1977), I, 6.

5. Issued in expensive and cheap editions, Summerly's *Home Treasury* had wide influence in both areas; Darton, *Children's Books,* 234–35.

6. Taylor, *Angel Makers,* 288–91, describes the hysteria that gripped whole communities and touched the upper orders as well.

7. Neuburg, *Penny Histories,* 72–75; Darton, *Children's Books,* 221–26.

8. Neuburg, *Penny Histories,* 75. Also see Henry Curwen, *History of Booksellers, The Old and the New* (London: Chatto and Windus, [*c.* 1873]), 379–98.

9. Manuscript in the Osborne Collection, Toronto Public Library, Toronto, Canada. Another notable contributor to original fairy tales was Horace Walpole, who wrote *Hieroglyphic Tales* (1772; pub., 1785), six tales in a Lilliputian edition of seven copies; see R. W. Ketton-Cremer, *Horace Walpole: A Biography* (New York: Longmans, Green and Co., 1953), 317–18.

10. Well-traveled and liberal Quakers, the Howitts wrote books about varied places, including translations from several tongues.

11. Thwaite, *From Primer to Pleasure,* 109.

12. Older children, especially boys, were allowed free access to the classics, but females and the young were discouraged on the grounds that such works were heathen and morally questionable, likely to endanger "weaker heads."

13. I am indebted to Barbara Dunlap for her insights into Yonge's work and for

information about audience reception.

14. Bayne-Powell, *The English Child*, 120–22.

15. Jones, *Hannah More*, 47–48.

16. Edgeworth's *Plays for Children* is listed in Robert A. Peddie and Q. Waddington, eds., *The English Catalogue of Books, 1801–1836* (London: Publishers' Circular, 1914), p. 178: "18mo 3*s*. 6*d*. Baldwin, June, 1817."

17. Orlando Hodgson, publisher and editor, who apparently specialized in dramas and songbooks as entertainments, also issued *Theatrical Characters* (London: Hodgson, *c*. 1860): "penny plain and twopence colored. A collection of prints [of dramas] with words and directionsn [*sic*]; comprising character portraits, stage fronts, scenes, etc.," to be "cut up and mounted for plays in the toy children's theatres." Today this is a rare work; one copy is in the Harvard Libraries.

18. The fear that social mushrooms might rise by advantageous marriages was not without foundation. Taylor suggests that such marriages were more frequent in the second half of the eighteenth century than at any other time in the age and cites two famous examples: The Earl of Peterborough married a favorite chorus dancer, the beautiful Anastasia Robinson, though he long kept the marriage secret and it is not clear that the countess was accepted; but the actress Elizabeth Farren was evidently everywhere received as the Countess of Derby (*Angel Makers*, 4–5). We may include the notorious Lady Emma Hamilton.

Selected Bibliography

SELECTED PRIMARY SOURCES

The Adventures of Jack the Broom Boy. London: T. & R. Hughes, 1807.

Aikin, Lucy. *Poetry for Children: Consisting of Short Pieces to be Committed to Memory*. London: Richard Phillips, 1801.

———. *Poetry For Children*. 2d ed. London: R. Phillipps, and Sold by B. Tabart, 1803.

The Alphabet of Nations. London: W. Tegg and Company, 1857.

Andersen, Hans Christian. *A Danish Story Book*. Trans. Charles Boner. London: J. Cundall, 1846.

———. *Wonderful Stories for Children*. Trans. Mary Howitt. London: Chapman and Hall, 1846.

———. *Shoes of Fortune and Other Stories*. Trans. C. Boner. London: Chapman and Hall, 1847.

———. *The Dream of Little Tuk, and Other Tales*. Trans. Charles Boner. London: Grant and Griffith, 1848.

Anecdotes and Adventures of Fifteen Gentlemen. London: E. Marshall, [*c.* 1821].

Anecdotes and Adventures of Fifteen Young Ladies. London: E. Marshall, [*c.* 1822].

B., J. L. *The Butterfly's Funeral, a sequel to the Butterfly's Ball & Grasshopper's Feast*. London: J. Wallis, 1808.

B., W. *The Elephant's Ball and Grand Fete Champetre*. London: Harris, 1807.

Bailey, Frederick W. N. *Blue Beard*. [A comic verse version.] London: Wm. S. Orme and Co., [1842].

———. *Drolleries for young England: a series of funny tales in rhyme*. London: Wm. S. Orme and Co., 1844.

Barbauld, Anna Laetitia (Aikin). *Lessons for Children*. Pt. 1, *For Children from Two to Three Years Old*. Pts. 2 and 3, *For Children Three Years Old*. Pt. 4, *For Children Three and Four Years Old*. London: J. Johnson, 1778–79.

———. *Hymns in Prose for Children*. London: J. Johnson, 1781.

Barton, R. C. *Chrysallina; or, The Butterfly's Gala, addressed to two little girls*. London: T. Boys, 1820.

Berquin, Arnaud. *L'Ami des Enfans*. Paris: Pissot and Theophile Barrois, Jan. 1782–Dec. 1783.

———. *L'Ami des Enfans*. 24 pts. in 12 vols. London: P. Elmsley, 1783.

———. *The Children's Friend*. 6 vols. London: T. Cadell and P. Elmsley, 1783–86.

———. *The Children's Friend*. Trans. Mark Anthony Meilan. 24 vols. London: J. Stockdale, 1786.

———. *The Looking-Glass for the Mind; or, Intellectual Mirror*. Trans. The Rev. W. D. Cooper. London: E. Newbery, 1787.

Blake, William. *Songs of Innocence*. London: W. Blake, 1789.

———. *Songs of Innocence & Experience*. London: W. Blake, 1794.

Boreman, Thomas. *A Description of Three Hundred Animals*. London: T. Boreman, 1730.

———. *A Description of a Great Variety of Animals and Vegetables*. London: Boreman, 1736.

———. *The Gigantick History of the Two Famous Giants, and Other Curiosities in Guildhall*. 2 vols. London: Boreman, 1740.

———. *Curiosities of the Tower of London*. 2 vols. London: Boreman, 1741.

———. *The History and Description of the Famous Cathedral of St. Paul's*. 2 vols. London: Boreman, 1741.

———. *The History of Cajanus the Swedish Giant*. London: Boreman, 1742.

———. *The History and Description of Westminster Abbey*. 3 vols. London: Boreman, 1742–43.

Bunyan, John. *The Pilgrim's Progress from this World, to that which is to come*. London: Nath. Ponder, 1678.

———. *The Christian Pilgrim: Containing an Account of . . . His Travels . . . to the New Jerusalem*. 1st American ed. 2 vols. Worcester, Mass.: Isaiah Thomas, 1798.

———. *The Illustrated Polyglot Pilgrim's Progress . . . in French and English*. New York: D. Appleton and Co., 1876.

———. *A Book for Boys and Girls; or, Country Rhimes for Children*. London: N. Ponder, 1686.

———. *Divine Emblems; or, Temporal Things Spiritualized*. [*A Book for Boys and Girls*, expanded and renamed.] London: R. Tookey, 1701.

———. *Divine Emblems*. 3d ed. [Illustrated.] London: [R. Tookey?], 1707.

———. *Divine Emblems*. [Another ed.] London: T. Bennett, [*c.* 1790].

Campe, Joachim Heinrich. *Robinson de Jungere*. Hamburg: Selbsverlag, 1779.

———. *Robinson the Younger*. Hamburg: n.p., 1781.

———. *The New Robinson Crusoe*. London: J. Stockdale, 1788.

Carroll, Lewis [Charles Lutwidge Dodgson]. *Alice's Adventures in Wonderland*. London: Macmillan and Co., [1865].

The Cat's Tea Party. London: Routledge and Sons, [*c.* 1871].

A Choice Collection of Riddles, Charades, Rebuses, &c. By Peter Puzzlewell, Esq. London: Elizabeth Newbery, 1792.

Cockle, Mrs. Mary. *The Fishes Grand Gala*. London: J. Harris, 1808.

———. *The Juvenile Journal; or, Tales of Truth*. London: C. Chapple, 1811.

The Comic Capering Willy Goat. London: G. Martin, [*c.* 1810].

Cooper, Mary. *Tommy Thumb's Pretty Song Book*. London: M. Cooper, 1744.

———. *Tommy Thumb's Song Book*. [Another ed.] Worcester, Mass.: Isaiah Thomas, 1788.

———. *Nancy Cock's Song Book*. London: M. Cooper, 1744.

———. *The Travels of Tom Thumb Over England and Wales*. London: M. Cooper, 1746.

———, ed. *The Court of Queen Mab*. [d'Aulnoy]. London: Cooper, 1752.

Cooper, Thomas. *The Child's New Play-Thing: Being A Spelling Book Intended To make Learning to Read a Diversion and not a Task*. London: T. Cooper, 1742.

The Court of Oberon; or, Temple of the Fairies. London: J. Harris, 1823.

Day, Thomas. *The History of Sandford and Merton*. London: J. Stockdale, Pt. I, 1783; Pt. II, 1786; Pt. III, 1789.

———. *The History of Little Jack*, in *The Children's Miscellany*. London: J. Stockdale, 1787.

———. *The History of Little Jack*. London: J. Stockdale, 1788.

———. *The Grateful Turk; or, the Advantages of Friendship*. Boston: J. White, 1796.

The Dog's Dinner Party. London: George Routledge and Sons, [*c.* 1870].

The Donkey's Party and Feast. [A papillonnade.] London: Dean and Son, [1855].

Dorset, Catherine Ann. *The Peacock "At Home": A Sequel To The Butterfly's Ball*. London: J. Harris, 1807.

———. *The Lion's Masquerade: A Sequel To The Peacock "At Home."* London: J. Harris, 1807.

———. *Think Before You Speak; or, The Three Wishes*. Philadelphia: Johnson and Warner, 1810.

———. *The Peacock and Parrot on Their Search for the Author of the Peacock at Home*. London: Harris, 1816.

———. *The Fancy Fair; or, Grand Gala at the Zoological Gardens*. London: Harris, 1838.

Edgeworth, Maria. *Parent's Assistant*. London: J. Johnson, 1795.

———. *Practical Education*. London: J. Johnson, 1798.

———. *Early Lessons*. London: J. Johnson, 1801.

———. *Moral Tales*. London: J. Johnson, 1801.

———. *Popular Tales*. London: J. Johnson, 1804.

———. *The Barring Out; or, Party Spirit*. 2d American ed. Philadelphia: Johnson and Warner, 1809.

———. *Comic Dramas*. London: R. Hunter, 1817.

———. *Plays for Children*. London: Baldwin, 1827.

Elliott, Mary (Belson). *Grateful Tributes . . . ; Containing . . . "My Father," "My Mother"* [*by Ann Taylor*], *"My Brother," "My Sister," "My Uncle," "My Aunt," "My Nanny," "My Bible," "My Grandfather," "My Grandmother," and "My Childhood"*. London: W. Darton, 1822.

———. *My Brother, My Aunt, My Grandmother, My Grandfather,* bound with Ann Taylor's *My Mother*. [*Title page missing. Illustrations by a single engraver. Hand colored. This volume from the author's collection.*] [*London?: n.p., c. 1815–35*].

The Emperor's Rout; or, The feast of the moths. [A papillonnade.] London: Tilt and Bogue, 1831, 1843.

The Famous Tommy Thumb's Little Story Book; Containing His Life and Surprising Adventures. London: Stanley Crowder; Salisbury: Benjamin Collins, [*c. 1760*].

Fenn, Ellenor. *Cobwebs to Catch Flies; or, Dialogues in Short Sentences, Adapted to Children from the Age of Three to Eight Years*. 2 vols. London: J. Marshall, 1783.

———. *Fables, By Mrs. Teachwell*. London: J. Marshall, 1783.

———. *Fables in Monosyllables by Mrs. Teachwell*. London: J. Marshall, 1783.

———. *School Occurrences*. London: J. Marshall, 1783.

———. *The Fairy Spectator; or, The Invisible Monitor*. London: J. Marshall, 1789.

Fielding, Sarah. *The Governess; or, Little Female Academy*. London: Printed for the Author and Sold by A. Millar, 1749.

———. *The Story of The cruel Giant Barbarico, The good Giant Benefico, and the pretty Dwarf Mignon*. Boston: Mein and Fleeming, and London: John Mein, 1768.

The Frisking, Barking, Lady's Lap-Dog, A Game of Forfeits. Illus. Robert Cruikshank. London: E. Marshall, [*c. 1820*].

The Gaping, Wide-mouthed, Waddling Frog. London: Dean and Munday, E. Marshall, [*c. 1815–20*].

Genlis, Stephanie, Contesse de. *Adèle et Théodore; or, Lettres sur l'éducation*. 3 vols. Paris: Lambert and Baudouin, 1782.

———. *Adelaide and Theodore*. London: Bathurst and Cadell, 1783.

Grand-Mamma; or, The Christning [*sic*] *"Not At Home."* London: John Harris, 1808.

Grandmamma's Nursery Rhymes. London: J. Fairburn, [*c. 1825*].

Grimm, M. M. *German Popular Stories. Translated from the Kinder und Haus Marchen*. 2 vols. London: C. Baldwin, 1823–26.

The History of Prince Lee Boo, a Native of the Pelew Islands. Brought to England by

Captain Wilson. London: E. Newbery, 1789.

The History of Sinbad, the Sailor. Containing An Account of his Seven Surprising Voyages. Glasgow: J. Lumsden and Son, 1819.

The History of Sixteen Wonderful Old Women. London: J. Harris, 1820.

The History of the Celebrated Nanny Goose. London: S. Hood, 1813. [An early version of "The Three Little Pigs" with a fox and geese.]

The History of the Prince Renardo and the Lady Goosiana. London: Fores, 1833. [An elaborate version of "The Three Little Pigs" with a fox and geese.]

Hodgson, Orlando. *Hodgson's Juvenile Dramas, Abridged and Adapted from the Original Editions.* 6 vols. London: Hodgson, 1822.

————. *Hodgson's Juvenile Drama* [*sic*], *A Collection of Plays.* London: Hodgson, [*c.* 1825].

Hofland, Barbara (Wreaks) (Hoole). *The Son of a Genius.* London: Harris, 1812.

————. *The Daughter of a Genius.* London: Harris, 1823.

The Hopping, Prating, Chattering Magpie. Illus. by R. Cruikshank. London: E. Marshall, [*c.* 1820].

The Horse's Levee; or, The Court of Pegasus. London: Harris, 1808.

Hugo, Victor. *Hans of Iceland.* [Illus. Geo. Cruikshank.] London: J. Robins and Co., 1825.

The Infant's Grammar; or, A Pic-Nic Party of the Parts of Speech. [Instructional papillonnade.] London: Harris, 1822.

The Jack Daw "At Home." London: A. K. Newman, [*c.* 1810].

Janeway, James. *A Token for Children; being an exact account of the conversion, holy and exemplary lives, and joyful deaths of several young children.* London: Dorman Newman, 1672.

————. *A Token for Children. The Second Part. Being a further account . . . of several other young children, not published in the first part.* London: D. Newman, 1672.

[Johnson, Richard] The Rev. Mr. Cooper. *The Looking-Glass for the Mind; or, Intellectual Mirror: Being an Elegant Collection of the Most Delightful Little Stories, And Interesting Tales . . . Translated from L'Ami Des Enfans. With Seventy-Four Cuts by I. Bewick.* London: E. Newbery, 1787. 17th ed., J. Harris, 1839.

————. *The Youthful Jester; or, Repository of wit and innocent amusement . . . humorous tales; merry jests, laughable anecdotes, and smart repartees . . . as innocent as it is entertaining.* London: J. Harris, 1804.

The Juvenile Numerator. London: Stevens and Co., 1810.

Kilner, Dorothy [M. P.]. *Little Stories for Little Folks.* London: Marshall, [*c.* 1781].

————. *The Village School; A Collection of Entertaining Histories.* 2 vols. London: Marshall, [*c.* 1783].

———. *The Life and Perambulation of a Mouse*. 2 vols. London: Marshall, [c. 1783].

Kilner, Mary Ann [S. S.]. *The Adventures of a Pincushion*. London: J. Marshall, [c. 1780].

———. *The Memoirs of a Peg-Top*. London: Marshall, [c. 1781].

———. *Jemima Placid; or, The Advantages of Good Nature*. London: Marshall, [c. 1783].

[Lamb, Charles]. *The King and Queen of Hearts*. London: Thomas Hodgkins [William Godwin], 1805.

———. *Adventures of Ulysses*. London: Hodgkins, 1808.

Lamb, Charles and Mary. *Tales from Shakespear* [sic]. *Designed for the Use of Young Persons*. 2 vols. London: [Godwin], 1807.

———. *Poetry for Children*. London: [Godwin], 1809.

Lear, Edward. *Book of Nonsense*. London: Thomas McLean, 1846.

———. *The Owl and the Pussycat*. London: Cundall and Son, 1872.

The Lilliputian Masquerade. Occasioned by the Conclusion of Peace between the Potent Nations, the Lilliputians and Tommythumbians. London: T. Carnan, 1783.

The Lioness's Ball; Being a Companion to the Lion's Masquerade. London: Harris, [1808].

The Lioness's Rout . . . A Sequel to The Butterfly's Ball. London: Tabart and Co.; J. Harris, 1808.

Little Rhymes for Little Folks. London: Harris, 1823.

The Lobster's Voyage to the Brazils. London: Harris, 1808.

M., A. D. *The Butterfly's Birthday, St. Valentine's Day, and the Whale's Ball*. London: John Harris, 1808.

Manager Strutt's Little Theatre. London: J. March, [c. 1840].

Marmaduke Multiply's Merry Method of Making Minor Mathematicians; or, The Multiplication Table. London: Harris, 1816.

Marryat, Frederick. *Frank Mildmay*. London: George Routledge and Sons, [1829].

———. *Peter Simple*. London: G. Routledge and Sons, [1833].

———. *Mr. Midshipman Easy*. London: Routledge and Sons, [1836].

———. *The Children of the New Forest*. 2 vols. London: H. Hurst, 1847.

Marshall, John. *Gaffer Goose's Golden Plaything*. London: Marshall, [c. 1780].

———. *Goody Goosecap*. London: Marshall, [c. 1780].

———. *The House That Jack Built, with some Account of Jack Jingle*. London: Marshall, [c. 1780].

———. *Jacky Dandy's Delight*. London: Marshall, [c. 1780].

———. *Nancy Cock's Pretty Song Book for All Little Misses and Masters*. London: John Marshall, [c. 1780].

———. *The Renowned History of Primrose Prettyface, who by her Sweetness of*

Temper and Love of Learning was raised from being . . . a Poor Cottager to Great Riches and to the Dignity of the Lady of the Manor. London: J. Marshall, 1785.

———. *The Renowned History of Primrose Prettyface.* [Another ed.] London: John Harris, 1802.

———. *The Renowned History of Primrose Prettyface.* [Another ed.] York: T. Wilson and R. Spence, 1804.

Martin, Sarah C. *The Comic Adventures of Old Mother Hubbard and her Dog.* London: J. Harris, 1805.

———. *Old Mother Hubbard and her Dog.* [A chapbook edition.] Designs by Geo. Cruikshank; engravings by Branstone. Banbury: J. G. Rusher, [*c.* 1814].

———. *A Continuation of the Comic Adventures of Old Mother Hubbard and Her Dog.* London: J. Harris, 1805.

———. *A Sequel to the Comic Adventures of Old Mother Hubbard.* London: J. Harris, 1806.

The Mermaid "At Home!" London: Harris, 1809.

Mirth without Mischief. Comtaining [*sic*] *the Twelve Days of Christmas.* London: J. Davenport for C. Sheppard, [*c.* 1780].

More, Hannah. *Village Politics. Addressed To All The Mechanics, Journeymen, And Day Labourers, In Great Britian. By Will Chip, A Country Carpenter.* Bath: Samuel Hazard, 1792.

———, ed. and contrib. *Cheap Repository Tracts.* London: J. Marshall; Bath: Samuel Hazard, 1795–98.

Mother Goose's Melody. Windsor, Vt.: Jesse Cochran, 1814.

Mother Goose's Quarto; or, Melodies Complete. Boston: Munroe and Francis, [*c.* 1825].

Mother Hubbard. London: John Evans, [*c.* 1770–90s].

Newbery, John. *A Little Pretty Pocket-Book.* London: J. Newbery, 1744.

———. [Christopher Smart?] *The Lilliputian Magazine.* London: J. Newbery, 1751–52.

———. *The Important Pocket Book; or, The Valentine's Ledger. For the Use of those who would live happily in this World, and in the Next.* [A moral-financial account book.] London: J. Newbery, [*c.* 1760s].

———. *The Newtonian System of Philosophy* (*The Philosophy of Tops and Balls*). By Tom Telescope, A.M. [O. Goldsmith? C. Smart?] London: J. Newbery, 1761.

———. *The Renowned History of Giles Gingerbread.* London: Newbery, 1764.

———. *The Fairing; or, A Golden Toy.* London: J. Newbery, [*c.* 1765].

———. [Oliver Goldsmith?] *The History of Little Goody Two-Shoes.* London: J. Newbery, 1765.

———. *Mother Goose's Melody; or, Sonnets for the Cradle.* London: J. Newbery, [*c.* 1760].

————. *Mother Goose's Melody.* [Another ed.] Worcester, Mass.: Isaiah Thomas, 1786.

————. *The Twelfth-Day Gift; or, The Grand Exhibition.* London: J. Newbery, [1767].

Nursery Poems. Banbury: J. G. Rusher, [*c.* 1840].

Nursery Rhymes. London: J. Catnach, [*c.* 1830].

Nursery Rhymes for Children. London: J. Fairburn, [c. 1825].

Nursery Rhymes from the Royal Collections. Banbury: J. G. Rusher, [*c.* 1840].

Nursery Songs. London: G. Ross, [*c.* 1812].

Nursery Songs. Banbury: J. G. Rusher, [*c.* 1840].

The Only True Mother Goose Melodies. Boston: Munroe and Francis, [*c.* 1843].

Oriental Tales. The Ruby Heart; or, Constantio and Selima; and The Enchanted Mirror. London: John Harris, 1802. 1st ed., E. Newbery, 1795.

Original Ditties for the Nursery. London: Harris, [*c.* 1805].

Peacock, Lucy. *The Adventures of the Six Princesses of Babylon.* London: T. Bensley and the Author, 1785.

————. *The Life of a Bee. Related by Herself.* London: J. Marshall, [*c.* 1788].

————. *The Visit for a Week . . . Original Tales.* London: Hookham and Carpenter, and for the Author, 1794.

————. *The Little Emigrant, A Tale.* London: R. and L. Peacock, 1802.

————, ed. *The Juvenile Magazine.* 2 vols. London: Marshall and Co., [1788].

The Peahen at Home; or, The Swan's Bridal Day. London: J. L. Marks, [*c.* 1840].

Pigweeney The Wise; or, The History of a Wolf and Three Pigs. Richmond: J. Darnill; London: Simpkin and Marshall, 1830. [Another version of "The Three Little Pigs."]

Polite Academy; or, School of Behaviour for Young Gentlemen and Ladies. Intended as a Foundation for good Manners and polite Address, in Masters and Misses. London: R. Baldwin; Salisbury: B. Collins, [*c.* 1760].

Polite Academy. [Another ed.] London: R. Baldwin; Salisbury: B. Collins, 1771.

Popular Tales of The Olden Time, Corrected and Adapted to Juvenile Readers of the Present Time, By a Lady ["Aladdin," "Ali Baba," "Jack and the Bean-Stalk," "Jack and the Giants," "The Gallant Little Tailor"]. London: Dean and Munday, [*c.* 1830].

Railway Alphabet. London: T. Dean and Son, [1852].

[Raspe, Rudolf Eric.] *Baron Munchausen's Narrative of his marvellous Travels and Campaigns.* [1st English ed.] London: Smith, 1785.

————. *Baron Munchausen's Narrative.* 2d ed. London: Smith, 1786.

————. *Gulliver Ressuscité, ou Les Voyages, Campagnes et Aventures Extraordinaires du Baron Munikhouson.* 2 Parts. Paris: Royez, 1787, 1786 [*sic*].

————. *Gulliver Revived; or, The Vice of Lying Properly Exposed.* London: G. Kearsley, 1789.

————. *The Surprising Adventures of the Renowned Baron Munchausen.* Gainsborough: Henry Mozley, 1812.

————. *The Surprising Adventures of Baron Munchausen.* [A chapbook.] London: For the Booksellers, 1816.

————. *The Travels and Surprising Adventures of Baron Munchausen.* With Five Woodcuts by Geo. Cruikshank. London: William Tegg, 1868.

Richardson, Samuel. *The Paths of Virtue Delineated: Pamela, Clarissa and Sir Charles Grandison.* London: R. Baldwin, 1756.

Ritson, Joseph, ed. *Gammer Gurton's Garland; or, The Nursery Parnassus; A Choice Collection of Pretty Songs and Verses, For All Little Children Who Can Neither Read Nor Run.* London: R. Christopher, 1784.

————. *Gammer Gurton's Garland.* [An enlarged ed.] London: Christopher and Jennett, [c. 1799].

Ritson, Joseph, and Francis Douce [?], eds. *Gammer Gurton's Garland.* [Enlarged ed.: Parts III and IV added.] London: R. Triphook, 1810.

Roscoe, William. *The Butterfly's Ball and the Grasshopper's Feast.* London: J. Harris, 1806.

————. *The Butterfly's Birthday.* London: Harris, 1809.

The Rose's Breakfast. London: J. Harris, 1808.

Rousseau, Jean-Jacques. *Émile; ou, de l'éducation.* 2 vols. Paris: Nelson, 1913.

The Royal Eagle's Feast and Ball. "By Jenny Wren who saw it all." [A papillonnade.] London: n.p., [c. 1810].

[Sharpe, Mrs. R. S.] *Dame Wiggins of Lee and her seven wonderful cats. A humorous tale.* London: A. K. Newman, [1823].

Sherwood, Mary Martha. *The History of the Fairchild Family.* London: John Hatchard, Pt. I, 1818; Pts. II & III, 1847.

Simple Simon. London: Cluer Dicey and Richard Marshall, 1764.

Sinclair, Catherine. *Holiday House.* London: Longman, Orme and Co., 1839.

Smart, Christopher. *Hymns, for the Amusement of Children.* London: Carnan and Newbery, 1771.

Songs for the Nursery; or, Mother Goose's Melodies. Boston: Thomas Fleet, 1719.

Strickland, Agnes. *The Rival Crusoes.* London: Harris, 1826.

Summerly, Felix [Sir Henry Cole]. *The Home Treasury of Books, Pictures, Toys.* London: J. Cundall, 1843–47.

Tabart, Benjamin. *A Collection of Popular Stories for the Nursery; Newly Translated and Revised from the French, Italian and Old English Writers.* Three parts; 35 "Lilliputian Folios." London: B. Tabart, 1804–9.

————, ed. *Songs for the Nursery Collected from the Works of the Most Renowned Poets.* London: Benjamin Tabart and Co., 1805.

————. *Songs for the Nursery.* [An enlarged ed.] London: William Darton, 1818.

————. *Popular Fairy Tales; or, A Lilliputian Library; Containing Twenty-Six*

Choice Pieces. London: B. Tabart, 1818.

Taylor, Ann. *Signor Topsy-Turvy's Wonderful Magic Lantern*. London: B. Tabart, [1810].

Taylor, Ann and Jane. *City Scenes; or, A Peep into London for Children*. London: Darton, 1801.

―――. *City Scenes*. [Revised ed.] London: Darton, Harvey and Darton, 1818.

―――. *Original Poems, for Infant Minds*. London: Darton, Pt. I, 1804; Pt. II, 1805.

―――. *Rhymes for the Nursery*. London: Darton, 1806.

Tom Thumb's Play Book. Boston: A. Barclay, 1771.

The Top Book of All, For Little Masters and Misses. London: S. Crowder; Salisbury: B. Collins, [*c.* 1760].

Trimmer, Sarah Kirby. *A Description Of A Set of Prints Of Scripture History: Contained In A Set of Easy Lessons*. London: Marshall, 1786.

―――. *A Description of a Set of Prints Taken from the New Testament*. 2 vols. London: J. Marshall, 1786.

―――. *Fabulous Histories. Designed For The Instruction Of Children, Respecting Their Treatment of Animals* [later *The History of the Robins*]. London: T. Longman, 1786.

―――. *A Description Of A Set Of Prints Of Ancient History*. 2 vols. London: J. Marshall, 1787.

―――. *A Description of a Set of Prints of Roman History*. 2 vols. London: J. Marshall, 1789.

―――. *A Description of a Set of Prints of English History*. 2 vols. London: J. Marshall, 1792.

―――. *Guardian of Education*. 5 vols. London: Hatchard, 1802–5.

―――. *A New Series of Prints, Accompanied By Easy Lessons: Consisting of Subjects Taken from The New Testament*. 2 vols. [40 plates engraved after William Blake ?] London: J. Harris, 1805.

―――. *A New Series of Prints, Accompanied By Easy Lessons: Being an Improved Edition of the First Set of Scripture Prints, from the Old Testament*. 2 vols., or bound in 1. [24 plates engraved by/after William Blake.] London: J. Harris, 1808.

Walpole, Horace. *Hieroglyphic Tales*. London: Printed for H. Walpole, 1785.

Watts, Isaac. *Divine Songs Attempted in Easy Language for the Use of Children*. London: M. Lawrence, 1715.

―――. *Dr. Watts's Celebrated Cradle Hymn*. London: J. Harris, 1812.

Wollstonecraft, Mary. *Original Stories from Real Life*. Plates by W. Blake. London: J. Johnson, 1788.

―――, trans. *Salzmann's Elements of Morality*. Plates by W. Blake. London: J. Johnson, 1790.

Wyss, Johann David. *The Family Robinson Crusoe*. 2 vols. London: M. J. Godwin and Co., 1814.

———. *The Swiss Family Robinson*. London: Godwin, 1818.

———. *The Swiss Family Robinson*. 6th ed. London: Baldwin, Cradock, and Joy, 1826.

Yonge, Charlotte. *The Heir of Redclyffe*. London: John W. Parker, 1853. 2 vols., Leipzig: B. Tauchnitz, 1853.

———. *The Daisy Chain*. London: J. W. Parker, 1856.

———. *Countess Kate*. London: J. and C. Mozley, 1862.

———, ed. *A Storehouse of Stories*. London and New York: Macmillan and Co., 1870.

———. *A Storehouse of Stories . . . The Second*. London and New York: Macmillan and Co., 1872.

SELECTED SECONDARY SOURCES

Bibliographies, Checklists, and Catalogues

British Museum General Catalogue of Printed Books to 1955. 265 vols. London: Trustees of the British Museum, 1960–67.

Gottlieb, Gerald. *Early Children's Books and their Illustration*. New York: Pierpont Morgan Library, 1975.

Gumachian et Cie. *Les Livres de l'Enfance du XV au XIX Siècle*. 2 vols. Paris: Gumachian, 1930.

Harris, G. Edward. *Contributions towards a Bibliography of the Taylors of Ongar and Stanford Rivers*. London: Crosby Lockwood, 1965.

Haviland, Virginia. *Children's Literature: A Guide to Reference Sources*. Washington: Library of Congress, 1966.

Low, Sampson. *The English Catalogue of Books Published from January 1835 to January 1863*. London: Low and Sampson, 1864.

Mahoney, Robert, and Betty Rizzo, eds. *Christopher Smart: An Annotated Bibliography, 1743–1983*. New York and London: Garland Publishing, 1984.

Moon, Marjorie. *John Harris's Books for Youth, 1801–1843*. Cambridge: Moon, in Association with Five Owls Press, 1976.

———. *Supplement to John Harris's Books for Youth, 1801–1843*. Richmond: Moon, in Association with Five Owls Press, 1983.

Neuburg, Victor. *Chapbooks: A guide to reference material in English, Scottish, and American chapbook literature of the Eighteenth and Nineteenth Centuries*. 2d ed. London: Woburn Press, 1972. 1st ed., 1964.

Peddie, Robert A., and Q. Waddington, eds. *The English Catalogue of Books, 1801–1836*. London: Publishers' Circular, 1914.

Rahn, Suzanne. *Children's Literature: An Annotated Bibliography of the History and Criticism.* New York: Garland, 1980.

Roscoe, Sidney. *John Newbery and His Successors, 1740–1814: A Bibliography.* Wormsley: Five Owls Press, 1973.

St. John, Judith. *The Osborne Collection of Early Children's Books, 1566–1910.* Toronto: Toronto Public Library, 1958, 1966.

Schiller, Justin G. *Realms of Childhood.* Catalogue 41. New York: Justin G. Schiller, 1983.

Watson, George, ed. *The New Cambridge Bibliography of English Literature,* Vols. 2 and 3. Cambridge: Cambridge University Press, 1971.

Contemporary Criticism

Barbauld, Anna Laetitia (Aikin). *The British Novelists.* 50 vols. London: F. C. and J. Rivington, 1810.

[Hailes, Nathaniel.] *The Juvenile Review; or, Moral and Critical Observations on Children's Books . . . a Guide for Parents and Teachers.* Two Parts. London: N. Hailes, 1817.

Malkin, Benjamin Heath. *A Father's Memoirs of His Child.* London: Longman, Hurst, Rees and Orme, 1806.

Trimmer, Sarah (Kirby). *The Guardian of Education.* 5 vols. London: J. Hatchard, 1802–5.

Recent Criticism and Background

Ashton, John. *Chapbooks of the Eighteenth Century.* London: Seven Dials Press, 1969.

Ashton, T. S. *The Industrial Revolution, 1760—1830.* Rev. ed. New York: Oxford University Press, 1964.

Avery, Gillian. *Nineteenth Century Children: Heroes and Heroines in English Children's Stories.* London: Hodder and Stoughton, 1965.

Babenroth, A. Charles. *English Childhood: Wordsworth's Treatment of Childhood in the Light of English Poetry from Prior to Crabbe.* New York: Columbia University Press, 1922.

Barry, Florence Valentine. *A Century of Children's Books.* London, 1922.

Bator, Robert, ed. *Signposts to Criticism of Children's Literature.* Chicago: American Library Association, 1983.

Bayne-Powell, Rosamond. *The English Child in the Eighteenth Century.* London: John Murray, 1939.

———. *Travellers in Eighteenth-Century England.* London: John Murray, 1951.

Bettelheim, Bruno. *The Uses of Enchantment: The Meaning and Importance of Fairy Tales.* New York: Vintage Books, Random House, 1977.

Bingham, Jane, and Grayce Scholt. *Fifteen Centuries of Children's Literature: An Annotated Chronology of British and American Works in Historical Context*. Westport, CT, and London: Greenwood Press, 1980.

Butler, Francelia, ed. *Master Works of Children's Literature, 1500–1739*. 7 vols. London: Stonehill and Chelsea House, 1983.

Carpenter, Humphery. *Secret Gardens: A Study of the Golden Age of Children's Literature*. London: Unwin, 1987.

Caulfield, Ernest. *The Infant Welfare Movement in the Eighteenth Century*. New York: P. B. Hoeber, 1931.

Cook, Elizabeth. *The Ordinary and the Fabulous: An Introduction to Myths, Legends, and Fairy Tales*. Cambridge: Cambridge University Press, 1971.

Coveney, Peter. *The Image of Childhood: The Individual and Society . . . in English Literature*. New York: Penguin Books, 1967.

Cunnington, Phillis, and Anne Buck. *Children's Costume in England: From the Fourteenth to the End of the Nineteenth Century*. New York: Barnes and Noble, 1965.

Cunnington, Phillis, and Catherine Lucas. *Costumes for Births, Marriages, and Deaths*. London: A. and C. Black, 1972.

Cutt, M. Nancy. *Mrs. Sherwood and Her Books for Children*. London: Oxford University Press, 1974.

Darton, F. J. Harvey. *The Life and Times of Mrs. Sherwood, 1775–1851*. London: Wells Gardner, 1910.

———. *Children's Books in England*. 3d ed. Revised by Brian Alderson. Cambridge: Cambridge University Press, 1982.

de Mause, Lloyd, ed. *The History of Childhood*. New York, San Francisco, and London: Harper and Row, 1975.

Erikson, Erik H. *Childhood and Society*. 2d ed. New York: W. W. Norton and Co., 1963.

Field, Louise F. *The Child and His Book*. London: Wells Gardner, [1892].

Frank, Francine, and F. Anshen. *Language and the Sexes*. Albany: State University of New York Press, 1983.

George, M. Dorothy. *English Social Life in the Eighteenth-Century*. London: Sheldon Press; New York: Macmillan Co., 1923.

———. *London Life in the Eighteenth Century*. New York: Knopf, 1925.

———. *England in Transition*. New York: Penguin Books, 1956.

Godfrey, Elizabeth [Jessie Bedford]. *English Children in the Olden Time*. London: Metheun and Co., 1907.

Hannas, Linda. *The English Jigsaw Puzzle, 1760–1890*. London: Wayland Publishers, 1972.

Harmon, Rebecca L. *Susanna: Mother to the Wesleys (1669–1742)*. London: Hodder and Stoughton, 1968.

Hecht, J. Jean. *The Domestic Servant Class in Eighteenth-Century England*. Routledge and Kegan Paul, 1956.

Jones, M. Gladys. *The Charity School Movement: A Study of Eighteenth-Century Puritanism in Action*. Cambridge: Cambridge University Press, 1938.

———. *Hannah More*. New York: Greenwood Press, 1968.

Lecky, William E. H. *The History of England in the Eighteenth Century*. 7 vols. London: Longmans, 1918–23.

Locke, John. *The Works of John Locke*. 10 vols. London: Thomas Tegg, 1823.

———. *Some Thoughts Concerning Education*. Ed. Rev. R. H. Quick. Cambridge: Cambridge University Press, 1902.

———. *An Essay Concerning Human Understanding*. Ed. John W. Yolton. London: J. M. Dent; New York: Dutton, 1961.

Lucas, Edward V., ed. *The Works of Charles and Mary Lamb*. 7 vols. London: Methuen and Co., 1903–5.

Lurie, Alison, and Justin G. Schiller, eds. *Classics of Children's Literature: 1621–1932*. 73 vols. New York: Garland Publishing, 1976–78.

MacDonald, Ruth K. *Literature for Children in England and America from 1646 to 1774*. Troy, NY: Whitston Publishing Company, 1982.

McConnell-Ginet, Sally, Ruth Borker, and Nelly Furman, eds. *Women and Language in Literature and Society*. New York: Praeger, 1980.

Mckendrick, Neil, ed. *Historical Perspectives: Studies in English Thought and Society in Honour of J. H. Plumb*. London: Europa, 1974.

Marshall, Dorothy. *The English Domestic Servant in History*. [London]: G. Philip for The Historical Association, 1949.

———. *English People in the Eighteenth Century*. London and New York: Longmans, Green, 1956.

———. *Eighteenth-Century England*. New York: D. McKay Co., 1962.

———. *Dr. Johnson's London*. New York: Wiley, 1968.

———. *Industrial England, 1776–1851*. London: Routledge and Kegan Paul, 1973.

Muir, Percival H. *English Children's Books from 1600 to 1900*. London: Batsford, 1954.

———. *Victorian Illustrated Books*. London: Batsford, 1971.

Neuburg, Victor. *The Penny Histories*, in *Milestones in Children's Literature*. General Editor, Brian Alderson. New York: Harcourt, Brace and World, 1968.

———. *Popular Education in Eighteenth-Century England*. London: Woburn Press, 1971.

Newman, Gerald. *The Rise of English Nationalism: A Cultural History, 1740–1830*. New York: St. Martin's Press, 1987.

Opie, Peter, and Iona Opie, eds. *The Oxford Dictionary of Nursery Rhymes*. Oxford: Oxford University Press, 1951.

Pickering, Samuel F., Jr. *John Locke and Children's Books in Eighteenth-Century*

England. Knoxville: University of Tennessee Press, 1981.

Pinchbeck, Ivy. *Women Workers and the Industrial Revolution, 1750–1850*. London: G. Routledge and Sons; New York: F. S. Crofts and Co., 1930.

Pinchbeck, Ivy, and Margaret Hewitt. *Children in English Society: From the Eighteenth Century to the Children's Act of 1948*. 2 vols. London: Routledge and Kegan Paul, 1969–73.

Plumb, J. H. *England in the Eighteenth Century*. Rev. ed. New York: Penguin Books, 1963.

———, ed. *Studies in the Social History of England: A Tribute to G. M. Trevelyan*. London and New York: Longmans, Green, 1955.

Rémise, Jacques. *The Golden Age of Toys*. Trans. D. B. Tubbs. New York: Time-Life Books, 1967.

Roscoe, Sidney, and R. A. Brimmell, eds. *James Lumsden & Son of Glasgow: Their Juvenile Books and Chapbooks*. Pinner: Private Libraries Association, 1981.

Rudé, George. *Wilkes and Liberty: A Social Study of 1763 to 1774*. London, Oxford, New York: Oxford University Press, 1972.

Sharp, Evelyn. *The London Child*. London: Bodley Head, 1927.

Sloane, William. *Children's Books in England and America in the Seventeenth Century*. New York: King's Crown Press, 1955.

Stannard, David E. *The Puritan Way of Death*. New York: Oxford University Press, 1977.

Stephen, Leslie. *English Literature and Society in the Eighteenth Century*. London: G. Duckworth, 1904.

———. *History of English Thought in the Eighteenth Century*. London: Macmillan, 1904.

Stone, Lawrence. *The Family, Sex, and Marriage in England, 1500–1800*. New York: Harper and Row, 1977.

Summerfield, Geoffrey. *Fantasy and Reason: Children's Literature in the Eighteenth Century*. Athens: University of Georgia Press, 1984.

Taylor, Gordon Rattray. *The Angel Makers*. New York: E. P. Dutton, 1974.

Thorne, Barrie, and Nancy Henley, eds. *Language and Sex: Difference and Domination*. Rowley, Mass.: Newbury House, 1975.

Thwaite, Mary F. *From Primer to Pleasure in Reading*. Rev. ed. Boston: Horn Book, 1972.

Townsend, John R. *Written for Children: An Outline of English-Language Children's Literature*. Rev. ed. Boston: Horn Book, 1983.

Trevelyan, G. M. *History of England*. New York and London: Longmans, Green, 1932.

———. *English Social History: A Survey of Six Centuries*. London: Longmans, Green, 1942.

————. *Illustrated English Social History.* 4 vols. London: Longmans, Green, 1949–52.

Tuberville, Arthur Stanley. *English Men and Manners in the Eighteenth Century.* New York: Oxford University Press, 1957.

————, ed. *Johnson's England: An Account of the Life and Manners of His Age.* 2 vols. Oxford: Clarendon Press, 1933.

Walton, C., and J. P. Anton, eds. *Philosophy and the Civilizing Arts.* Athens: Ohio University Press, 1974.

Whalley, Joyce. *Cobwebs to Catch Flies: Illustrated Books for the Nursery and School-room, 1700–1800.* Berkeley and Los Angeles: University of California Press, 1975.

Whiteley, J. H. *Wesley's England: A Survey of Eighteenth-Century Social and Cultural Conditions.* London: Epworth Press, 1945.

Zipes, Jack. *Breaking the Spell: Radical Theories of Folk and Fairy Tales.* Austin: University of Texas Press, 1979.

————. *Fairy Tales and the Art of Subversion.* New York: Wildman Press, 1982.

————. *The Trials and Tribulations of Little Red Riding Hood: Versions of the Tale in Socio-cultural Perspective.* South Hadley, Mass.: J. F. Bergin Publishers, 1983.

Sources of the Illustrations

Illustrations not otherwise credited are from my own collection.

1. [Charles Perrault.] *Histoires ou Contes du Temps Passé. Avec des Moralitez.* [?Amsterdam: ?Jacques Desbordes], 1700. PML 85504. The Pierpont Morgan Library, New York.

2. *The New Tom Thumb, as Related by Margery Meanwell.* London: Harris, 1838.

3. *Histoire Naturelle des Animaux.* [France: n.p., *c.* 1850–60]. [Pictorial cover detached from its own and affixed to this edition: Tours: Alfred Mame et Fils, 1865.]

4. *A Silver Hornbook.* [?England: ?Late seventeenth century.] PML 19007. The Pierpont Morgan Library, New York.

5. Sarah Kirby Trimmer. *A New Series of Prints, Accompanied by Easy Lessons . . . from the Old Testament.* London: J. Harris, 1808.

6. The Rev. Isaac Taylor. *Scenes in America, for the Amusement and Instruction of Little Tarry-At-Home Travellers.* London: Harris and Son, 1821.

7. *A New Hieroglyphical Bible for the Amusement and Instruction of Youth.* Cooperstown, [N. Y.]: H. and E. Phinney, 1842.

8. *The Childrens Bible.* London and Dublin: Ann Law, 1763. PML 85502. The Pierpont Morgan Library, New York.

9. John Bunyan. *The Illustrated Polyglot Pilgrim's Progress . . . in English and French.* New York: D. Appleton and Co., 1876.

10. *The Popular Story of Blue Beard; or, Female Curiosity.* London: Ryle and Co. [successor to Catnach], [*c.* 1846].

11. *Popular Tales of the Olden Time, Corrected and Adapted to Juvenile Readers of the Present Time, By a Lady.* London: Dean and Munday, [*c.* 1830].

12. *A Silver Hornbook.* [?England: ?Late seventeenth century.] PML 19007. The Pierpont Morgan Library, New York.

13. *A New Hieroglyphical Bible.* Cooperstown, [N. Y.]: H. and E. Phinney, 1842.

14. [Oliver Goldsmith.] *An History of the Lives, Actions, Travels, Sufferings, And Deaths of the Most Eminent Martyrs, and Primitive Fathers of the Church.* London: J. Newbery, 1764. PML 85501. The Pierpont Morgan Library, New York.

15. Trimmer. *A New Series of Prints, Accompanied by Easy Lessons . . . from the Old Testament.* London: J. Harris, 1808.

16. [John Bunyan.] *The Christian Pilgrim: Containing an Account of the Wonderful Adventures and Miraculous Escapes of a Christian, in his Travels from the Land of Destruction to the New Jerusalem.* First American Edition. 2 vols. Worcester: Isaiah Thomas, 1798. PML 85505. The Pierpont Morgan Library, New York.

17. [?Benjamin Harris.] *The New-England Primer Enlarged: For The More Easy Attaining the True Reading of English. To Which Is Added, The Assembly of Divines and Mr. Cotton's Catechisms.* Boston: T. and J. Fleet, 1763. E–3/89/E Not. Acc. The Pierpont Morgan Library, New York.

18. *Biblia; or, A Practical Summary of Ye Old And New Testaments.* London: R. Wilkin, 1727. PML 65843. The Pierpont Morgan Library, New York.

19. *A New Hieroglyphical Bible.* Coopers-

town, [N. Y.]: H. and E. Phinney, 1842.

20. Isaac Watts. *Dr. Watts's Celebrated Cradle Hymn, Illustrated with Appropriate Engravings*. London: J. Harris, 1812. PML 85528. The Pierpont Morgan Library, New York.

21. John Oakman et al. *Moral Songs Intended as a Companion to Dr. Watts's Divine Songs*. London: Darton and Harvey, [c. 1802]. Reprinted in A. W. Tuer, *Pages and Pictures from Forgotten Children's Books*. London: Leadenhall Press, 1898–99.

22. [Nathaniel Cotton.] *Visions in Verse, for the Entertainment and Instruction of Younger Minds*. London: Vernor, Hood, and Sharpe, 1808.

23. *A Primer, for the Use of the Mohawk Children, To Acquire the Spelling and Reading of their own, as well as to get acquainted with the English, Tongue; which for that Purpose is put on the opposite Page*. London: C. Buckton, 1786. PML 85496. The Pierpont Morgan Library, New York.

24. *Martin's New Battledoor of Natural History*. London: G. Martin, [about 1810]. PML 81638. The Pierpont Morgan Library, New York.

25. *Les Dictz Des Oiseaux* [sic] *et Des Bestes*. Châlons-sur-Marne: Étienne Bally, [?about 1493]. PML 47197. The Pierpont Morgan Library, New York.

26. Edward Topsell. *The Historie of Foure-Footed Beasts and Serpents*. London: G. Sawbridge, 1658. PML 32303. The Pierpont Morgan Library, New York.

27. Johann Amos Comenius. *Orbis Sensualium Pictus. Translated by Charles Hoole, M. A., for the Use of Young Latin Scholars*. New York: T. & J. Swords, 1810. PML 53872. The Pierpont Morgan Library, New York.

28. John Bunyan. *Divine Emblems; or, Temporal Things Spiritualized. Calculated for the Use of Young People*. London: T. Bennett . . . , [about 1790]. PML 66116. The Pierpont Morgan Library, New York.

29. L. C. D. E. M. [i.e., Louis Couvay, Docteur en Medecine]. *Méthode Nouvelle et Très-Exacte, Pour Enseigner et Apprendre La Premiere Partie De Despautere*. Paris: Jean Gaillard, 1649. PML 81156. The Pierpont

Morgan Library, New York.

30. [Hans Holbein.] *Emblems of Mortality; Representing, In Upwards of Fifty Cuts, Death Seizing All Ranks and Degrees of People. . . . Intended as well for the Information of the Curious, as the Instruction and Entertainment of Youth*. London: T. Hodgson, 1789. E-2/51-/E) Toovey Collection. The Pierpont Morgan Library, New York.

31. *Aesop's Fables With His Life: In English, French & Latin*. London: Printed by William Godbid for Francis Barlow, 1666. PML 64797. The Pierpont Morgan Library, New York.

32. *Aesop's Fables, In English and Latin, Interlineary, for the Benefit of those Who Not Having a Master, Would Learn Either of These Tongues*. [?Edited by John Locke.] London: A. and J. Churchil, 1703. PML 65064. The Pierpont Morgan Library, New York.

33. [Aesop.] *Select Fables, In Three Parts*. Newcastle: T. Saint, 1784. PML 52926. The Pierpont Morgan Library, New York.

34 and 34a. [Robert Dodsley.] *Select Fables of Esop and Other Fabulists*. Birmingham: Printed by John Baskerville, for R. and J. Dodsley, 1761. PML 60342. The Pierpont Morgan Library, New York.

35. "Solomon Winlove" [i.e., ?Oliver Goldsmith]. *Moral Lectures*. London: F. Newbery, 1769. PML 85484. The Pierpont Morgan Library, New York.

36 and 36a. [R. Ransome.] *The Good Boy's Soliloquy; Containing his Parents' Instructions Relative to his Disposition and Manners*. London: W. Darton, Junr., 1811. PML 80883. The Pierpont Morgan Library, New York.

37. Philip Dormer Stanhope, 4th Earl of Chesterfield. *Letters Written By the . . . Earl of Chesterfield, to his Son, Philip Stanhope, . . . Together with Several Other Pieces on Various Subjects, Published by Mrs. Eugenia Stanhope*. London: J. Dodsley, 1774. PML 65626–27. The Pierpont Morgan Library, New York.

38. *A Pleasant Song of the Valiant Deeds of Chivalry, Atchieved by that Noble Knight*

Sir Guy of Warwick. [?London: ?about 1700]. ECB)43 Broadside. The Pierpont Morgan Library, New York.

39. *The History of Valentine and Orson*. [London]: Printed for the Company of Walking Stationers, [about 1790]. PML 81637. The Pierpont Morgan Library, New York.

40. B. P. *Gesta Romanorum; or, Fifty-Eight Histories Originally (As 'Tis Said) Collected from The Roman Records. With Applications or Morals for the Suppressing Vice, and Encouraging Virtue and the Love of God*. London: G Conyers, [?about 1720]. PML 85482. The Pierpont Morgan Library, New York.

41. *Popular Tales of the Olden Time*. London: Dean and Munday, [c. 1830].

42. [Charles Perrault.] *Histoires ou Contes du Temps Passé*. [?Amsterdam: ?Jaques Desbordes], 1700. PML 85504. The Pierpont Morgan Library, New York.

43. *Fat and Lean; or, The Fairy Queen, Exhibiting the Effects of Moral Magic, by the Ring and the Three Mirrors*. Chelmsford: I. Marsden, [c. 1815].

44. *The Sleeping Beauty of the Wood*. Glasgow: Printed for the Booksellers, [c. 1840–55].

45. *Park's Entertaining History of Tom Thumb*. London: A. Parks, [c. 1830s].

46. R. R[ansome]. *The Invited Alphabet; or, The Address of A to B; Containing his Friendly Proposal for the Amusement and Instruction of Good Children*. London: W. Darton, Jun., [?about 1804]. PML 85492. The Pierpont Morgan Library, New York.

47. *The Youth's Natural History of Animals*. New York: Mahlon Day, 1829.

48. *A Month's Vacation . . . with an Entertaining Description of the Principal Places of Amusement . . . in London*. London: William Cole, n.d. Reprinted in A. W. Tuer, *Forgotten Children's Books*. London, 1898–99.

49. *The Life and History of A, Apple-Pie . . . eaten by twenty-six young ladies and gentlemen*. London: Dean and Munday, and A. K. Newman and Co., [c. 1835–40]. Reprinted in A. W. Tuer, *Forgotten Children's Books*. London, 1898–99.

50, 51, and 52. Oliver Goldsmith. *Dr. Goldsmith's Celebrated Elegy on that Glory of Her Sex, Mrs. Mary Blaize*. London: J. Harris, 1808.

53. "Toby Ticklepitcher." *The Hobby-Horse; or, Christmas Companion: Containing . . . the Song of a Cock and a Bull, a Canterbury Story, and a Tale of a Tub. Faithfully copied from the original Manuscript, in the Vatican Library*. London: E. Newbery, 1784. PML 81588. The Pierpont Morgan Library, New York.

54. *A Pretty Book of Pictures for Little Masters and Misses; or, Tommy Trip's History of Beasts and Birds . . . To which is prefixed The History of Little Tom himself, of his Dog Jouler, and of Woglog the great Giant*. 9th ed. London: J. Newbery, 1767. Reprinted in A. W. Tuer, *Stories from Old-Fashioned Children's Books*. London: Leadenhall Press, 1899–1900.

55. *The Lilliputian Magazine; or, Children's Repository*. London: W. Tringham, [c. 1800s]. Reprinted in A. W. Tuer, *Forgotten Children's Books*. London, 1898–99.

56. Jefferys Taylor. *The Farm: A New Account of Rural Toils and Produce*. London: John Harris, 1834.

57. [Ann Taylor.] *Signor Topsy-Turvy's Wonderful Magic Lantern; or, The World Turn'd Upside Down*. London: B. Tabart, [1810].

58. *Whittington and His Cat*. London: John Harris, [1827]. PML 81678. The Pierpont Morgan Library, New York.

59. Tom Telescope. [i.e., ?Oliver Goldsmith ?John Newbery] *The Newtonian System of Philosophy*. London: J. Newbery, 1761. PML 85536. The Pierpont Morgan Library, New York.

60. *Rainsford Villa; or, Juvenile Independence. A Tale*. London: J. Harris and Son, 1823. Reprinted in A. W. Tuer, *Forgotten Children's Books*. London, 1898–99.

61 and 62. [?John Newbery.] [*The Renowned History of Giles Gingerbread.*] [London: John Newbery, ?1766 or earlier.] PML 81624. The Pierpont Morgan Library, New York.

63. Benjamin Franklin. *The Art of Making Money Plenty, in Every Man's Pocket. By*

Dr. Franklin. London: Darton, Harvey and Darton, 1817. PML 85545. The Pierpont Morgan Library, New York.

64. *The French History Briefly Told, from Early Times to the Present Period.* London: John Harris, 1833.

65. [Rudolf Eric Raspe.] *The Travels and Surprising Adventures of Baron Munchausen.* Illustrated by G[eorge] Cruikshank. London: William Tegg, 1868.

66. J. Aspin. *Ancient Customs, Sports, and Pastimes, of the English.* 2d ed. London: John Harris, 1835.

67. *The Children's Cabinet; or, A Key to Natural History.* London: Laurie and Whittle, 1798. PML 83915. The Pierpont Morgan Library, New York.

68. *The Youth's Natural History of Animals.* New York, 1829.

69. [Richard Scrafton Sharpe.] *Old Friends in a New Dress; or, Familiar Fables in Verse.* London: Harvey and Darton, and William Darton, 1820. PML 85487. The Pierpont Morgan Library, New York.

70. Henry Fielding. *The History of Tom Jones, A Foundling. Abridged from the Works of Henry Fielding, Esq.* London: E. Newbery, 1784. PML 85553. The Pierpont Morgan Library, New York.

71. Arabella Argus. *The Juvenile Spectator: Being Observations on the Tempers, Manners, and Foibles of Various Young Persons.* Parts I and II. London: W. Darton, 1813–12 [*sic*].

72. *Park's Entertaining History of Tom Thumb.* London: A. Parks, [*c.* 1830s].

73. [Daniel Defoe.] *The Life and Adventures of Robinson Crusoe of York, Mariner.* London: William Darton, 1823. PML 81161. The Pierpont Morgan Library, New York.

74 and 75. [Raspe.] *The Travels and Surprising Adventures of Baron Munchausen.* London: William Tegg, 1868.

76. Samuel Richardson. *Clarissa; or, the History of a Young Lady . . . Abridged from the Works of Samuel Richardson, Esq.* London: E. Newbery, [about 1780]. PML 85586. The Pierpont Morgan Library, New York.

77 and 78. *The Renowned History of Primrose Prettyface, who . . . was raised . . . to . . . the Dignity of Lady of the Manor.* Cuts by Bewick. York: T. Wilson and R. Spence, 1804. Reprinted in A. W. Tuer, *Old-Fashioned Children's Books.* London, 1899–1900.

79, 80, and 81. [Ellenor Fenn.] *Cobwebs to Catch Flies; or, Dialogues in Short Sentences Adapted to Children from the Age of Three to Eight Years.* 2 vols., bound as one. London: Baldwin and Cradock, 1833.

82. Trimmer. *A New Series of Prints, Accompanied by Easy Lessons . . . from the Old Testament.* London: J. Harris, 1808.

83. Sarah Trimmer. *A Series of Prints . . . to Illustrate the Old Testament and Scriptures Lessons . . . from the Old Testament.* London: Baldwin and Cradock, and N. Hailes, 1829.

84. Sarah Trimmer. *A New Series of Prints . . . from the New Testament.* London: J. Harris, 1805.

85. [Fenn.] *Cobwebs to Catch Flies.* London: Baldwin and Cradock, 1833.

86. Elizabeth Sandham. *The Bee and Butterfly; or, Industry and Idleness.* London: A. K. Newman and Co., 1836.

87. The Rev. Isaac Taylor. *The Mine.* 4th ed. London: John Harris, 1832.

88. [M. P. (i.e., Dorothy Kilner)] *The Life and Perambulation of a Mouse.* London: John Marshall and Co., 1783. PML 85514. The Pierpont Morgan Library, New York.

89 and 90. [Sarah Trimmer.] *Fabulous Histories, by Mrs. Trimmer; or, The History of the Robins. Designed for the Instruction of Children, Respecting Their Treatment of Animals. Illustrated with Twelve Plates.* London: J. F. Dove, 1833.

91. [Edward Augustus Kendall.] *Keeper's Travels in Search of His Master.* 2d American ed. Philadelphia: Johnson and Warner, 1808.

92. *The Juvenile Journal; or, Tales of Truth. By Mrs. Cockle.* 2d ed. London: C. Chapple, 1811.

93. [Daniel Defoe.] *La Vie et Les Avantures Surprenantes de Robinson Crusoe.* Am-

sterdam: L'Honore and Chatelain, 1720–1721. PML 85526.1. The Pierpont Morgan Library, New York.

94. [Thomas Day.] *The History of Sandford and Merton*. 3 vols. London: J. Stockdale, 1783, 1786, 1789. PML 85516.1–3. The Pierpont Morgan Library, New York.

94a. [Day.] *The History of Sandford & [sic] Merton*. 3 vols. London: J. Stockdale, 1801. Reprinted in A. W. Tuer, *Forgotten Children's Books*. London, 1898–99.

95. Johann David Wyss [with Johann Rudolf Wyss]. *The Swiss Family Robinson; or, Adventures of A Father and Mother and Four Sons in a Desert Island*. 6th ed. London: Baldwin, Cradock, and Joy, 1826.

96. *The History of Prince Lee Boo, A Native of the Pelew Islands*. 7th ed. London: J. Harris, 1827.

97. Argus. *The Juvenile Spectator*. London: W. Darton, 1813–1812 [sic].

98. [Thomas Day.] *The Grateful Turk; or, The Advantages of Friendship*. Boston: J. White, 1796. PML 81564. The Pierpont Morgan Library, New York.

99 and 100. The Rev. W. D. Cooper [Richard Johnson]. *The Looking-Glass for the Mind; or, Intellectual Mirror*. With 74 cuts by Bewick. 17th ed. London: John Harris, G. Whittaker, Harvey and Co., et al., 1827.

101. Maria Edgeworth. *The Parent's Assistant; or, Stories for Children*. Vol. 5. 3d ed. London: J. Johnson, 1800.

102. Maria Edgeworth. *The Barring Out; or, Party Spirit*. 2d American ed. Philadelphia: Johnson and Warner, 1809.

103. Edgeworth. *The Parent's Assistant*. Vol. 4. 3d ed. London: J. Johnson, 1800.

104. [Mary Pilkington, ed.] *Pity's Gift: A Collection of Interesting Tales; to Excite the Compassion of Youth for the Animal Creation*. London: T. W. Longman, 1798.

105. [Johnson.] *The Looking-Glass for the Mind*. London: John Harris et al., 1827.

106. Clara Hall. *The Young Gentleman's Library*. London: A. K. Newman and Company, [c. 1820s].

107. Argus. *The Juvenile Spectator*. Part II. London: W. Darton, 1812.

108. [Thomas Beddoes?] *The History of Isaac Jenkins, To Which Are Added, A Friendly Gift to Servants and Apprentices, and The Brazier, or, Mutual Gratitude*. Dublin: R. D. Webb, 1831.

109. [Mary Martha] Sherwood. *The History of Little George and His Penny, The Lady in the Arbour, The Rosebuds, and Poor Burruff*. London: Houlston and Co., n.d.

110 and 111. [Beddoes?] *The History of Isaac Jenkins*. Dublin: R. D. Webb, 1831.

112. [Elizabeth] Sandham. *The Adopted Daughter, A Tale for Young Persons*. London: J. Harris, 1815.

113. [Barbara] Hofland. *The Son of a Genius; a Tale for Youth*. London: J. Harris and Son, 1822.

114. Mary Belson [Elliott]. *Simple Truths, In Verse; For the Amusement and Instruction of Children, at an Early Age*. 3d ed. London: W. Darton, 1822.

115. Sherwood. *The History of Little George and His Penny*. 19th ed. Londc Houlston and Co., n.d.

116. [Lucy Butt] Cameron. *The Careless Little Boy*. London: Houlston and Stoneman, n.d.

117. Sherwood. *The Lady in the Arbour*. London: Houlston and Co., n.d.

118. [Mary Martha] Sherwood. *The Little Woodman, and his Dog Caesar*. London: Houlston and Son, 1834.

119. [Mrs. (Mary Martha Butt) Sherwood.] *The History of Little Henry and His Bearer*. Wellington: F. Houlston and Son, 1814. PML 85525. The Pierpont Morgan Library, New York.

120. *The Popular Story of Blue Beard*. London: Ryle and Co., [c. 1846].

121. Clara Reeve. *The Old English Baron: A Gothic Story, from an Ancient Manuscript*. London: For the Booksellers; Colliergate, York: J. Kendrew, 1813.

122. *Popular Tales of the Olden Time*. London: Dean and Munday, [c. 1830].

123. [William Wordsworth.] *The Little Maid and the Gentleman; or, We Are Seven*. York: J. Kendrew, [about 1820]. PML 81566. The Pierpont Morgan Library, New York.

124. [Sarah Catherine Martin.] *The Comic Adventures of Old Mother Hubbard and her Dog*. [London: J. Harris, 1806.]

125. [Taylor.] *Signor Topsy-Turvy's Wonderful Magic Lantern*. London: B. Tabart, [1810].

126 and 127. [Ann Taylor.] *My Mother*, bound with [Mary (Belson) Elliott,] *My Brother, My Aunt, My Grandmother, My Grandfather*. [London?: n.p., c. 1815–35].

128. *The History of Sixteen Wonderful Old Women*. London: John Harris, 1820. Reprinted in A. W. Tuer, *Forgotten Children's Books*. London, 1898–99.

128 a. *The History of Sixteen Wonderful Old Women*. London: John Harris, 1820. Reprinted in A. W. Tuer, *Forgotten Children's Books*. London, 1898–99.

129. *Marmaduke Multiply's Merry Method of Making Minor Mathematicians; or, The Multiplication Table*. Boston: Munroe and Francis, [c. 1840–50].

130. *A Good Child's Book of Stops*. [London?: n.p., c. 1830s]. Reprinted in A. W. Tuer, *Forgotten Children's Books*. London, 1898–99.

131. [William Roscoe.] *The Butterfly's Ball and the Grasshopper's Feast*. London: Harris, 1807. Reprinted in A. W. Tuer, *Forgotten Children's Books*. London, 1898–99.

132 and 133. [Catherine Ann Dorset.] *The Peacock "At Home." Twentieth Edition. The Butterfly's Ball; An Original Poem by Mr. Roscoe. And The Fancy Fair; or, Grand Gala at the Zoological Gardens*. London: John Harris, 1838.

132 a. *The Lobster's Voyage to the Brazils*. London: John Harris, 1808. Reprinted in A. W. Tuer, *Forgotten Children's Books*. London, 1898–99.

134. [Dorset.] *The Peacock "At Home": A Sequel to the Butterfly's Ball*. London: John Harris, 1807. Reprinted in A. W. Tuer, *Forgotten Children's Books*. London, 1898–99.

135 and 136. W. B. *The Elephant's Ball and Grand Fête Champetre*. London: J. Harris, 1807. Reprinted in A. W. Tuer, *Forgotten Children's Books*. London, 1898–99.

137. Catherine Ann Dorset. *The Lion's Masquerade. A Sequel to the Peacock "At Home."* London: J. Harris, 1807. Reprinted in A. W. Tuer, *Forgotten Children's Books*. London, 1898–99.

138. [Catherine Ann Dorset.] *Think Before You Speak; or, The Three Wishes. A Tale*. Philadelphia: Johnson and Warner, 1810.

139. [Christopher Smart.] *Hymns, for the Amusement of Children*. Dublin: T. Walker, [?about 1772]. PML 81627. The Pierpont Morgan Library, New York.

140. *The Court of Oberon; or, Temple of the Fairies*. London: John Harris, 1823. Reprinted in A. W. Tuer, *Forgotten Children's Books*. London, 1898–99.

141. [Marie Le Prince de Beaumont.] Autograph manuscript, illustrated, of *Beauty and the Beast, A Fairy Tale*. [Translated from the French by Adelaide Doyle. Illustrated by Richard Doyle.] 1842. MA 2756. The Pierpont Morgan Library, New York.

142. Victor Hugo. *Hans of Iceland*. London: J. Robins and Co., 1825.

143 and 144. *Popular Tales of the Olden Time*. London: Dean and Munday, [c. 1830].

145. B.A.T. *The History of Mother Twaddle, and the Marvelous Atchievements of Her Son Jack*. London: J. Harris, 1807. PML 84100. The Pierpont Morgan Library, New York.

148. *Park's Entertaining History of Tom Thumb*. London: A. Parks, [c. 1830s].

149. *The New History of Tom Thumb. As Related by Margery Meanwell*. London: Harris, 1838.

150. Catherine Sinclair. *Holiday House*. Edinburgh: William Whyte and Co., 1851.

151. [Charles Lamb.] *The King and Queen of Hearts: With the Rogueries of the Knave Who Stole The Queen's Pies*. London: M. J. Godwin, 1806. PML 19273. The Pierpont Morgan Library, New York. *Knave Who Stole The Queen's Pies*. London: M. J. Godwin, 1806. PML 19273. The Pierpont Morgan Library, New York.

152 and 153. Hans Christian Andersen. *The Shoes of Fortune and Other Stories*. Translated by C. Boner. Drawings by Otto

Speckter. London: Chapman and Hall, 1847.

154. Hans Christian Andersen. *The Dream of Little Tuk, and Other Tales*. Translated by Charles Boner. Illustrated by Count Pocci. London: Grant and Griffith, successors to John Harris, 1848.

155 and 156. The Rev. Isaac Taylor. *Scenes in Asia, for the Amusement and Instruction of Little Tarry-At-Home Travellers*. London: Harris and Son, 1821.

157. *The Ocean; A Description of the Wonders of the Sea*. London: John Harris, 1833.

158. Frederick Marryat. *Masterman Ready; or, The Wreck of the Pacific. Written for Young People*. London: Longman, Orme, Brown, Green, and Longmans, 1841–1842. PML 85529. The Pierpont Morgan Library, New York.

159. *Popular Tales of the Olden Time*. London: Dean and Munday, [c. 1830].

160. Andersen. *The Dream of Little Tuk*. London: Grant and Griffith, 1848.

Index

The numbers in boldface type refer to illustration numbers.